T

DRUIDS

FIG. I.—JOHN AUBREY, 1626-1697

FROM THE DRAWING IN THE ASHMOLEAN MUSEUM

THE
DRUIDS

T. D. KENDRICK

SENATE

The Druids

First published in 1927 by Methuen & Co. Ltd, London

This edition published in 1994 by Senate, an imprint of
Studio Editions Ltd, Princess House, 50 Eastcastle Street,
London W1N 7AP, England

ISBN 1 85958 036 X
Printed and bound in Guernsey by
The Guernsey Press Co Ltd

THIS BOOK

IS ASCRIBED TO

THE MEMORY OF

FANNY SOWTER

PREFACE

IF it were not that I very much dislike long titles, I would call this book *An Introduction to the Study of Ancient Druids and Ancient Druidism*, for that is what it is really intended to be. Frankly, its main purpose is to provide a complete and well-documented summary of the whole of the pertinent material upon which a study of this subject should properly be based ; and in order not to mask what I hope is a sober outline of fact, I have deliberately omitted various tempting discussions and elaborations of uncertainties. Thus I have not allowed myself to deal *seriatim* and fully with the many theories of the origin of druidism ; while, as for my own speculation on this matter, I have whittled it down to a statement of opinion so brief that it enters the field with what must be surely a minimum of offensive and defensive armour.

I hope that the manner in which I have presented my material will demonstrate, as the salient lesson of this book, that an essential preliminary qualification for the study of druids and druidism is a general knowledge of the racial history and prehistory, and social atmosphere, of early Gallic and British civilisation. This method of approach is so important, that I should like to say a word about books for the benefit of those who are unacquainted with the literature of the subject.

To gain the necessary general information there are two

works of outstanding importance to serve as guides : firstly, Dr. Rice Holmes's *Cæsar's Conquest of Gaul* (2nd ed., Oxford, 1911), and the companion volume, *Ancient Britain and the Invasions of Julius Cæsar* (Oxford, 1907) ; and, secondly, the colossal *Histoire de la Gaule* (5ᵉ ed., Paris, 1924, especially Vols. I, II, III, and VI) by M. Camille Jullian. These books will also introduce the reader to the major problems affecting the religious life of the peoples concerned, and he may then turn to the more detailed studies of these problems. Here there are two excellent English works easily available, namely, Dr. J. A. MacCulloch's *The Religion of the Ancient Celts* (Edinburgh, 1911), and Dr. MacBain's *Celtic Mythology and Religion* (Stirling, 1917). Conjointly, he should acquaint himself with the shorter authoritative articles on druidism, such as that by Dr. MacCulloch in Hastings' *Encyclopædia of Religion and Ethics*, that by E. C. Quiggin in the *Encyclopædia Britannica*, and the sections by M. Camille Jullian and Sir Edward Anwyl in the *Cambridge Mediæval History* (II, chap. xv, " Keltic Heathenism in Gaul," p. 460, and " Keltic Heathenism in the British Isles," p. 472).

Only after a careful general preparation of this kind, is it safe to venture into the vast and dangerous literary quagmire that awaits the student in the single good bibliography of the subject (*Druids and Druidism ; A List of References*, New York Public Library, 1920). This most useful catalogue by Dr. G. F. Black is an invaluable index of the *quantity* of the writings upon our subject, but not, of course, of their *quality* (though Dr. Black has very properly censured as worthless some of the material included in his list) ; and it behoves the student, therefore, to make his way circumspectly through the three hundred and more entries. The truth is that a prodigious amount of rubbish has been written about druidism, particularly that worst and insidious variety that masquerades as deep and recondite learning. Here I have given abundant references to the many helpful and important works that are to be consulted on the special problems that arise in the course of our enquiry, and I hope the reader will accept them as a general guide to the trustworthy literature. If they are thought to be insufficient, let him consult the fuller pages of M. Camille Jullian.

In writing this book I have had no assistance, except for some kindly advice from Mr. Robin Flower of the British Museum. But I want very gratefully to acknowledge my indebtedness to Professor H. J. Rose for some valuable criticisms made when my manuscript was complete. Although these referred principally to doubtful readings of passages in the classical authorities, I have benefited very considerably throughout the whole book from Professor Rose's comments.

For permission to reproduce illustrations already published I desire to express my best thanks to the Council of the Wiltshire Archæological and Natural History Society (Figs. 1 and 45); to the Trustees of the British Museum (Fig. 9 (1, 2, 7) and Fig. 25); to the Council of the Royal Irish Academy (Figs. 11 and 12); to M. Ernest Leroux (Figs. 16 and 23, both from M. A. Blanchet's *Traité des Monnaies Gauloises*); to the Council of the Society of Antiquaries of Scotland (Fig. 20); to M. G. Demonmerot, on behalf of the late M. René Gadant (Fig. 21); to the Société Éduenne (Fig. 26); to the Council of the Royal Archæological Institute (Fig. 35); to M. Gamber (Fig. 40, from *L'Homme Préhistorique*); to Mr. R. Hansford Worth and the Council of the Devonshire Association (Figs. 41 and 49); to the Council of the British Archæological Association (Fig. 47); and to the Société Polymathique du Morbihan (Fig. 50).

T. D. KENDRICK

LONDON, *June, 1927*

CONTENTS

LIST OF ILLUSTRATIONS

xiii

THE DRUIDS

CHAPTER I

TRADITION

THERE is little need to remark upon the inextin-
guishable affection with which the druids are still
regarded in the popular imagination. The antiquary in his travels, or for that matter any curious layman,
must inevitably be aware of the renown they enjoy ; for the
signs of it are constantly encountered in the narratives of
guides and guide-books, and in the place-names of the
country-side ; while it is not uncommon to hear that some
of the supposed ceremonies of the druids have been re-
enacted with appropriate pomp by societies professing to
continue the ancient functions of the order. A visitor to the
Chislehurst Caves in Kent—to take one example out of the
many that offer themselves in this connection—will discover
that there is attached to these artificial galleries, which are
relatively of quite modern date, a complicated system of
legend glorifying the druids not only as the singing priests
of a subterranean chapel,[1] but also as the makers of the
prehistoric flint implements found in the neighbourhood.
In fact, it may truly be said that the unlettered public has
accepted, as a simple solution of the mysteries of very remote
antiquity, a primary division of nearly all our ancient remains
earlier than Saxon times into " Roman " and " Druidic," so
that the druids are rapidly becoming synonymous with the
Ancient Britons, that is to say, the pre-Roman population
of this country. As a counter to this, the learned from time

[1] Cf. the description of the caves in *Journ. Brit. Arch. Assoc.*,
IX (1903), 147.

to time assert that the current notions concerning the druids are mistaken ; but in spite of all their endeavours the priest-hood has lost little, if any, prestige, and continues securely enthroned in the fancy of the people.

This general faith in the druids, so widely held throughout the country and so difficult to disturb, invites discussion at the outset of a book dealing with the priesthood as it is known to us in antiquity. For it may reasonably be asked whether the popular beliefs ought not to affect the manner whereby the problem is approached, whether they do not place it in a sense outside the scope of a merely archæological dissertation. In a word, is it possible that the people possess through the agency of folk-memory a dim and mysterious knowledge of the druids that should over-rule any theoretical conclusions in opposition to the popular notions ?

As a matter of fact, it cannot seriously be maintained that such knowledge exists. Folk-memory may, of course, be a significant factor in many of the problems in which the antiquary is interested, but here it would be little short of amazing if it had existed in such a precise and informative manner over a period that is now about 2000 years in length. For it would not be an instance of haphazard memory of forgotten days preserved in names and customs no longer understood, whereby one might conceivably achieve contact with the times of the druids, but an instance of deliberate and uninterrupted knowledge that unfortunately only made itself manifest in quite recent times (as will soon be shown), and that, equally unfortunately, is partly in conflict with the archæological evidence.

The soundest argument against the possibility that such folk-memory existed is the positive knowledge we possess of the growth of the beliefs in question, and in the first chapter I propose to prove their modernity. This can best be achieved, *firstly*, by considering one especially deep-rooted notion about the druids, namely, the theory that it was they who built and used prehistoric rough stone monuments ; and, *secondly*, by a general study of their appearances in popular literature.

One reason why archæologists are not very successful in correcting the general opinion of the druids, or in showing that some of its more extravagant implications are ridiculous, is that it was they themselves, or rather their ancestors in archæology, who implanted the current notions. Doubtless the culprits did not anticipate the far-reaching results of the magnification of an obscure priesthood, but the fact remains that as the result of an archæological discourse the druids at one bound came not only into their own, but into a great deal more than their own ; and it looks as though they are likely to hold on to it.

Of course, it is not a very difficult thing to establish eccentric ideas concerning the distant past, but as a rule these find favour only in a strictly limited section of the community ; for a time they may be firmly believed, and they may even be persistent, but they are only current among a few dabblers in learning, and seldom attract any wide notice. It is obvious, therefore, that there must be some strong appeal to common sense, or the satisfaction of a solution to a definite puzzle, if an idea is to be popularly comprehended and accepted ; and it is because these advantages could be pleaded on behalf of the druids, that they hold their present high place in the general estimate of our ancient history and prehistory.

For there happened to be a focus upon which their claims could be centred, a reason for the revived memory of them, and this was provided by the mysterious but well-known rough stone monuments that are still plentiful throughout the land, chambers built of enormous slabs of stone, and circles and alignments of massive uprights or great recumbent boulders. Nothing was known as to the use of these or their origin, and when the druids were paraded as their probable builders the attraction of priests without temples to temples without priests proved irresistible.[1] And so it came about that all the protests of modern learning are

---

[1] Dr. Joseph Anderson noticed the significance of the entries for stone circles in the early indexes to Archæologia ; in 1809 it was simply *Stones, Circles of*, but in 1844 this was altered to *Stones, Circles of, v. Druids*.

insufficient to re-name the Druids' Altars and Druids' Temples of our country-side ; they are the names bestowed by the people at the bidding of earlier archæologists, and they are at once explanatory and satisfying ; wherefore it is evident that *dolmen, cromlech, megalithic monument,* and the like, have small chance of becoming popular substitutes.

This widely held belief that it was the druids who built the stone monuments is the subject that it is convenient to discuss first of all ; and to illustrate the genesis of the idea, that is to say, the manner of the druidic revival in its archæological sense, it is necessary to consider in some detail the historical aspect of a special problem of British archæology, that of the famous megalithic pile, Stonehenge. Nowadays there is nothing more druidic than Stonehenge ; in fact, it is so signally and sacredly druidic that some modern druids think it proper that a portion of the ashes of their deceased brethren should be buried within its precincts. It is all the more interesting, therefore, to find that for a long while its druidic character was absolutely unsuspected, for this must surely rob the modern notion of all traditional value.

The first unmistakable reference to the monument occurs in the 11th century in the writings of Henry of Huntingdon, who was content simply to catalogue it as one of the marvels of this island, though he remarked at the same time that its origin was unknown. A century later, however, we come upon the account of the building of Stonehenge related by Geoffrey of Monmouth, an exciting legend about the transport of the stones from Ireland by Merlin to form the memorial erected by Aurelius Ambrosius to the victims of Hengist's treachery in A.D. 470. This story was current for about 500 years, and is repeated in the poetry of Alexander Neckham (1157-1217), in Langtoft's chronicles (*c.* 1300), and in the works of several much later writers. A slight variation in the legend was made by Polydore Vergil at the beginning of the 16th century, for this writer affirmed that the monument was simply the sepulchre of Ambrosius ; but the first published theory running counter to Geoffrey's version is that of Edmund Bolton, who proposed in 1624 that Stonehenge was the tomb of Boadicea.[1] And it is evident that the Merlin story was wellnigh forgotten about this time, because even such an inquisitive and diligent person as the antiquary Camden, who can be trusted to have ferreted out any surviving folklore, was quite at a loss to explain the monument, and had nothing better to repeat than a vague rumour that the stones themselves had been artificially composed of sand and glue.

Therefore, so far as tradition is concerned, all that there is to go upon is this 12th century story recounted by Geoffrey ; and, accordingly, it becomes important to enquire whether Merlin was supposed by the mediæval historians to have been a druid. I am not disposed to shirk the issue by saying that Merlin was largely a creature of Geoffrey's imagination ; but to maintain that this author's account of the origin of Stonehenge is evidence of its traditional association with the druids seems to me, even on the most charitable view of the tale that can be taken, to be absolutely beyond the warrant of the facts.

Actually, the Merlin stories form a group that originally concerned two distinct persons, one a 6th century Welsh prince, Myrddin ab Morfryn, and the other Vortigern's prophet, Ambrosius, who figures in the *Historia Britonum* of " Nennius." Geoffrey used the name Merlinus for both these persons, and then proceeded to combine the stories about them as though they referred to a single individual. The Welsh prince is certainly the hero of his later *Vita Merlini*, but in the earlier *Historia Regum Britanniæ* it is Ambrosius who is uppermost in his mind ; in fact, in his first work he plainly says that Ambrosius was another name for Merlin.[2]

---

[1] The name is, I admit, indefensible, except on the grounds of euphony and popularity. But though I am prepared to champion most forlorn causes, I confess it seems hopeless now to substitute the appalling, yet more correct, Boudicca or Buddug.

[2] *Hist. Reg. Brit.*, VI, 19. On this subject see J. J. Parry, *The Vita Merlini*, Illinois, 1925, p. 113 ; Hans Matter, *Englische Gründungssagen von Geoffrey of Monmouth bis zur Renaissance* in *Anglistische Forschungen*, Hft. 58, Heidelberg, 1922, pp. 149 ff. ; W. W. Newell, *Publications of the Modern Language Assoc. of America*, XX

Now there is not one word about druidical training nor practice either in the *Historia* or in the *Vita*. In the last-named work it is said of Merlin *rex erat et vates*, he was a king and a prophet ; while in the *Historia* he is simply a prophet, only distinguished by his strange birth and his superior utterances from the other magicians of Vortigern. And these, it should be noted, share the name *magi* with other wise men living outside the druidic lands, the sooth-sayers of the Trojan settlers in Italy, for example.

In order, therefore, to give a druidic flavour to this story about Stonehenge, we must say that the tale relates to the Ambrosius of " Nennius," and that the dual rôle of sorcerer and adviser played by this person at the court of Vortigern in the 5th century suggests the degraded duties that might have appertained to the surviving druids, if there were any in England, at so late a date. But in " Nennius," it must be remembered, the word *magi* is used for such seers, and not druids ; so that even if it be granted that this Ambrosius was a druid in its ultimate sense of a simple magician, Geoffrey's tale is nevertheless separated by a period of about eight centuries from the last mention of the word druid in Gaul. And we are even further removed from the real and organised druidism that was flourishing in this country before the Roman occupation, of which it is very obvious neither Geoffrey nor " Nennius " knew anything at all.

But this is not everything. Geoffrey himself describes his Merlin-Ambrosius person as the son of a Christian prin-cess [1] who had been visited by an incubus ; [2] and if we go further back for information about his birth, and what manner of man he was, that is to say, if we enquire in the *Historia* of " Nennius," [3] we get still further away from the druids, for it is therein related that he was sprung from Roman parents of consular rank.

It is almost impossible, therefore, to see any trace in this story of Geoffrey's that can reasonably be held to reflect the

(N.S. XIII), Baltimore, 1905, No. 19—*Doubts Concerning the British History attributed to Nennius*, pp. 647 ff.

[1] *Hist. Reg. Brit.*, VI, 17.   [2] *Ibid.*, VI, 18.
[3] Nennius, *Hist. Brit.*, 42 (Stevenson, 1838).

tradition of a druidic origin of Stonehenge. Nor, in truth, can it even be said that there is anything in the legend to suggest that the monument was popularly connected with the *religious* ceremonies of the ancient Britons ; for it will have been noticed that in the tale it is explained simply as a memorial to dead heroes.

But whether one attaches any importance to it or not, this story represents the only popular belief ever current, so far as one can tell, about the monument before the beginning of the 17th century. At that time King James I became interested in Stonehenge, and the enquiries that he caused to be made into the origin of this astonishing ruin gave rise to a long series of theoretical disquisitions whose purport has considerable bearing upon our special subject, the growth of the current notion that it was the druids who built it. The first attempt to solve the mystery was made by Inigo Jones, the architect-general, who was ordered to the task by the King himself. Jones prepared a treatise on the subject that was drawn up in 1620 and published some thirty years later. At the outset he discusses the possibility of a druidic origin, but he does not bring this forward as a theory favoured by others or supported by any sort of tradition ; he mentions it incidentally as a supposition of his own, and it is dismissed in a page as an exceedingly improbable alternative to his decided opinion that the monument was Roman.

This disquisition was followed in 1663 by the admirable essay of Dr. Charleton, a court physician, who, though " reputed to have over-valued his Parts and Performances," was nevertheless acknowledged to be a person of great learning. He contended that the monument was built by the Danes for the consecration of their kings, a most popular conclusion in the days of a recently revived monarchy :—

Nor is thy Stone-Heng a less wonder grown,
Though once a Temple thought, now prov'd a Throne.
Since we, who are so bless'd with Monarchy,
Must gladly learn from thy Discovery,
That great Respects not only have been found
Where Gods were Worshipp'd, but where Kings were Crown'd.

But Dr. Charleton never even bothered his head with a possible druidic origin ; he was only at pains to disprove the Roman theory of Inigo Jones, and quite clearly the druids were not reckoned in his day as serious candidates for the honour of having built Stonehenge. Nor are they as much as mentioned in the tremendously vigorous counterblast prepared by John Webb, a relation by marriage and former pupil of Inigo Jones, who undertook to restore Stonehenge to the Romans ; this, I think, is really significant, because he goes out of his way to quote Dr. Aylett Sammes as supporting the theory of a Phœnician origin, Bishop Nicholson as thinking the monument Saxon, Aubrey as believing it to be British, and Bolton's guess that it was the tomb of Boadicea. Aubrey, as we shall see, did believe that the druids built Stonehenge, but his views and arguments were unpublished, and Webb knew nothing of them ; consequently there is not a word for or against the druids in his long and involved work.

The first person, then, to claim Stonehenge for the druids was the excellent and entertaining antiquary, John Aubrey (1626-1697), the portrait of whom is reproduced as the frontispiece. A mere statement of his opinion was published in Gibson's edition of *Camden's Britannia* in 1695, but his celebrated disquisition upon Stonehenge and Avebury was never given to the world, apparently because he was not satisfied with his knowledge of the rough stone monuments in other districts. This is a great pity, since it must have been a refreshing and intelligent document, far pleasanter reading than the angry and laboured arguments of Jones, Charleton, and Webb. "I come in the rear of all," wrote Aubrey, "by comparative arguments to give clear evidence that these monuments (Avebury, Stonehenge, and the like) were Pagan temples ; which was not made out before ; and have also with humble submission to better judgment, offered a probability that they were Temples of the Druids. . . . This enquiry, I must confess, is a groping in the dark ; but although I have not brought it into clear light, yet can I affirm that I have brought it from an utter darkness to a thin mist, and have gone further in this essay than anyone before me." [1] This is an admirable mood, and it is not surprising to find that both in description and conjecture he had written with care and acumen. For he was never obsessed with his druidic theory ; indeed, he seems at one time to have decided that the monuments were merely sepulchres, and was probably turned to his final opinion by Camden's remarks on the name Cerrig-y-Drudion. But what we shall notice with interest is that he himself was clearly of the opinion that he was the very first to think that Stonehenge was a druidic temple, for it is unlikely that we should have had such humble talk if there had been a scrap of folklore that could have been used as warrant for his view.

Although it was never completely published and explained, Aubrey's conclusion seems to have had more effect than there is controversy to show. I think there is no doubt that he influenced Dr. Plot, the historian of Staffordshire ; and Toland (1670-1722), who wrote a curious and rambling history of the druids, pays a pretty tribute to him as the only man he had met in his early days who, beside himself, had a right notion of these matters. And so, when the next and chief protagonist of the druids appears, there was no longer need to prove that Stonehenge was the work of this priesthood ; instead, it is tacitly assumed. Part of this assurance may be ascribed to the natural ebullience of the new author ; but if views other than his own held the day, he was not the one to pass them by unchallenged, and I am inclined to think that William Stukeley owed something of the startling success of his writings upon the druids to the increasingly favourable reception, just before his own day, of Aubrey's hypothesis. Not that there can have been direct influence, for Stukeley was but ten years old in 1697 when Aubrey died, and when his famous works upon Stonehenge and Avebury appeared in 1740 and 1743, he makes no acknowledgment of indebtedness to his predecessor ; indeed, the allusions to Aubrey in Stukeley's abundant writings are few and of the briefest sort.

[1] Aubrey, *Topographical Collections*, ed. J. E. Jackson, Devizes, 1862, p. 317.

If Aubrey was a somewhat diffident protagonist, Stukeley, at any rate, was headstrong and whole-hearted. The druids absorbed him. He even erected his own private druidic temple, a sylvan one, in his garden at Grantham; and his friends nicknamed him Chyndonax. With admirable ingenuity he mixed together a splendid hotch-potch of invention and surmise until he had brewed the legend of a community of all-powerful priests of an ultimate Phœnician origin, and professing the patriarchal religion of Abraham, who built stone temples in the form of sacred serpents; *Dracontia*, he said these serpent-fanes were called, though he had no authority at all in antiquity for the word in a

FIG. 2.—Medal with bust of Stukeley (obverse), and Stonehenge (reverse).

temple sense. And not only did he twist words, but he is also said to have twisted the very stones themselves to suit his theory, when he attempted the diagrammatic reconstruction of the remains; even Sir Richard Colt Hoare, who followed Stukeley and accepted most of his conclusions, was sometimes far from satisfied with the doctor's surveys and descriptions. But it is only fair to add that although he has been occasionally convicted of curling a tail out of a straight line of stones, or discovering the head of a snake where others have not been able to find anything at all, he has nevertheless won modern approval as a field-worker, for it is not very long ago that a particular series of measurements made by him had by chance to be repeated, whereupon the surveyors were able to record unequivocal testimony to the accuracy of the 18th century antiquary;[1] and there is certain positive achievement to his credit in this respect, for it was he who first pointed out the existence of the avenue and the cursus at Stonehenge, and who first grappled with the problem of the relation between the monument and the adjacent barrows.

But even so, I imagine present-day enthusiasts for the druids are not likely to praise over loudly the man who so nobly furthered the renaissance of their cult, since the imaginative doctor-clergyman is an advocate of dubious repute, and I doubt if any modern druid would be wise to appeal to Stukeley's archæological authority in the matter of stone monuments ; for it would not be difficult to compile an ugly little catalogue of his mistakes, and the outspoken aspersions of his contemporaries[2] and successors upon his over-confident method; and, although he must be freely pardoned for it, it is not easy to forget that it was he who stood sponsor for a document that later proved to be one of the most harmful forgeries that have ever been perpetrated, a none too happy augury for his pet theory.

But whether he was a good or a bad antiquary hardly matters ; it is enough that he was in earnest and that he was successful in the propagation of his doctrine ; more suddenly and completely successful than any other archæological teacher I can call to mind. No one seems to have disputed his main conclusion, although in the instance of Stonehenge an attempt was made to give it an astronomical flavour in 1771 by the Glasgow vaccinator, John Smith, the first of the exponents of the famous theory that the plan of the monument is in deliberate relation with the movements of heavenly bodies. This author dissented from Stukeley on certain minor points ; for instance, he did not believe that the altar stone was used for human sacrifice, his reason being simply that the altar would not bear fire. He tried

[1] See Mr. O. G. S. Crawford's remarks in *The Observer*, Sept. 23, 1923.

[2] The poet Gray, for instance, more than once refers uncompromisingly to Stukeley's " nonsense."

a fragment of it in a crucible and found that it first of all changed colour and then was reduced to a powder ; " very unfit surely for burnt offerings ! " he says.[1] And there were other variations of Stukeley's thesis, such as that of the Bath architect, John Wood, who hazarded that although Stonehenge was druidical, it was really a lunar temple with Diana as its goddess. In fact, the first directly opposed view was not put forward until almost exactly fifty years after Stukeley had published his book on Stonehenge ; this was the theory of John Pinkerton, a Scottish historian, who argued that the monument was Gothic.[2]

It was not only in Great Britain that Stukeley's notion found favour. Toland tells us that in his time none of the French megalithic monuments were attributed to the druids, but in 1805, when Cambry published his famous *Monumens Celtiques*, we find that he advocates the druidic origin of all the continental rough stone monuments. It is true that he does not directly express his indebtedness to Stukeley, but the reverend doctor is mentioned in such a way that there is little doubt that his writings must have provided the mainspring of Cambry's arguments.

If we except Pinkerton's work, we may say that Stukeley's theory held the field without a rival. Certainly no one seriously attempted to challenge the druids as builders of Stonehenge and other monuments, and they continued in splendid possession for wellnigh a hundred years after Stukeley's time. And it was natural enough that during this length of time popular fancy should adopt them as obviously the ideal priests for the tenantless altars and temples ; thus, with leisure to work its way unopposed throughout all the land, and with the argument of scholars in its support, the familiar fiction was formidable indeed ;

---

[1] Poor Stonehenge ! John Evelyn found the stone so hard that *all his strength with a hammer* could not detach a fragment.—*Diary*, July 22, 1654.

[2] Pinkerton was not really the first in the field with an alternative opinion, for John Bryant, in his *Analysis of Antient Mythology* (1776), suggests Stonehenge was much older than the druid theory implied ; but he only devoted a line or two to the subject, and can hardly be called the champion of a rival theory.

and there is nothing remarkable in its becoming at the beginning of the 19th century an article of general belief.

The moral of this story of the disputed origin of Stonehenge is very obviously that the now famous druidic theory, whether it be right or wrong, is not based on any sort of tradition, but is merely an invention of the late 17th century that was very successfully propagated during the next hundred years. In fact, before this period [1] the only person who seems to have considered it even as remotely likely was Inigo Jones, and he very summarily rejects it at the outset of his enquiry. It would be possible to cite other instances of what may be termed the pre-druidic notion of our megalithic monuments, such as that of the celebrated Kit's Coty House, near Maidstone in Kent. Quite recently I have seen this once more claimed for the druids, since it has the appearance of being the ruins of a small chamber (Fig. 38, p. 167), the kind of thing supposed by the modern friends of the order to have been either a sort of observatory or a cell of initiation. But I would point out that there is at least nothing traditional about this contention, for it differs *in toto* from the popular belief of other days ; this is related to us by Camden and by Stow, and their version is to the effect that the Coty was erected to mark the burial-place of a British prince Catigern, who fell near the site when fighting against the Saxons in the 5th century A.D. The druid theory, therefore, is simply a rival and subsequent *guess*, and it will later be shown that there are excellent archæological reasons proving that both guesses are wrong.

It is hardly necessary to add that there is little or no corroborative evidence suggesting that a prolonged folk-memory actually existed.[2] Thus I have not been able to discover any antique place-names embodying the notion of

---

[1] Cf. the testimony of Schedius and of Pufendorf (p. 21) and my remark about de Brebeuf (p. 24).

[2] This has, of course, been tested several times. In 1766 Professor Garden of Aberdeen, describing the stone circles of his district, treats the question of their origin in scientific fashion. He concludes : " I have found nothing hitherto, either in the names of these monuments or the tradition that goes about them, which doth particularly relate to the Druids or point them out."—*Archæologia*, I, 341.

druidic origin attached to sites of megalithic monuments. In this connection the most notorious name is Cerrig-y-Drudion in Denbighshire, for the second word is sometimes mis-spelt Druidion, and an inevitable confusion with the druids, initiated by the celebrated antiquary Camden (1551-1623), has resulted. Actually the name means *stones of the heroes*, and nothing more ; the megalithic monuments to which it refers have now disappeared, but a tradition in respect of one of them has survived, and it has nothing whatever to do with the druids, the legend being that it was used as a prison for the victims of the monstress Cynric Rwth. I have also come across Tre'r Dryw, translated Druidstown, in Anglesey, recently quoted again as an example, for there are said to be stone monuments near by ; but it is hardly possible to admit this instance, because the ancient meaning of Dryw is *wren*, and not druid, which is a more or less modern connotation.[1]   In England we have

---

[1] There is, however, a connection between wrens and druids, since the wren was a prophetic bird (see *Cormac's Glossary*, 60 ; on the word *dryw* see *Rev. Celtique*, XX, 340, and XLIII, 453).   Rowland (*Mona Antiqua*) spelt the name Tre'r Drew and translated it Druid's Mansion, claiming it was the site of the Archdruid's dwelling.   The word Drew does, of course, occur in the names of places where there are megaliths, as at Stanton Drew, but it should be no longer necessary to point out that it is merely a personal name, and not a variant of druid.   There are three examples, and in each instance it can be shown that the land belonged to a family called Drew (see Rev. J. E. Jackson in *Aubrey's Topographical Coll. for Wilts*, Devizes, 1862, p. 103, for the references to all three sites ; also Thurnam, in *Wilts. Arch. Mag.*, III (1856), 168 ; and Crawford, *Long Barrows of the Cotswolds*, 231).   The only place I know where tradition may really keep alive the memory of a druidic place of worship is at Chartres, and there it has nothing to do with megalithic remains.   But it is a fact that in the cathedral crypt one may visit a recess in the foundation of the masonry now called the Druids' Grotto, and, more important, a stela probably of Gaulish, i.e. druidic, date.   Legend has it that in pagan times the druids worshipped here the Mother of God (*la Vierge devant enfanter* or *Virgo paritura*), and up to the end of the 18th century a wooden image existed that was supposed to be the object of their adoration, though it was really of early mediæval date.   Legend also places the site of this druid worship at Fermincourt, near Dreux (Cochin, *Mem. Acad. Celt.*, IV, 1809), and this must surely add considerable interest to the fact that the first printed

Stoke Druid in Gloucestershire as a place-name, where megalithic remains are to be found, and if it could be traced back
beyond the period of the archæological advertisement of the
druids we might see in it some evidence of folklore. But
at the moment I have not succeeded in tracing it back at
all, and I am rather impressed by the fact that it seems to
have been quite unknown to Seyer, the historian of Bristol,
who described this particular ruined structure in considerable
detail in the year 1821.

Up to this point I have only attempted to show that in
disputing the claim that the druids built the stone monuments one is not adventuring against a formidable display
of folk-knowledge. There is, of course, a great deal more to
be said on the archæological aspect of the subject, and it is
possible that it may not be necessary to insist upon a complete divorce of the druids from all their " temples." But
here I am concerned solely with the traditional value of the
theory of druidic origin, and it will be convenient to postpone
further discussion for a later chapter.

The next point I want to make is that the theories of
Aubrey and Stukeley, however well they may explain many
modern notions, are not wholly responsible for them. To
discover the ultimate cause of the revival of interest in these
priests, and the secret of the success of such theories, it is
essential to search further than among the pronouncements
of individuals and to take stock of the altering outlook of
the times in which they were promulgated. This, I think,
can best be appreciated after a short survey of the rôle
played by the druids in literature.

At the end of the 4th century A.D. the word *druid* still
survived in the general literature of Roman Gaul, for it
occurs twice in the poems of Ausonius (see p. 97) in an
adjectival form that must clearly have been intelligible at
any rate to the professors to whom the poem is addressed.
But after the decline of the Empire and the passing of

book dealing with the druids (see below, p. 18) was written by a
priest of Dreux. It must also be remembered that this is the district
wherein the ancient druids held their annual assemblies (Caesar,
B.G., VI, 13).

Western Europe into the hands of the Teutonic immigrants, the traditional history of Gaul, and the works of the classical historians, were rapidly and completely forgotten ; so that as a result the druids do not re-appear again in any literature for a good many hundred years.

The word finally comes to light once more in the mediæval manuscripts of Ireland, where it had in all probability never ceased to circulate in the vulgar tongue,[1] while a supposed variant form, *derwydd*, is also found in a few early poems of the Welsh bards. In the 14th century, for example, the Irish scribe who translated the *Historia Britonum* of "Nennius" uses "druid" as the equivalent of *magi*, i.e. seers or magicians, in the original ; and there is no doubt that at about that time, and before it, the word was well known to the Irish clerks.

But in the original *Historia*, written about A.D. 800, the magicians of the 5th century king Vortigern were not called druids ; the Venerable Bede did not write of them in his *Ecclesiastical History*, and there is no mention of them

---

[1] It is to my mind much less likely that it was merely a borrowing by learned scribes from classical sources, or that the word was in any sense a Gallo-Roman importation. I am quite prepared to believe that in one form or another the name druid may have remained current in common Keltic speech ; but from the 5th century onwards there is no evidence that it had any significant traditional association with the ancient druids ; it merely referred to a person pre-eminent for magic or poetry. The etymology of the word is still uncertain. The orthodox view (Thurneysen, see Holder, *Altceltische Sprachschatz, s.v. druida*, D'Arbois de Jubainville, *Cours de la littérature celtique*, VI, 93, n. 2, and *Revue Celtique*, XXXI (1908), p. 83) takes *dru* as a strengthening prefix and *uid* as "knowing," so that a *druid* was a "very wise man." M. Camille Jullian, however, remarks (*Hist. de la Gaule*, II, p. 85, n. 7) that one should not exclude the possible significance of Pliny's fanciful derivation from the Greek δρῦς (see p. 89) ; for who knows, he asks, that the Gauls did not use a radical sounding like δρῦς as a word for oak. Dr. R. Much is of the same opinion, and called attention (*Mitt. Anthr.*, Wien, XXXVIII (1908), p. 46) to the Welsh *derw* (= oaks) (cf. Evans, *Welsh Dict., s.v. Derwydd*). On the other hand, Dr. Goldman suggested (*Mitt. Anthr.*, Wien, *ib.*, p. 47) an ingenious and not impossible Etruscan origin for the word, that would then signify "skilled in sacred things."

at all in any of the Saxon or early mediæval chronicles and romances. In England and on the continent, in fact, the Teutonic invasions had effectively obliterated all common knowledge of the ancient priesthood, and it stood little chance of revival as long as the church, the official fount of historical information, ignored the one possible source of enlightenment, the early Roman historians. This state of affairs is plainly revealed in the grossly unhistorical treatment of the subject-matter of the Arthurian cycle, wherein the druids might reasonably have found mention had the mediæval authors consulted the classical material relating to the periods they were describing.

Thus, except for the occasional use of the name in a debased sense by the Irish schoolmen, and, more doubtfully, by the Welsh bards, it seems safe to say that throughout a long period from the 4th to the 16th century the original druids of antiquity had wellnigh passed from man's memory.

At length, however, the time came that the common classical sources of information were more frequently consulted, and as an inevitable consequence the knowledge that there had once been priests called druids gradually became general among educated folk. And if one watches for the early mentions of the druids in popular work, it can fairly easily be seen that their name creeps in rather as a morsel of this casual erudition than as a concession to vulgar predilection.

In England the period of oblivion from the 4th century onwards is not interrupted, to the best of my knowledge, until the year 1509, when the druids were included in the complement of Barclay's *Ship of Fools ;* but they only get in at second-hand, and four lines is their portion :—

> Or as the Druydans rennyth in vayne about
>   In theyr mad festes upon the hylle of yde
> Makynge theyr sacrafyce with furour noyse and shout
>   Whan theyr madnes settyth theyr wyt asyde.

On the continent they were brought once more, after their long oblivion, to the notice of scholars by the *Annales Boiorum* of Aventinus (Johann Turmaier), who completed this celebrated work about the year 1521. The druids are described as Gaulish philosophers driven out of Gaul into Germany by the Emperor Tiberius, and this is really all that Aventinus has to say about them ; but the *Annales* are so frequently quoted by later writers,[1] that the book may in justice be signalled as the starting-point [2] of the awakening interest in the druids that resulted from the renaissance of learning.

It would be difficult to imagine Rabelais omitting any discoverable name, so that it is not surprising that he should mention the ancient druids two or three times in *Pantagruel*, that was written about 1532. His source was obviously Cæsar, as can be seen from the passage, " If you fancy Mercury (*sic*) to be the first inventor of arts as our ancient Druids believed of old," [3] for it is borrowed directly from the Sixth Book of the *Gallic War*.

In the half-century after the appearance of *Pantagruel*, there were published several learned treatises of antiquarian interest in which reference was made to the druids. The first of which I have record was a book in French verse by Jean Le Febure of Dreux, called *Les Fleurs et Antiquités des Gaules*, published in 1532 ; this must have been a very interesting book, and a very important one in the druidical bibliography, since it is said to have been principally devoted to a description of the druids, or ancient philosophers of Gaul ; but, unfortunately, there does not seem to be any copy still existing.[4] The next important book appeared over forty years later ; [5] this was the *Historiæ Brytannicæ Defensio*

---

[1] It seems to have been Aventinus who started the curious legend about the druid's shoe. See *Annales*, ed. Cisner, Frankfurt, 1627, p. 68 ; and, in the same work, *Nomenclatura, s.v. Druides*.

[2] There was nothing about the druids in the *Germaniæ Exegeseos* (Hagenoae, 1518) of Franciscus Irenicus.

[3] Rabelais, *Oeuvres*, ed. Moland, Paris, 1884, p. 454. Cf. *B.G.*, VI, 17, " Minervam operum atque artificiorum initia tradere."

[4] See *Bibliotheque de la Croix du Maine* (ed. de Juvigny, Paris, 1772, I, 495). Le Febure was a priest and a native of Dreux. The work was apparently unknown to Cochin, who wrote an article on the antiquities of Dreux (*Mem. de l'Acad. celtique*, IV (1809), 453).

[5] In the meantime Leland had compiled an excellent summary of the classical references to druids and druidism, but this remained

(1573), by Sir John Price, who suggested that as *pryduides* (*prydydd*, a poet) was an alternative name for the Welsh bards, these must be the same folk as those called druids by the ancients. This volume was accompanied by the *De Mona Druidum Insula* of Humphrey Llwyd, in which one or two of the classical references to druidism were repeated. Four years afterwards, in 1577, Holinshed offered some fanciful remarks about what he termed the *Druyish* religion, but he was evidently aware that ordinary people knew nothing whatever about the priests themselves ; and the same may be said of that careful antiquary Camden (1586), who can be trusted to have recorded any folklore that came to his ears.

In the meantime Étienne Forcadel had published his *De Gallorum Imperio* (1579), a book that set forth much of the classical information about the druids ; and this was followed in France by the *Histoire de l'Estat et Republique des Druides* (1585) of Noel Taillepied, an amusing book that describes the druids as an aristocracy ruling Gaul from about the year 2800 after the creation of the world (i.e. roughly 1200 B.C.) to the year A.D. 16.

But all these works were heavy antiquarian treatises and the next popular reference to the druids after their mention in the works of Rabelais seems to be that in the *Felicitie of Man* (1598), by Barckley, who speaks of a woman " that was a Soothsayer of them which were called Druides," an explanatory remark that illustrates tolerably well my contention that the word druid reappears in literature as the result of the increased attention given by scholars to the classical historians, and not as a contribution from popular traditional knowledge.

in MS. until the 18th cent. (*Commentarii de Scriptoribus Britannicis*, Oxford, 1709, Chaps. I-III). Leland assumed that druidism flourished in England until the conversion of Lucius Magnus to Christianity (see Geoffrey of Monmouth, *Hist. Reg. Brit.*, IV, 19-VI, 1) ; Merlin he classed as a bard, or possibly (he suggests) a *vates*. Another work that appeared in this interval was the *De Prisca Celtopædia* of Picard de Tontry (1556) ; it is cited by Jullian, *Hist. de la Gaule*, II, p. 86, n. 2 (5th ed.), but I have not seen it myself.

As a matter of fact, at this period the only practical interest taken in the druids seems to have been aroused by the French antiquary Guenebauld, who claimed that he had found the tomb of an archdruid called Chyndonax. This discovery was a very exciting affair that attracted considerable attention ; it took place in 1598 on Guenebauld's vineyard near a Roman road in the vicinity of Dijon, and consisted of a cylindrical stone coffer, about a foot in height, that contained a glass cinerary urn. On the base of the coffer was a Greek inscription mentioning Mithras and also a name interpreted by Guenebauld as Chyndonax, who, because he was described as a chief priest, was assumed to have been necessarily an important druid. Guenebauld himself published this find some years later in a delightful little book, complete with illustrations, which seems, since it is of earlier date than Sir Thomas Browne's *Hydrotaphia*, to be one of the first treatises in the history of transalpine archæology that dealt with the problems of a single excavation. The authenticity of the inscription has been questioned, although it is rather difficult to understand why, and, needless to say, the coffer itself is now lost ; but as a Roman cemetery, whose existence was unknown to Guenebauld, was discovered over 200 years later on the site, the funeral apparatus must have been genuine enough. However this may be, Chyndonax the Druid became a real person to a great many people at the end of the 16th century and at the beginning of the 17th ; and on more than one occasion he was saluted in verse :—

> Felicem Druydam, qui tot post saecula vivit,
> Quemque per ora virum fata volare jubent !

But this, as I have said, is the only instance at so early a date where any sort of popular attention seems to have been devoted to the druids ; and even after this discovery I daresay that outside Burgundy no one bothered about Chyndonax except a few scholars and theological disputants.

By this time, however, the learned world was beginning to occupy itself seriously in the problems of druidism, and throughout the 17th century, just as in the later half

FIG. 3.—TITLE-PAGE OF *DE DIS GERMANIS*, BY SCHEDIUS

of the 16th, a number of works appeared that dealt with the priesthood. But books of this kind are evidence of nothing more than an academic study of the classical historians ; and the manner in which the subject is approached, at any rate in the first half of the century, makes it tolerably clear that it was deemed to be one not as yet generally familiar.

The first work in the new century that treated of the druids was an oration of Francois Meinard, the Frisian, that was printed in 1615,[1] and set forth the claims of the druidic mistletoe to be henceforth regarded as the emblem of jurisprudence. But much more important was the great work *De Dis Germanis*,[2] by the German youth Elias Schedius (1615-1641), in which as many as twenty-six chapters were devoted to a study of druidism ; for Schedius believed that the Germans had had their druids just like the Kelts. Two chapters deal with the probable kind of altar used by the druids, and it is important to remark, in view of the modern superstition on this subject, that in the 17th century *turf*, and not *stone*, was thought to be the chosen material. This notion of a turf altar in the middle of a grove is re-stated in an engaging pamphlet on the druids by the diplomat Esaias Pufendorf of Chemnitz, a work written as a university thesis, and first printed in 1650.[3] Pufendorf's charming study had the luck to be brilliantly translated in the last century by Edmund Goldschmid,[4] and in its English form his little book deserves to be better known.

The next work of interest here was the *Originum Gallicarum Liber* of the Dutchman, Marcus Boxhorn, that was published at Amsterdam in 1654 ; the greater part of it is philological and not directly concerned with the druids, but it contains an appendix in the form of a long Latin poem

[1] *Orationes Legitimae : I. Oratio solemnis de visco Druidarum iurisprudentiae symbolo.* Poitiers, 1615.

[2] Amsterdam, 1648. The earlier and gloriously illustrated book by Cluverius, *Germania Antiqua* (Lugduni Batavorum, 1616), contains only two or three brief references to the druids.

[3] It was later included in the *Opuscula a iuvene lucubrata*, Halae Hermundurorum, 1699.

[4] Privately printed. Edinburgh, 1886.

that purports to set forth a system of druidic philosophy. A continental work of greater significance appeared two years later ; this was written by Jean Picard of Tours,[1] who treated the problem of the druids in a severely historical fashion, transcribing in full many of the classical references to them. In the meantime, a short article, *De Origine Druidum*, by Henry Jacob, a Fellow of Merton College, had been published in England in the *Delphi Phœnicizantes* (Oxford, 1655), a work of which Edmund Dickinson claimed to be the author ; and a few years later another little book on druidism, also in Latin, came from Oxford ; it was written by Thomas Smith of Magdalen,[2] and its principal interest is that it names Camden, the 16th century antiquary, as the pioneer in the revival of the study of the druids. There is yet a third Oxford book to be mentioned, namely, *The Court of the Gentiles*,[3] by Theophilus Gale, for it contained a short section on the druids, and, since it was written in English, may well have given them some publicity.

But at this period the druids were no longer in need of such advertisement—at any rate in this country. For the 17th century had witnessed, as well as the continued interest of scholars, the gradual spreading in England of a vague popular notion of the druids as the ancient poet-priests of Britain. This recognition was not directly due to any one scholar's work, and I am inclined to think it must be almost wholly ascribed to the choice by Beaumont and Fletcher of an Early British theme for a tragedy. The performance in 1618 of *Bonduca* must have presented a picture of the druids in a form that could not fail to win for them a considerable

---

[1] *De Prisca Celtopaedia*, Paris, 1556.

[2] *Syntagma de Druidum moribus ac institutis*, London, 1664.

[3] Oxford, 1669 and 1671. See Pt. II, Bk. I, Ch. V, 78-82. There were one or two other works on the druids published in the closing years of the century. Of these the *De Philosophia Celtica* of J. C. Kuhn (1676) is a dull tract of fourteen pages ; there was also the *Disputatio de Gallorum veterum Druidibus* (Upsala, 1689), by Peter Lägerlof (a work I have not seen). More interesting than Kuhn's book, though not much longer, was the *Veterum Instituta Druidum*, by Elias Eyring (1697) ; this includes a reading of the suspected inscription (Orelli, 2200) from the Moselle (p. 100).

amount of popular attention, and from that date onwards it is idle to pretend that their name could not have been generally familiar. Thus it is possible that when Henry Jacob wrote in the middle of the 17th century that there was no one in whose ears their fame had not resounded,[1] he may well have been referring to something more than their repute in the world of scholars.

Bonduca, then, is certainly a landmark in the story of the revival of popular interest in the druids. Of course, the part played in it by the druids is indirectly a result of the labours of scholars, because these had enabled Fletcher to use the works of the classical writers, especially Tacitus, as sources for his story ; whereas Shakespeare, because he had taken the story of his *Cymbeline* largely from mediæval romances, consequently did not bring the druids at all into his play dealing with the same period.

The first scene of the third act of *Bonduca* is laid in a *Temple of the Druids*, and begins with a solemn entry of the druids singing ; and it will be noticed that song seems to be their principal function. " Now sing, ye Druides ! " commands Caratach ; and in another place Bonduca exclaims—

> Rise from the dust, ye relics of the dead,
> Whose noble deeds our holy druids sing.

And in the first act Caratach refers to

> The holy Druides composing songs,
> Of everlasting life to victory.

This notion of the druids as being primarily bards gained further currency in Milton's *Lycidas* (1637) :—

> Where were ye, Nymphs, when the remorseless deep
> Clos'd o'er the head of your lov'd Lycidas ?
> For neither were ye playing on the steep,
> Where your old Bards, the famous druids, ly—

and in England it remained firmly established for close upon a hundred years.

In France, on the other hand, it is likely that a popular knowledge of the druids was achieved more slowly, and, when

---

[1] *Loc. cit.*, p. 33.

established, it was probably a more precise notion of them than that obtaining in this country. The principal factor must have been the translation of Lucan's *Pharsalia* by de Brebeuf (1656), for this would render the well-known passage describing the druids (p. 88) familiar in substance to a good many Frenchmen. And it is interesting to note, as an appendix to a subject already mentioned, that at this period in the 17th century the current idea in France must still have been that groves, and not stone temples, were the places of worship of these priests.[1]

> Au milieu du silence et des bois solitaires
> La Nature en secret leur ouvre ses mystères.

As a reinforcement of this view (which was already clearly established in Pufendorf's *Dissertatio*, and in the earlier work of Schedius), the same poem contains the famous and magnificent description of the horrible druidic forest at Marseilles, so fearsome a place that—

> Les voisins de ce bois si sauvage et si sombre
> Laissent à ses Démons son horreur et son ombre,
> Et le Druide craint en abordant ces lieux
> D'y voir ce qu'il adore et d'y trouver ses Dieux.

But in England, as I say, the idea of the druids as a kind of prophetic bard prevailed for a hundred years after Milton wrote *Lycidas*. It is true that at the beginning of the 18th century Addison refers once in the *Tatler* [2] to the " Druid of the family " in a context that shows he was using the word in the sense of a priest ; but William Diaper, in 1713, returned to the more popular notion—

> With sacred miselto the Druids crown'd
> Sung with the Nymphs, and danced the pleasing Round.[3]

[1] The grove-idea was always more popular in France than in England. Courier, for instance, in one of the *Censeur* letters of 1819, mentions a " M. Marcellus," who regarded his native forests as a memorial of the druids, and would not allow a single tree to be cut. P.-L. Courier, *Lettres au redacteur du Censeur*, V, Nov. 1819. For that matter, it is still current in France and in the wooded districts of Northern Spain (especially in Galicia, so my friend Dr. Pericot tells me).

[2] *Tatler*, No. 255 (1710).

[3] *Dryades : or the Nymphs' Prophecy*, London, 1713, p. 15.

And so did Thomas Coke in 1726—

> Thrice happy land [Kent], 'tis here the Druids sing,

and—

> He walked a God amids't th' admiring Throng,
> The darling Subject of the Druids' Song.[1]

In the middle of the 18th century there took place that very remarkable revival of interests in the druids upon which I have already commented in connection with the theories of the origin of Stonehenge. Aubrey, who first suggested the druids as builders of the monument, had died in 1697, and it was not until over forty years later that Stukeley's famous exposition appeared to achieve for this theory almost universal acclamation and acceptance. But in the meantime the ground had been prepared by the publication of several books of antiquarian argument and disquisition that differed from those of the preceding century in that they were intended for a wider public than the few students of the ponderous Latin treatises of earlier days. One of the first was Thomas Brown's dissertation on Mona that was included in Sacheverell's *Account of the Isle of Man* (1702), and another was Henry Rowland's *Mona Antiqua Restaurata* (1723). In 1726 came Toland's *History of the Druids*, and a year afterwards France had *La religion des Gaulois tirée des plus pures sources de l'antiquité*, by Dom Martin (1727). By the turn of the half-century there had also appeared the important work of Frick (1744), that included reprints of several earlier essays on druidism, Sir Thomas Carte's *History of England* (1747), containing a full account of the druidic order as it was known to the ancient writers, and Simon Pelloutier's *Histoire des Celtes*, which, curiously enough, had very little to say about druids.

A point had clearly been reached, therefore, when a knowledge of the druids was no longer an incidental product of historical research among the classical authors, but was in itself the subject of a fairly general interest, a period, that is to say, wherein most educated folk would have some knowledge of the ancient Keltic inhabitants of the country.

[1] *The Bath*, Dublin, 1726, p. 3.

Now within twenty years of the publication of Stukeley's book on Avebury in 1743, Gray's famous poem, *The Bard*, had appeared, Mason had published his *Caractacus*, and, more important even than *The Bard*, Macpherson's *Ossian* (" Fingal," 1761) was in circulation, a work there and then destined to compel the chiefs of literary Europe, either in angry defiance or in triumphant delight, to an investigation of the mythology of the ancient Keltic world.

There was nothing about druidism in *Ossian*, there was nothing directly about druidism in *The Bard*, but they advanced the cause of the druids and promoted a popular affection for them more thoroughly than any archæological treatise could have done. It is, in fact, to this early *romantic* poetry that we should properly attribute the astonishing success of the laborious theories of Stukeley and other archæologists. Such poetry was an evidence of the turning of men's minds away from the old familiar classical mythology and the rigours of the classical formulæ in letters and art ; and the signal for a movement towards the freedom of Keltic wildness, of the chill grand landscapes of the north peopled with hoary bards and with rude chieftains, and the mysterious haunting creatures of Keltic mythology.[1]

The Romantic Movement, then, is the ultimate cause of the revived interest in the druids that we have witnessed in the 18th century, the secret of that strange power they have exercised ever since over popular fancy. The string of books concerning them, and the list of allusions to them in general literature that followed the turning-point in the story of the revival (1750), are much too long to be recited here. But as evidence of their renown soon after this date, it will suffice to mention the production at the Théâtre-Français in 1772 of a tragedy, *Les Druides*, by Le Blanc de Guillet (Antoine Blanc), and of Fisher's *Masque of the Druids*, at Covent Garden (1774 and 1775), and the revival of *Bonduca* in 1778.

Their fame, however, was destined to be even greater

[1] On this subject see the excellent little book, *The Celtic Revival in English Literature*, by E. D. Snyder (Cambridge, Mass., 1923). I most gratefully acknowledge my indebtedness to this work for many of the references quoted here.

than that afforded them by the theatre. For not only was
their ancient glory recalled, but their religion also ; and it
had many votaries. An important factor in the romantic
movement had been the renewed study of Welsh bardic
poetry,[1] promoted chiefly by Lewis Morris (1700-1765) and
Evan Evans (1731-1789), and it was not very long before
it was suggested that the mediæval bards were the repositories and servants of an ancient and mystical religion, of
druidism, in fact. The tenets of this Bardism were formulated
in 1792 by William Owen Pugh in *Llywarc Hen*, but the chief
exponent of the new faith was Iolo Morganwy (1746-1826),
who not only accepted the greater part of the bardic traditions as a survival from the days of the druids, but also
claimed that he himself was directly descended from them.

The supposed bardic religion was eventually developed
into a system in which druidism, so far as it is discoverable
in the classical sources, and the patriarchal faith of the
Scriptures were ingeniously combined. At the beginning of
the 19th century this helio-arkite theology was most successfully championed by the Rev. Edward Davies,[2] and afterwards by Algernon Herbert,[3] who gave it the name by which
it is now known, neo-druidism. But there is no need to
describe its later progress and complicated ramifications ; it
will be sufficient to remark that an important general consequence of the movement was the conversion of the ancient
bardic *gorsedd* into a *druidic* institution, so that the gathering
of the poets at the Eisteddfod became a full-dress ceremony
of the druids, and was, and still is, particularly effective in
keeping their memory fresh in the popular imagination.

It is necessary, however, to say a word about the basic
assumption that the mediæval Welsh bards were a direct
continuation of the druidic hierarchy, for this is not by any
means an extravagant or ridiculous belief. The druids of
old were very closely connected with the bardic profession ;
much of their lore was doubtless transmitted by means of

---

[1] The story of this revival is outlined by Sir J. Morris-Jones in
Y Cymmrodor, 28 (1918), p. 10 ff.
[2] *Celtic Researches* (1804) ; *Mythology of the British Druids* (1809).
[3] *The Neo-Druidic Heresy* (1838).

poetry, they are more than once named together with the bards, and it is even possible that as their sacerdotal powers vanished they may have been to some extent merged in the bardic class. Moreover, as Matthew Arnold pointed out,[1] the very fact of the existence of an elaborate poetical system right at the beginning of the mediæval literary history of Wales seems to indicate a clear and persistent tradition of an older poetical period, and one is irresistibly led to think of the druidic system described by Cæsar. But such considerations cannot be taken to imply that the servile Keltic bard of the kind known to us in the Middle Ages was necessarily descended from bards included in the druidic order. For whatever the druids may have been, or may have become, professional bardism is something recognisable and distinct. Even in their distant past the Kelts seem to have employed poets in a purely secular capacity, and who were in no way concerned with the druidic functions (see p. 134) ; thus it is obvious that the survival of the calling of the professional bard is only a token of ancient Keltic custom, and not a proof of connection with druidism.

The most that can reasonably be claimed is that *some* bards of special distinction may have been possessed of the remnants of the druidic doctrines. But even on this point the evidence is not convincing, and it would be almost impossible to demonstrate that any of the mediæval Welsh poets and poetasters were the conscious possessors of a scrap of the ancient druidic lore. The existing manuscripts of their poems do not date back beyond the 12th century, and it may be safely said that there is nothing in the poetry of that period, even in those of the pieces that have a traditional flavour of the earlier centuries, or in those that are ascribed to 6th century bards, to warrant the belief that the poets themselves knew anything at all about ancient druidism as an organised religion. All that can be adduced on this score is that in the 12th century and afterwards the bards sometimes, not very frequently, called themselves *derwyddon*, which may, or may not, be a form of *druids ;* but, to my

---

[1] *On the Study of Keltic Literature* (Works, ed. 1903, V, p. 45).

mind, there is not the slightest suggestion that those to whom the term was applied enjoyed the reputation of being members of, or even connected with, the ancient priesthood.

This question of Bardism and Druidism has already been treated in thorough fashion by writers of much learning,[1] and I do not propose to pursue the enquiry here. But I cannot help remarking with regret that Neo-druidism, with all its extravagances and impostures, has rendered the delightful study of Keltic tradition in Wales a wearisome and ungrateful task for a student in earnest search of druidic survival. I believe myself that bardic tradition and bardic custom is the most important of the several fields in which one might legitimately seek to achieve contact with real druidism. But the blundering enthusiasm that pretends this contact is already proved, and the consequent prejudice of scholars against enquiry in this direction, are indeed formidable obstacles in the way of an ordinary examination of the material.

In this chapter I have tried to test several methods whereby one might forge a link, traditionally, with the druids, and I have not been able to claim any success. It is necessary, therefore, to add that I have no special reason for wanting to prove that such a link cannot exist. But I am impressed by the remarkable stirring of popular opinion engendered by Romanticism, which I believe to be directly responsible for the many druid-cults of to-day ; and this must of necessity lead to a profound suspicion of every alleged tradition that has become involved with the movement.

To sum up, I think it may be said that the testimony of the druidical literature is plain enough. For England it has shown that the Saxon invasion blotted out the memory of the druids, leaving, so far as our records go, no trace of them in popular tradition, either as regards sites of their former worship or vestiges of their lore ; and it has shown that a knowledge of the former existence of the priesthood was

---

[1] D. W. Nash, *Taliesin : or the Bards and Druids of Britain*, London, 1858, esp. pp. 330 ff. ; Matthew Arnold, *loc. cit.*, pp. 26 ff. ; Jules Leflocq, *Etudes de mythologie celtique*, Orleans, 1869, pp. 115 ff. ; Thomas Stephens, *Literature of the Kymry*, London, 1876, pp. 84 ff.

regained slowly and laboriously in the 16th century as a result of the return to the study of the ancient historians. And it has shown that the theory, now so popular, that the druids built the megalithic monuments, was an invention of the late 17th century, successfully promulgated, in the succeeding century, by Romanticism.

With this much achieved as a preliminary, we can proceed to a study of the druids in antiquity.

CHAPTER II

PREHISTORY

FROM the ancient historians we gather this much about original druidism—that Britain was reputed to be its fountain-head, and that its priests in Gaul were famous as philosophers as early as the beginning of the 2nd century B.C. As a matter of fact, all that we hear directly of the British druids is that there were priests of that name in Anglesey in the 1st century A.D. ; but there was a great deal written about the Gallic druids, who continued to be very important persons up to the time of Cæsar, although their power vanished soon afterwards.

To this little stock of knowledge is added the statement that there were no druids in the lands of the Germans ; and it is also to be remarked that there is no literary evidence of their existence either in Italy or in Spain.

Thus it may be said that the period of their greatest ascendancy lies within the compass of the first few centuries B.C., and that their influence was confined to Gaul and Britain. As a corollary of this, it is usually held that they were the priests of the Kelts, or rather of the British and Gallic sections of the Keltic-speaking peoples. For the period of their maximum influence corresponds reasonably closely with that of the Keltic supremacy in Western Europe ; and the word druid itself, in related forms such as *drui, drai, draoi*, and *dryw*, is current in modern and mediæval Keltic tongues.

The subject of the connection between the Kelts and the druids is of great importance as regards the origin of druidism, and its study is certainly one of the principal interests of this book ; but it is not one that can be directly approached. In fact, it will be best to reserve the debate of this problem until after the discharge of the two other tasks that confront the student of the ancient druids. For, first of all, it is necessary to become acquainted with the peoples who inhabited Gaul and Britain at the time of, and before, the druids, and at the same time to take stock of the outside influences likely to have affected their behaviour and beliefs ; then, secondly, we must examine in detail the classical evidence relating to the druids themselves. Only after these preliminary investigations can we attempt to set forth our knowledge of druidism in general terms, and to discuss its origin in the light of the ethnological and historical material at our command.

In this chapter I propose to deal with the first of these matters, namely, the ancient population of the lands wherein druidism manifested itself. But to avoid an unprofitably long diversion from the main subject, I shall not attempt a summary of the whole prehistory of the area ; instead, I shall take up the story at a point in the Bronze Age somewhere about 1500 B.C., that is to say, at a period after the savage cultures of the Stone Age hunting folk had been superseded by the higher agricultural civilisation of the Bronze Age.

This civilisation was introduced gradually, and not everywhere in the same manner nor by the same people. Ultimately, it must be attributed to the influence of the still higher civilisations of the East ; but in Western Europe it is only a faint and distant reflection of Mesopotamian, Egyptian, and Ægean cultures, and we have no practical interest either in this remote origin, or in the complicated borrowings whereby it was eventually transmitted into our northern lands.

Naturally, in Gaul and in Britain the Bronze Age was ushered in with the inevitable disturbance and traffic consequent upon so notable a cultural advance. But after the stimulus afforded to Western European civilisation by the initial spread of new ideas, and after the economic upheaval caused by the propagation of a new source of wealth, there

FIG. 4.—Map of Gaul and Britain.

was gradually developed a group of agricultural peoples who possessed the land in a prosperous and relatively unadventurous peace.

It is important for our purpose to understand that this Bronze Age population of Gaul and Britain was in reality a composite of separate cultures of varying degrees of development. No doubt the major element in the population may everywhere have been the descendants of the ancient Stone Age folk ; and, accordingly, it is possible that there existed sufficiently strong racial and linguistic affinities throughout the whole area to justify the inclusion of all its occupants in a single Bronze Age civilisation. But a single civilisation may consist of provinces that vary according to the different influences exerted upon each ; and it is a fact that the provinces of Bronze Age Gaul were far from being alike.

To the west of the Seine and the Rhône the indigenous folk had been very largely affected by the activity of the metal trade in Spain and Portugal, and the coming and going of traffic along the Atlantic trade-route that had united the megalithic cultures of the Peninsula, of Western and South-Western France, and of Britain and Ireland. Together, these regions formed a *western province* that remained a cultural entity throughout the Bronze Age ; though towards the end of the period Spanish influence lessened, as its component cultures grew more and more self-centred, while the cultures of Brittany and of Ireland became increasingly important. But such fluctuations could not break the link forged by the traffic and exploration of the earlier megalithic period in the dawn of the Metal Era, and for many centuries to come new fashions and new customs could travel rapidly from one end of the province to the other. Furthermore, we must not fail to observe that the connection with Spain made all parts of it accessible to influences from outside travelling either along the North African coast or directly across the Mediterranean.

A second, or *south-eastern*, archæological province of the Bronze Age in Gaul was the country lying between the Rhône from Lyon to the sea and the modern French-Italian frontier.[1] Here there was no trace of the great megalithic culture that had flourished in the western province, and the affinities of the people were directed towards the neighbouring cultures of the Genoese Gulf and the plain of Northern Italy. The province is, in fact, Transalpine Liguria, and its people may be safely called Ligurians. It is they who are famous for the extraordinary number of bronze sickles that have been found in their territory, so notable a quantity that it is customary to speak of them as the most industriously agricultural people of prehistoric Europe.

The third, or *eastern*, province lay north of the bend of the Rhône, and occupied the greater part of eastern and North-Eastern France. It was not, at any rate at first, a culture equally distributed, and many districts of this vast area, as, for example, the Sénonais, seemed to have lagged behind in a wretched flint-culture ; but as one approaches the Rhône and the Rhine, especially in the advanced Bronze Age, one encounters the remains of a flourishing people whose culture was undeniably affected both by the adjacent Ligurians and also by the Bronze Age peoples of Eastern Germany. This province, therefore, while it certainly possessed a virile indigenous population (see p. 70), was the gateway into Gaul of the transrhenan cultures, and, as such, it was destined to play a very important part in the formation of the later Gallic civilisation.

Our own island presents a meeting-ground of the extended cultures of the western and the eastern provinces ; for Brittany and Ireland, on the one hand, and North-Eastern Gaul on the other, were all instrumental in the formation of the British Bronze Age culture. As a natural consequence of this twofold source, the British culture is unequal, Cornwall, for instance, showing close affinities with Brittany, while in East Anglia there are plainer signs of Rhineland influence. But it is a mistake to suppose because of the somewhat arbitrary distribution of various Bronze Age customs and small commodities that the country was overrun

---

[1] This culture may well have extended further northwards ; for a summary of the evidence, see René Gadant, *La Religion des Éduens et le monument de Mavilly*. Autun, 1922.

by invasions corresponding with every change of fashion. Thus the alteration in burial methods following the introduction of cremation is simply due to the gradual spread of the custom from Brittany and the Channel Islands,[1] and is, at first, commonest in South-West England, where it is impossible to correlate it with a distinct superposed culture-complex, such as one should be able to recognise if the rite had been introduced by an invading folk. On the other hand, the invention of the socket for axes and other articles was probably brought to our country along the Rhine trade-route, just in the same way as a few of the exotic *winged* axes, or occasional axes of Italian type, also travelled north.

However, of all the lands we have considered, that is to say, of Gaul and Britain and Ireland, the district furthest removed during the Bronze Age from the immediate invasion of new customs, new inventions, and new philosophies, was our own island. Whatever novelty of thought, or change in attitude towards the sacred, came to this country from the outer world must have been transmitted through the medium of the adjacent cultures of Ireland and of Gaul, and no innovation would be likely to have reached our shores until it had first been digested by the outside Bronze Age world. That is to say, Britain would be less susceptible to important and revolutionary innovation during the second millenium B.C. than any other part of the future lands of the druids ; it was, in fact, the district best suited by virtue of its position for the formation of a specialised religion, and its conservation throughout this period. This is a point on which stress may reasonably be laid, seeing that Britain happens to be the land in which, so Cæsar was told, the druidical *disciplina*, or doctrine, originated.

[1] It may be ultimately due to Alpine influence exerted along the famous trade-route, Swiss Lakes, Pressigny (i.e. Central France), Brittany. The leaf-shaped sword is another invasion-bogey of the British Bronze Age, but this, having first of all been copied from North Italian or Central European models, became the common property of the whole of the northern provinces of Europe, and its dissemination throughout the west seems to be a natural and inevitable consequence of the normal Bronze Age traffic.

Of the other provinces, it is to be noted that many writers have emphasized the peaceful domestic character of the Ligurian culture, some arguing on the grounds of their supposed religion, and others on the composition of the bronze hoards found in their territory. In the last respect, a famous example is the Briod (Jura) [1] hoard of 269 pieces of bronze, whereof 256 were sickles and only three were weapons (one fragment of a sword and two small spearheads) ; and another is the Larnaud (Jura) [2] hoard of 1485 pieces, among which there were not more than 126 fragments of swords and spearheads. Of course, an argument based on the composition of these and other hoards is not entirely convincing ; a good deal depends on whether the axe be styled a weapon or not, and whether the hoards compared are of approximately equal date ; nevertheless, the preponderance of the agricultural implements in this area [3] deserves to be contrasted with finds in other lands like the great hoard of over a hundred bronze swords and daggers from Huelva,[4] in the south of Spain, or such British hoards as that found at Blackmoor,[5] in Hampshire, where a collection of 61 pieces included only five objects that were not parts of swords or spears. And if it be right to assume on these grounds that the Ligurians were an essentially peaceful people, we may conjecture further that they had nothing to do with the origin of druidism. For one of the principal objects of the druidical doctrine, so we are told, was the encouragement of bravery in war, and we are left in no doubt about the sympathy of the druids with military ideals ; so that it looks as though their religion could hardly have been developed on Ligurian soil.

[1] *Congr. préhist. de France*, 9 Sess. (1913), Lons-le-Saunier, p. 443.
[2] *Ibid.*, p. 451.
[3] Similar hoards have been found outside the area, but they were probably Ligurian importations. An example is the hoard of 92 sickles found at Bösel, Kr. Lüchow, in the north German plain.
[4] *Revue Archéologique*, 5, S. XVIII (1923), 222 ; *Bol. R. Acad. Hist.* (Madrid), LXXXIII (1923), 89 ; *Actas y Mem. Soc. Española de Antropologia*, II (1923), 37 ; *Buttleti Assoc. Catalana d'Antropologia*, II (1924), 223.
[5] Evans, *Ancient Bronze Impts.*, London, 1881, pp. 460 and 464.

The end of the Bronze Age is a notable period in the prehistory of Gaul, because it witnessed the domination of the transrhenan cultures not only in the Seine and Rhône valleys, but even as far west as the valley of the Upper Loire. This was in part the consequence of the general community between the province of Eastern Gaul and the Rhineland that is noticeable in the earlier stages of the Bronze Age ; but, more directly, it was the consequence of the arrival within the area of a new folk, called the Urn-Field People, whose distinctive culture, characterised by extensive cemeteries of cremated burials in urns, had been developed in that portion of Central Europe comprised by the lands of modern South-East Germany (Thuringia, Saxony, and Prussian Silesia), North-West Czecho-Slovakia, Austria, and Hungary.

For a long time the people inhabiting this east-central district of Europe had been in a close trade-connection with South-West Germany and the Rhineland, and also with the Ligurians in North Italy ; but at the close of the Bronze Age, i.e. about 1000 B.C., there was an actual progression of the people themselves westwards. This began by a movement into South-West Germany, the Rhineland, and Switzerland, and into Central Gaul as far as the Loire, while at much the same time related peoples also descended the valley of the Rhône and settled in South-Western France and across the Pyrenees in Catalonia.[1]

The arrival of these Urn-Field folk took place at very much the same time as the introduction of the use of iron into Western Europe ; and the cultures that resulted from their immigration belong properly to the earliest, or *Hallstatt*, division of the Iron Age. This word Hallstatt is the name of a village in the Austrian Tyrol where a rich cemetery of the first Iron culture has been brought to light, and it is universally applied to corresponding culture-stages everywhere else in the west of Europe. It is simply a convenient ticket for a particular grade of culture, and it may be freely used if it be understood that it does not carry with it ulterior

---

[1] *Buttleti Assoc. Catalana d'Antropologia*, III (1925), 212.

implications either of racial affinity or even of complete cultural identity.

The use of a new metal, and of a new name for the changed civilisation that coincides with its introduction, sounds as though the close of the Bronze Age in Gaul had witnessed a wholesale revolution in the arts of life, instigated by conquering hordes endowed with superior equipment. In reality nothing of the sort occurred. The first Hallstatt culture of Gaul was simply a continuation of the Bronze Age civilisation, with the difference that the Urn-Field peoples had added a sufficient element of East European novelty to make it an integral part of a single early Iron Age civilisation extending from France to Austria. But, essentially, Gaul had experienced no marked ethnographical change ; and in no sense had it been overrun by a *new* Hallstatt folk. Instead, its changed culture was slowly evolved from Bronze Age beginnings on its confines, whence it spread only gradually throughout its extent.

On the other hand, we must take stock of an important cultural development in North-Western Germany that becomes manifest about the same time as the formation of the Hallstatt cultures in the Alpine countries, that is to say, in the 1st and 2nd centuries of the first millennium B.C. This was the incursion into the Lower Rhineland of a culture seemingly developed in North and Eastern Germany that was characterised amongst other things by a peculiar domestic pottery, consisting chiefly of wide-mouthed vessels of coarse, gritty ware with a frilled lip,[1] pots with the body, or lower portion covered by comb-ornament, and big vessels with a " smeared " or " rustic " surface.[2] Although it was born of

[1] For an account of this *Harpstedt* pottery, see R. Stampfuss in *Mannus*, XVII (1926), 287.

[2] In Germany this " frill-comb-smear " pottery (abundantly represented in the North German museums) belongs to the late Bronze Age and early Iron Age. I have made a fairly thorough study of it, and I am satisfied it is identical with certain English ceramic types ; it represents, in fact, the first pottery, since the early Bronze Age beakers, that is sufficiently peculiar, and sufficiently alike on both sides of the Channel, to suggest an *invasion*. But I wish I could feel equally sure of its date and manner ; I suggest about 600 B.C.

the distinct *northern* Bronze Age province of Europe, it is difficult to say whether this culture really represents a people of separate race, as has been claimed, from the Bronze Age population of Southern and Western Germany ; but that is a problem that need not be immediately discussed, and it is only necessary to remark that these folk, whoever they were, after they had subsequently absorbed something of the Hallstatt culture in the Rhineland, adventured, or perhaps were driven, into North-Eastern Gaul and across the sea into this country.

The date of their arrival in force on the English shores, if we may judge by the chronology of their expansion on the continent, and the mixed character of their pottery in the English settlements, cannot have been earlier than about 600 B.C. To what extent these newcomers occupied the country, I am not prepared to say ; but as the pottery finds showing the most striking affinities with those on the conti- nent (Fig. 5) seem limited to the Thames valley, Kent, and Sussex, it is possible that the invaders were forced to remain content with a holding in the south-eastern counties. Yet one cannot deny that after their coming fashions derived from the Rhineland headquarters of the Western European Iron Age civilisation influenced British cultures much further afield.

It must be borne in mind, however, that this invasion was not the only herald of the Iron Age in Britain. Intimate relations with the continent had existed during the Bronze Age, above all in the Atlantic or *western* province, and importations of continental Iron Age manufactures, some of which must have reached us before the Rhineland folk crossed to our shores, are of regular occurrence in Britain and Ireland. Therefore, although Rhineland types are

(above), though it may be that the invaders reached Kent very much earlier, and that 600 B.C. was merely the time when their influence was beginning to make itself felt inland. All the other so-called " Hallstatt " wares in this country belong either to the finer wares associated with this " frill-comb-smear " pottery in Germany, or to a slovenly and degenerate variety, including debased Bronze Age forms, that was common all over North-Western Europe at the close of the Bronze Age, and that lasted on well into the Iron Age.

clearly recognisable in other English Hallstatt settlements, as in Hampshire and Wiltshire, the predominant types in these districts are (in my view) more likely to have been derived at second hand from the Gallic Hallstatt cultures

FIG. 5.—"Frill-comb-smear" pottery found in England: 1, 2, 3, 4 from Margate; 5 from Sussex; 6 from Berkshire. (1, 2, and 3 are × ¼: 4, 5, and 6 are × ⅛.)

by means of an already established cross-Channel traffic, which linked the whole of Western Gaul from the Pyrenees to the Channel Islands with Britain and Ireland, than to have been formed by the district imposition of a Rhineland culture. As an instance of this traffic, one may recall the fact that Brittany exported into England a number of the typical Breton socketed axes with square section and straight sides (Fig. 6) ; and that these implements date from a period in the Breton prehistory when such patently Hallstatt forms were in use as the Kerhon urn [1] (Fig. 8), which, when found, contained no less than 170 of them, or that from Bogoudonou (Fig. 8) that contained over 90. Indeed, Hallstatt pottery of this and of other kinds is by no means unusual in Brittany and the Channel Isles, so that traffic in the western Bronze Age province is demonstrably a probable source of part, at any rate, of the British Iron Age culture.

It seems, then, that although the turn of the second-first millennia B.C. is an important date for Gaul, marking, as I say, the first real aggression of the transrhenan cultures, it is nevertheless *ethnologically* much less important for this island than is commonly supposed, though *culturally*, of course, it is certainly significant as the period of the introduction of socketed axes, leaf-shaped swords, and some of the new pottery fashions of the Iron Age. But it is difficult to give credit to the widely held view that this period about 1000 B.C. was remarkable for a great invasion of continental pre-Iron Age folk who interrupted and altered the British Bronze Age cultures ; instead, the evidence is better read as suggesting that our shores remained inviolate from everything but the ordinary traffic of cross-Channel commerce for another three or four hundred years after this time.[2]

We may say, therefore, that during the developed Bronze

---

[1] *Bull. Soc. Polymathique du Morbihan*, 1896, p. 147 ; *Rev. d'École d'Anthr.*, 1896, p. 452.

[2] I admit that the cross-Channel traffic between Brittany and Southern England may have been less peaceful than my remarks suggest, and a reasonable amount of evidence is forthcoming to support the notion of an invasion of Wessex about this time. But it was a localised movement, and I have not thought it worth while to discuss the possibility at length here (a great deal depends on the chronology of the southern earthworks supposed to have been connected with the invasion). All I am trying to do in this chapter is to call attention to the major ethnological changes in Gaul and Britain.

FIG. 6.—HOARD OF SOCKETED BRONZE AXES OF BRITTANY TYPE
FOUND AT NETHER WALLOP, HANTS ($\frac{1}{3}$)

FIG. 7.—MODEL OF DESTROYED TEMPLE, ODILIENBERG, ALSACE
(AFTER FORRER)

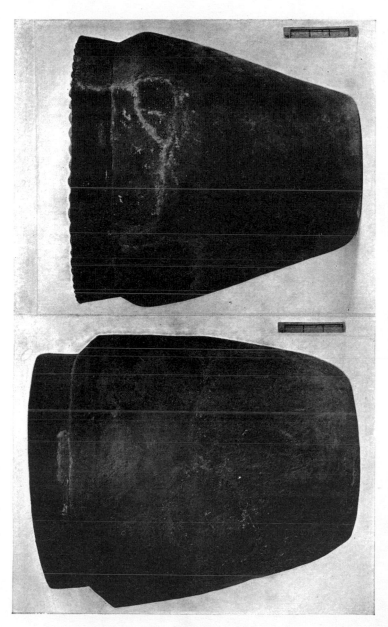

FIG. 8.—POTTERY VESSELS FROM BOGOUDONOU (LEFT), KERHON (RIGHT), BRITTANY, FOUND CONTAINING HOARDS OF BRONZE AXES ($\frac{1}{5}$)

Age and the first half of the early Iron Age, roughly from 1500 to 500 B.C., the general distribution of the population in Gaul and Britain remained static, and that the only movements of significant importance for our special enquiry were the arrival of the Urn-Field peoples on the confines of Gaul about 1000 B.C., and an incursion of foreigners from the Rhineland into England somewhere about 600 B.C.

Turning to the second half of the early Iron Age, that is to say, the five centuries before the beginning of the Christian era, we find ourselves already within measurable reach of the druids themselves. This stretch of time is called the *La Tène* period, the name being borrowed from that of a site on Lake Neuchâtel, where the typical culture of these centuries was first identified. The new culture is a witness to the achievement of the complete cultural unity throughout a single Iron Age civilisation, extending from the north of France to Hungary, that had been begun some 500 years earlier by the arrival of the Urn-Field people from Central into Western Europe. It is nothing more than a natural development from the culture of the Hallstatt folk, who had now become part of an immense and homogeneous Central European province ; in fact, the only notable distinction between the new culture and that of the Hallstatt folk, apart from the inevitably altered fashions in arms and trinkets, was the development of a lavish scroll decoration that, though in a slight measure influenced by details of classical ornament, was, as a whole, conceived in an entirely barbarian—one might almost say oriental—spirit [1] (Fig. 9).

The most notable event in the La Tène period was the sudden expansion of the culture beyond its homeland limits. This certainly began as early as 500 B.C., but the beginning

[1] I am convinced that it is a mistake to say that the La Tène scroll-ornament is largely a result of the influence of classical art. It must be remembered that the borrowing of certain details from Greek art is a minor matter, and what should be studied is the general *spirit* of the art. Here the affinities are " Scythian " rather than Greek. See the remarkable essay by Bruno Brehm in Strzygowski's *Heidnisches und Christliches um das Jahr* 1000, Vienna, 1926, p. 37. I have to thank my friend Professor Alföldi for calling my attention to this paper.

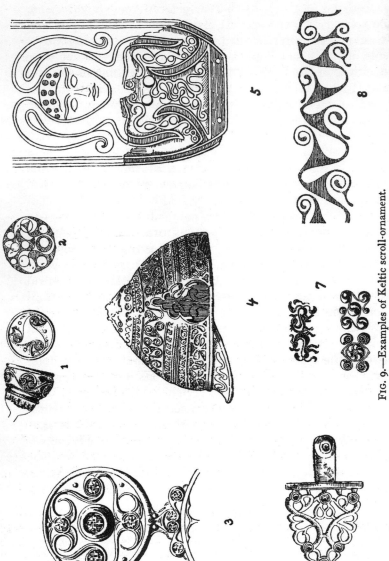

FIG. 9.—Examples of Keltic scroll-ornament.

1, Terminal of gold torc, Somerset; 2, Detail of bronze mirror, Cornwall; 3, Detail of bronze shield, Thames; 4, Helmet from Amfreville, Eure, France; 5, Detail of bronze belt, Waldalgesheim, Coblenz; 6, Openwork bronze, Ardennes; 7, Detail of bucket, Aylesford, Kent; 8, Painted frieze on pottery vase, Marne.

of the 3rd century B.C. was the period of the greatest movement and of the furthest enterprise. From the Alpine lands
these folk poured forth in armed bands, sometimes as would-
be colonists, sometimes as homeless and vagrant wanderers.
They swept down upon the Mediterranean coast of France
and advanced into Spain ; they streamed across the Alps
into Italy, capturing Rome in 390 B.C. ; and in the 3rd
century others of their race advanced eastwards into the
Balkans, where they devastated Thrace, Macedonia, and
Thessaly, and pillaged Delphi (279 B.C.). Some of these
last wanderers even found their way across into Asia Minor,
where they were employed as mercenaries ; and as witness
to their adventures so far afield, it is said that potsherds of
middle La Tène character have been found on the site of
the ancient Hatti (modern Boghasköj), near Angora.

Right at the beginning of the period the north of France
was very quickly occupied by the new culture, and it was
not long before this had crossed the Channel. But the
exact course of events in the north-western area is rather
hard to follow.

The Champagne district of France is thought to be the
starting-point of the English culture, for it is impossible to
remain unimpressed by the resemblance between the Yorkshire chariot-burials and the fifty or more discovered in the
Marne area and east of the Marne towards the Rhineland.
But the Marne burials are early (La Tène I), and if the culture
they represented spread suddenly northwards, as the Yorkshire burials suggest, it is a curious thing that to the north
and north-west of the Marne there should be none of the
beautiful painted pottery that distinguished the earliest and,
in lesser degree, the middle La Tène culture in the Marne
area itself.

This reads as though the La Tène invasion of England—
and it is impossible to doubt that there was such an invasion
—took place after the painted pottery period. But against
this view must be set the evidence of the bronze brooches
found in this country, for there are many more of the earlier
(La Tène I) type than of the later (La Tène II) variety. Of
course, it is conceivable that such small articles as brooches

were trifles acquired in the course of normal merchandise, but the occurrence of the La Tène I type in the Yorkshire area, where the chariot-burials were found, seems to add to the probability that the La Tène culture was forcibly imposed on this country during the 5th-4th centuries B.C. On this view, it might be urged that in this country the early painted pottery of the continent was translated into a ware with similar curvilinear decoration that was not painted, but outlined by grooves and filled-in by incised dashes or hatched lines.[1] This sort of pottery is common in Brittany and Southern England (Fig. 10), and its technique was a familiar decorative method of the old western province of the Bronze

FIG. 10.—Upper portion of vase with scroll-ornament, from Margate (⅓).

Age (though it was not, of course, the exclusive property of this area) ; it certainly dates back to the time of the megaliths in Spain and in Brittany, and lasted throughout the Bronze Age ; while in England this technique, in a crude form and applied to chevron and triangle patterns, was practised at the beginning of the Iron Age, as can be seen in the finds from the famous Wiltshire settlement at All Cannings Cross.

But if England was invaded at this early period, Ireland seems to have escaped until a little later, for that country

[1] Unfortunately, the only dateable sherds of this ware in Britain are late (La Tène III) ; but there is a good deal that is not dated, and in Brittany it is much earlier (La Tène I).

has no La Tène I brooches. On the other hand, she can show some very peculiar pottery (Fig. 11) that is unlike anything in our own island, though allied to a series in the Marne-Breton culture, and she possesses spearheads ornamented on the wings [1] in the continental fashion that are not found in England ; and added to this there are a number of other objects, sculptured boulders and so forth, that do

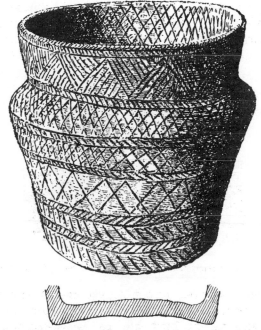

FIG. 11.—Small urn found near Tykillen, Co. Wexford, Ireland ($\frac{1}{2}$).

not occur in the English culture. All this very much suggests that the La Tène culture of Ireland was derived directly from the continent and independently of Britain ; and such points of resemblance between the cultures of the two islands as is afforded by the ornamental sword-scabbards must be ascribed either to the common origin of the La Tène style, or to commerce across St. George's Channel.

[1] *Proc. R. Irish Acad.*, XXXVIII (1910), C, 102, Fig. 2.

This suggests that the La Tène culture reached England about 400 B.C., and Ireland about 350 or 350 B.C., as independent movements from the continent. And since nothing has hitherto come to light in Ireland that could reasonably be read as evidence of an invasion in the Hallstatt period,[1] it looks as though in that country the La Tène people were the first to interrupt the original Bronze Age civilisation ; indeed, it is possible that an archæologist familiar with Bronze Age pottery in Ireland, and the La Tène wares in the Marne district, would be able to find some support for this contention in a study of the pottery fashions represented

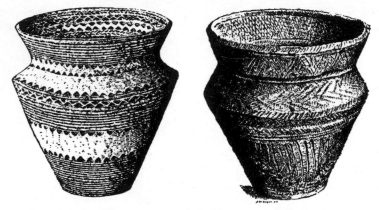

FIG. 12.—Pottery vessels from Greenhills, Tallaght, Co. Dublin (¼).

by the Greenhills urns [2] (Fig. 12) from Tallaght, Co. Dublin, for they seem to me to reveal fairly clearly a fusion between local Bronze Age and continental La Tène forms.

There is still one more cultural change to be noted before this hasty survey of the ethnology of the druidic lands is complete ; but it only concerns North-Eastern France and South-Eastern England. What happened was that towards the middle of the La Tène period the great culture of the

---

[1] For a review of the Hallstatt material found in Ireland, see E. C. R. Armstrong, *Journ. R. Soc. Antiquaries of Ireland*, LIV (1924), p. 1.

[2] *Proc. R. Irish Acad.*, XXI, 3 S. v, (1898-1900), 338.

Marne began to break up, as the cremation-burials of a new folk appeared side by side with the accustomed inhumations of the district ; these cremations afterwards became more and more frequent until, at about the end of the 2nd century B.C. they altogether supplanted the older method of interment, and an altered culture possessed the area. In the middle of the 1st century B.C. offshoots, of which this changed civilisation of Northern France is plainly parent, made their appearance in the south-eastern counties of England, and have been recognised in the cremation-graves of Aylesford and Swarling in Kent, at Welwyn in Hertfordshire, and a number of other cemeteries in an area that includes Suffolk and Cambridgeshire, and extends as far north as Northamptonshire.[1]

It is now time to attempt a re-statement in racial terms of the story of these archæological changes, and to do this it will be easier to follow in a reverse order the events we have described. We may begin, therefore, in the 1st century B.C., when the people of Gaul were divided into the three groups that have been immortalised in the famous generalisation of Cæsar. Probably the boundaries of these groups were ill-defined, and there is no doubt that the folk within them were far from being homogeneous ; but, nevertheless, in essence each group represented a distinct race, or mingling of races, and a distinct language. One such group was a confederacy of tribes settled between the Garonne and the Pyrenees, and known as the Aquitani ; these people presented a composite of various racial elements derived partly from the native Bronze Age inhabitants of the area, partly from the Iberians (a short and swarthy folk who were themselves the children of the Spanish Bronze Age and had lately spread across the Pyrenees into the south of Gaul), partly from the ancient Ligurians (some of whom are known to have moved westwards across the Rhône), and, finally, from the invaders who had transferred the Hallstatt, and afterwards the La Tène, culture across France into Spain.

[1] For a detailed study of this culture as represented in England, see *Reports Search Comm. Soc. Antiquaries of London*, V (1925)— " Swarling Cemetery."

In Cæsar's time a folk akin to these last-named invaders, and now grafted upon the native population, was established throughout the second province of Gaul, which extended from Liguria in the south-east throughout the plains of Central France to the Atlantic in the north-west, and was known by the name of the Keltæ. The third province stretched northwards beyond the Seine and the Marne to the Rhine, and was inhabited by the Belgæ.

The changed culture in North-Eastern France that we have just said succeeded the famous Marne culture, which was of a pure La Tène character, was that of the Belgæ ; they were a tall, fair people, according to the ancient historians, who did not differ in any remarkable way from their near neighbours in Gaul. But Cæsar was told [1] that they were of German origin, and this plainly means that the early cremation-graves noticed as unusual among the Marne inhumations of the middle La Tène period must have been the graves of invading Germans, and that the whole province ultimately acquired a German character.

Now the Germans, so we are told, had no druids,[2] and the formation of the Belgic culture, and certainly its advent into England, took place after druidism was already established, because it was known to the Greek writer Sotion of Alexandria as early as about 200 B.C.[3] Therefore, although the German incursion across the eastern frontier of Gaul, and the subsequent sustained aggression on their part, was a very important factor in Gallic and British early history, it can have no bearing on the problem of druidic origins ; and, consequently, the development of the Belgic culture has no immediate interest for us.

The Aquitani, too, seem as little likely to be concerned with the origin of druidism. There were no druids, so far as we can tell, in Italy nor in Spain, so that the Ligurian [4] and Iberian elements in the population suggest that Aquitania was not a hopeful ground for the development of the druidic religion. Moreover, the earliest reference to the druids

---

[1] *B.G.*, ii, 4, 1.   [2] See p. 79.   [3] See p. 74.
[4] Cf. my earlier remark about the Ligurians (p. 37).

assigns them to the Kelts and the Galatæ, and, in spite of
the formidable mountain of argument that has been devoted
to the elucidation of what precisely the classical writers
meant by these terms, it may be safely asserted that had
Sotion intended to convey that the druids were the *philosophers* of people so well known in the Greek world as the
Ligurians or the Iberians, he would certainly have named
them expressly, instead of attributing them to a people who
must either have been the Keltæ of Gaul, or the related folk
representing the extended La Tène culture (Galatæ), which,
as we have seen, had been carried eastward into the Balkans
and Asia Minor.   It is quite true that there were also Kelts
in Aquitania, and there may even have been druids there
when Sotion wrote, but I repeat that a Greek author would
not name the Kelts as representing the native Mediterranean
inhabitants of south-west Gaul ; and, accordingly, their
presence can only serve to divert our interest to the Keltic
province itself.

   This lies as a solid wedge driven through the old Bronze
Age provinces and destroying their unity, for the south-
eastern (Ligurian) province, and the north-eastern province
(before the formation of the Belgic culture), were both absorbed into the Keltic world, while the western province
was completely sundered.   Indeed, if we add to this that
the Kelts had also penetrated southwards, that they had
crossed over into Britain and Ireland, and that they had
spread eastwards through the Balkans, we might describe
them more picturesquely as having *exploded* over Europe,
shattering and altering the old-established cultural provinces.

   But it would be a mistake to suppose that this new
Keltic culture was carried everywhere by people of identical
race, or that it anywhere represented a pure racial type.
The most that can be said on the last score is that nearest to
the centre of expansion tallness and fairness seem to have
been predominating characteristics of the invaders, and that
a tall, fair man was certainly the classical notion of the
average Kelt ; while, in addition to this, all bearers of the
name spoke the same, or variations of the same, tongue.
But every one knows that community of language is no sign

of racial identity, and it may be taken for granted that in Cæsar's time the people who called themselves Kelts were of a very mixed character, and included a large element of subjugated folk of a shorter and darker strain.

I have already digressed sufficiently far from our main subject, and to proceed further in this matter of the Kelts is to become entangled in one of the most difficult problems of prehistoric ethnology in Europe ; but, as was said at the beginning of this chapter, the Kelts and the druids are inseparably connected, so that we cannot well avoid a brief reference to the probable origin of this people.

The view I take is that a correlation between language-distribution, particularly as discoverable by means of place-names,[1] and the distribution of archæological cultures, justifies the general contention that the Kelts were a people of La Tène culture who, expanding from Central Europe, introduced the Keltic language into Gaul, Britain, and Ireland, Spain, Italy, the Balkans, and Asia Minor.   And if this much be granted, then, on my own showing, the cradle of the race lies somewhere between Gaul and Hungary, and the people were a mixed folk sprung of the mixed Hallstatt races, who were themselves products of the varied Bronze Age folk.   We are bound, therefore, to go a step further and ask what is the specially Keltic element operating in the formation of this culture of the La Tène period that distinguished its bearers so decisively from other peoples like the Germans, and that led to the development of their own peculiar tongue ?

In all the length of the prehistoric period there seems to be only one racial strain in this area that can explain such a differentiation from the adjacent and cognate cultures ; and that was provided by the Urn-Field people.   Their coming, at the end of the Bronze Age, afforded a link with Central Europe that is sufficiently strong to account for the origin in lands nearer the Alps of what may be described as a distinctive westernmost branch of the great family of

---

[1] See the instructive table in Dottin, *Manuel pour servir à l'étude de l'Antiquité Celtique*, Paris (1906), p. 337.

peoples speaking an indo-germanic tongue. And to my mind the notion that the Urn-Field folk were, so to speak, the stimulus that led to the origin of the Kelts, is corroborated by the well-attested circumstance that the Keltic language is more closely allied to the ancient Italian tongue than to any other ; [1] for this affinity is of high antiquity (as may be judged from the fact that the Latins and the Kelts did not have the same word for iron), and must be attributed to the close connection existing between North Italy and East Central Europe, the home of the Urn-Field culture, at the end of the Bronze Age. And it also seems to add to the probability that the Kelts were cradled in the south German plain, that is to say, between the Swiss Lakes and the Bohemian Forest, rather than to the north between the Rhine and the Elbe.

It may be said, then, that one peculiarity of the huge La Tène province, that was founded on the Bronze Age and Hallstatt civilisations and that extended from France to Hungary, was the special local development and general use of a language of indo-germanic character whose elements were, I suspect, first introduced into the western districts of the province by the Urn-Field peoples. But this is only half an explanation of the problem, for the Kelts were not Keltic because they spoke an indo-germanic tongue. We must also take into account, therefore, a second, and more important, peculiarity of the province, and that was an astonishingly successful consolidation within itself, whereby it was welded into a cultural whole, a prosperous and homogeneous confederacy of similar tribes. Now these two peculiarities taken together are sufficient, I think, to explain the origin of the Kelts, which, on this view, must simply be ascribed to the laborious achievement of interior solidarity in a province that had first of all been stimulated by the eastward movement of a folk of novel culture. This does not mean, however, that the Urn-Field people are to be called Kelts, although their arrival in the Alpine lands was the

---

[1] See A. Walde, *Uber älteste sprachliche Beziehungen zw. Kelten u. Italikern.*, Innsbruck, 1917 ; also Ebert's *Reallexikon, s.v. Kelten B and Italiker B ;* but cf. J. Vendryes in *Rev. Celtique*, XLII, 379.

factor that made this solidarity ultimately possible ; nor even that the term can be applied to the Hallstatt folk. These early people were only the ancestors of the Kelts, and not the Kelts themselves ; [1] and the name should properly be reserved for the folk of developed national and linguistic characteristics who do not appear until the period of the evolution of the La Tène from the Hallstatt civilisation.

The clue, therefore, to the secret of the origin of the Kelts lies in what I have called the La Tène consolidation, and I think it an error to search further back in antiquity in the hope of finding them as a ready-made specialised people. Consequently, our special interest in them does not demand a more detailed treatment of the subject, and we may pass immediately to another aspect of the Keltic problem that has to be noticed here since it is so frequently stressed by writers seeking to give a precise account of the Keltic expansion.

Linguistically, the ancient Kelts of Western Europe are usually divided into two branches, the one (Brythonic) including the people of Gaul and the greater part of Britain, and the other (Goidelic) comprising the inhabitants of Ireland, and of the Scottish Highlands, and the Isle of Man. It is rather difficult to be certain about the other Kelts outside Gaul, but it is supposed that both in Spain, and also in the direction of the eastward expansion towards Greece, the Keltic tongue was of the Goidelic, or Irish type, and it has been shown that the speakers of the early Latin dialects in Italy also possessed some of its most important characteristics.

The difference between Goidelic and Brythonic speech depends on one or two grammatical and phonetic peculiarities, the principal distinction being that Goidelic is labio-velar, and thus preserved the indo-germanic q, whereas the tendency of Brythonic tongue was to be labial, so that this q was generally, but not always,[2] changed into pp or p.

---

[1] The Kelts, and their country Keltica, seem to have been known by name to the Greeks about 500 B.C. But we do not know the significance of the terms at that time, so that our argument is not affected.

[2] The Coligny calendar, for instance (see p. 116), has q-forms. On this subject see Walde, *op. cit.*, p. 57, n. 1.

Thus the indo-germanic root-word for horse *ekŭos* (to take the stock example) remains *equus* in Latin, is *ech* in Old Irish, but became *epos* in Gaul. And this last modification was characteristic not only of Keltic speech in Gaul and Britain, but also of the Oscan and Umbrian dialects in Italy.

The main interest for us is that the Goidelic variety of the Keltic speech was spoken in Ireland, while in Britain the other variety was adopted. This certainly seems to add strength to the notion already expressed that Ireland obtained the Keltic culture independently from the continent ; but, in truth, one should hesitate to claim even this much on the basis of a mere dialectical difference, and to proceed further and to attempt to define the course of events by invasion-series of Q-Kelts and P-Kelts is to place far too heavy a strain on the subtle and delicate machinery of philological science.[1] It must be sufficient to say, irrespective of the probable dates of the invasions, that the Keltic-speaking folk who went to Ireland had been in a position to preserve, and were able to enforce, the speech of the Keltic homeland in a purer form than that imposed by the Keltic-speaking people who had crossed to England.

Many factors might have operated to bring such a state of affairs about ; the geographical isolation, for instance, of the bearers of the new tongue before their ultimate migration, or, alternatively, the opportunity of immediate communication with the language-centre ; or, perhaps, the inclination of the natives who received the new language towards particular vowel and consonantal forms, or their disinclination from others. Obviously, therefore, utmost care must be exercised before trying to convert such phonetic changes into invasion-terms, and I have no intention of interrupting this account of ancient Gaul and Britain by a debate on the merits of this particular labiovelar-labial variation. It is worth while, however, to recall Professor Eoin MacNeill's warning in this very connection. He

---

[1] If the reader would like an example of the permissible deductions regarding folk-movements to be obtained from philological data, he should consult the section in the *Cambridge Ancient History* (IV, 456) on the co- and no-peoples in Italy.

remarks [1] that in all the western dialects of Latin, that grew into the romance languages, the initial *w* of Germanic speech was changed into *gw*, and that this change took place in Welsh and Spanish, but not in Irish. But this does not prove, he points out, that the Welsh are more nearly akin to the Spaniards than they are to the Irish, nor, if history happened to be silent, would it prove that Britain after the Roman occupation was peopled by a Spanish invasion that did not extend to Ireland.

In studying the growth of a religious system we have to take into account not only the cultural evolution in the province concerned, but also the probable influences exerted upon it by the thought and opinion of the outside world. Thus something must be added to the foregoing story of the early inhabitants of Gaul and Britain ; for what has been said hitherto of the increasing domination throughout the first millennium B.C. of the transrhenan barbarians, culminating in the actual incursion of these folk into our area, is, as it were, only the salient fact suggested by the local prehistory of our provinces, and the sketch must be completed by a word as to their relations with the more highly developed civilisations of the eastern Mediterranean and the Ægean Sea.

Whatever may have been the racial origin of the later Stone Age (neolithic) folk inhabiting North-Western Europe, there is hardly any room for doubt that their culture, which is now known to us chiefly in the terms of their progress in craftsmanship, was mainly derived from the splendid civilisations of the near East. For Mesopotamia and Egypt are, I am convinced, the ultimate source of all that was notable among the changes in European culture that took place between the close of the old Stone Age (palæolithic) and a point when the Bronze Age was already established ; and of the innovations due to their influence I think it is fair to name agriculture as the most remarkable example.

But to say this much does not in the least imply that any Sumerian or Egyptian ever set foot in our area, nor

---

[1] *Phases of Irish History*, Dublin, 1919, p. 46.

does the gradual transmission of their culture, which is patently independent of folk-movement, imply the simultaneous procession of their philosophical or religious thought. For our special enquiry, it cannot be too strongly insisted, we are not concerned with cultural influences of this kind, which were exerted at a distance ; we have only to discover cases of definite contact between the ancient inhabitants of our area and the peoples of other lands. There is not, as a matter of fact, a scrap of evidence suggesting any direct imposition of an eastern culture upon Gaul and Britain, and whatever cultural improvement came from such a source, that is from Mesopotamia or from Egypt, must be attributed not to colonisation, nor even to far-flung trade, but to the natural and inevitable *fire-bucket* progress of ideas, *culture-creep*, that all ages have witnessed and that can still be observed in action to-day.

There is no need, of course, to deny all possibility of an uncertain and shadowy connection between the ancient East and our area after the northern Bronze Age had begun. But it is disappointing that there should be no trace of Egyptian or other wanderers on the south coast of France or in Spain, where relics of them might legitimately be expected, and that we should have no better tangible evidence of their probable influence upon our civilisation than a number of little segmented faience beads that are found in our English barrows and are supposed to have been made in Egypt somewhere about 1300 B.C.[1] But these beads are never found with other Egyptian grave-furniture, so that it is obvious they do not represent the burials of Egyptians themselves, but were merely an easily portable merchandise ; and certainly they do not justify us entertaining the notion that the neolithic or Bronze Age religion of Britain might have been accepted by the natives at Egyptian dictation.

[1] It is not by any means certain that they *were* made in Egypt (see *British Museum Bronze Age Guide* (1920), p. 89). It is a curious thing that they do not seem to have exact parallels in Egypt, but perhaps they were made solely for export (probably in Alexandria). For a decided opinion as to their Egyptian origin, see Sayce, *Reminiscences*, 405.

A more direct outside influence than the remote and second-hand stimulus from Asia or Africa was exerted from the coasts and islands of the Ægean Sea ; and there is little doubt in my mind, to take a single example, that the main inspiration of Western European Copper Age and Bronze Age pottery was derived from the Ægean wares current in the 3rd and 2nd millennia, B.C.   This affected our area from two directions, firstly by the medium of the Danube valley, and secondly, but less noticeably, across the Mediterranean and along the Atlantic trade-route.   But here again it would be very difficult to demonstrate in the case of Gaul and Britain an actual intrusion of folk from the Ægean at this early period, and the most that we can claim is that in the Danubian area the connection with the Ægean was sufficiently intimate to have resulted in a spiritual community that might later have influenced Western European belief at the time of the formation of the Keltic culture. But to say even this much is to venture on dangerous ground, for the mere copying of fashions is no proof of sympathy in beliefs ; and it will be wiser, having noticed the uncertain chance whereby Ægean thought might be transmitted to North-Western Europe, to proceed without further comment to the instances of certain contact between the Western Mediterranean and the outside world.

The first people who assuredly ventured from a distance into the West were the Phœnicians.   At the end of the 2nd millennium and the beginning of the 1st, the weakness of the Egyptian and Assyrian Empires was turned to account by the kings of Tyre, who were thereby enabled to found a nation of considerable commercial importance, whose colonies and trading-stations (Fig. 13) were established in Asia Minor, on the African coast, in Cyprus, Malta, Sicily, Sardinia, and finally in Spain.   Carthage was founded by this folk about 814 B.C., and their famous Spanish station, Gades (Cadiz), in the 8th century ; so that at the beginning of the 1st millennium we meet for the first time an incontrovertible instance of the presence of foreigners from distant lands at the Mediterranean doorway into Gaul. But it is wellnigh certain that Gaul was unaffected.

Phœnician influence in Spain is measurable and indubitable, and it is discernible in the Balearic Isles and in Sardinia, but the coasts of Gaul have not as yet afforded any evidence of the visits of these newcomers to the West ; [1] and beyond the obvious fact that at the later period of Carthaginian supremacy these coasts lay open to the raids of Punic pirates or to the occasional visits of Punic traders, there is nothing here for our comment.

I suppose a digression is still necessary in order to remark that there is no evidence whatever that the Phœnicians

¡FIG. 13.—Map of Mediterranean basin, showing the Phœnician colonies.

came as far north as the Isles of Scilly or the south-west of England ; and it may be assumed that if they required any of the produce of these northern regions in addition to that obtainable in the rich markets of their assured colonies and trading-stations, it would reach them only indirectly after serial transportations. Here again it is not *impossible*

[1] For references to finds of supposed Phœnician origin in Gaul, see Déchelette, *Manuel, II*, Pt. I, p. 29, notes 1 and 2 ; and Jullian, *Histoire de la Gaule*, I, 187. But cf. Dr. Hall's remarks, *Ancient Hist. of the Near East* (6th ed., 1924), p. 523, n. 1 ; and Myres, *Camb. Anc. Hist.*, III, 641.

that the Phœnicians themselves should have ventured so
far to the north ; we can only say that after plenty of
excavation in England and in Scilly it is a fact that no
trace of them has been found, nor a trace of any culture
even remotely resembling theirs.[1]   And there is something
else to remember.   Three or four centuries later when the
Phœnician thalassocracy no longer existed, and Carthage
alone represented its former might, two Punic admirals
were sent on voyages of discovery.   One of them, Hanno,
went southwards to explore Africa, and the other, Himilco,
sailed through the Strait of Gibraltar northwards up the
Atlantic coast of Spain.   After almost incredible delays he
at length reached the Isle of Ouessant off the Brittany
promontory, which, together with the adjacent islands, is
said to have been a native depot for the metal trade from
Cornwall.   Himilco's story, so far as it is recoverable from
the verse of Avienus,[2] with its tales of the dangers of the
long calms and the thick fogs, of the vast masses of floating
seaweed that stayed his progress, of the enormous tracts
where the waters scarcely covered the sandy floor of the
ocean, and of the giant and savage beasts that beset his
boat, demonstrates very effectively the justness of the remark
that such a voyage must have been very much the same
sort of expedition into the unknown as was the voyage of
Columbus to America,[3] or its comparison with modern polar
exploration ; [4] and no one could reasonably pretend that
Himilco was simply supposed to be re-visiting the trading-
posts of his Phœnician ancestors.

It was not the Phœnicians who first confronted the
remote and barbarian folk of Gaul with a higher civilisation ;

---

[1] My friend, Mr. George Bonsor, who is intimately acquainted
with Phœnician problems in Spain, once came to England to conduct
a search for traces of them in Scilly and Cornwall, a search that
included numerous excavations.   He found a good deal of material
he was not looking for, but nothing Phœnician !

[2] The best text, with critical notes by Schulten, is in *Fontes
Hispaniæ Antiquæ* (Schulten and Bosch), *Fasc.* 1, Avieni Ora Mari-
tima.

[3] Jullian, *Histoire de la Gaule*, I, 385.

[4] Déchelette, *Manuel*, II, Pt. I, 30.

it was the Greeks. At the end of the 8th century B.C. the great colonising movement of the Ionian Greeks had begun, and in the 7th century the Phocæans, following in the wake of the famous voyage of the Samian Kolaios,[1] were already crossing to explore the markets of the West. It was they, so Herodotus says,[2] who first made the Greeks acquainted with the Adriatic, Tyrrhenia (Etruria), and with Iberia ; and they remained a great sea-power until the end of the 6th century. During this period they not only established themselves in Spain,[3] where they were

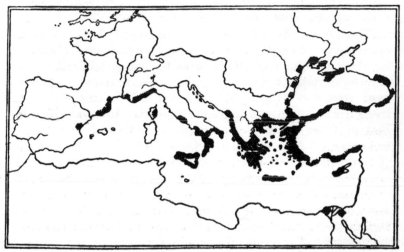

FIG. 14.—Map of the Mediterranean basin, showing the Greek colonies.

speedily involved with the Phœnician, or rather the Carth-aginian interests, but also they founded a colony in Gaul itself, no doubt being driven northwards to the Rhône mouth as a result of the rivalry in the southern markets (Fig. 14).

The foundation of the Greek colony at Massilia (Mar-seilles) about the year 600 B.C. is the beginning of the direct intrusion of the alien and greater outside world into the

---

[1] Herodotus, IV, 152. [2] I, 163.
[3] See the instructive little book by Rhys Carpenter, *The Greeks in Spain*, Bryn Mawr, 1925.

lands we have termed the druidic provinces ; and such a settlement of a new people, the spread of their stations along the Riviera, and their up-river traffic to Arles and Avignon, is clearly an event of dramatic importance in the story of Gaul.

It would be an exaggeration to say that the influence of the Greeks had immediate effect throughout all Gaul, or even that it is discernible at any great distance from the coastal area in the first century or so after the foundation of the colony. But, in general, the result of the arrival of the Greeks, and of their long sojourn on these shores, was a profound alteration of the Gallic civilisation.

Naturally, this is especially noticeable in the native arts and crafts. Masonry, that is to say, scientific and accurate building with squared stones of easily manageable size, was one of the many things that the barbarians learnt. In stone-work they had hitherto been familiar only with the clumsy megalithic architecture of the early Bronze Age, which at the best of times was only practicable in certain districts, and was now but seldom employed,[1] or such simple devices as the construction of revetments of stone slabs. But now they were able to learn to build properly in the manner of the Greeks, and it is an interesting fact that in their first and simplest attempts to copy the newcomers, as in the building of certain *oppidum* walls, a trick of Greek (and Etruscan) construction has been noticed more than once,[2] namely, the cutting of expanding mortices in the stone blocks which were then held together by wooden tenons cut with similarly expanding ends (Fig. 15). And in addition to building, which the barbarians eventually applied to houses and towns, another very important innovation was that they

[1] Megalithic architecture was still used occasionally for funeral monuments in Western and Southern Gaul in the Hallstatt period. On the other hand, I think that *cyclopean* building, as seen in Catalonia, is largely a Greek innovation. Cf. Bosch Gimpera, *Problemes d'historia antiga i d'arqueologia Tarragonina, Butlleti Arqueologic.* Tarragona, 1925.

[2] Déchelette, *Manuel*, II, Pt. 3, 995, and n. 1. I have seen this mortice-style in a Greek context at Ampurias, Spain.

learnt after some centuries to copy and use the Greek coinage system (Fig. 16).

Justinus has summed up the effect of Greek influence from Massilia in a well-known passage that, though it may

FIG. 15.—Wooden tenons and fish-tailed mortices on stone blocks, Odilienberg, Alsace (*after Forrer*).

seem to suffer from an excess of enthusiasm, is none the less almost exactly true. The Gauls learnt, he says,[1] a more civilised way of life that tempered their former barbarity ; they were taught to cultivate their lands, to prune the vine

FIG. 16.—Stater of Philip of Macedon (top left) and Gallic coins made in imitation (⅓).

and plant the olive, and also to enclose their towns with walls. They learnt, moreover, to live according to laws, and such a high degree of civilisation was attained that it seemed as though it was not Greece that had come to Gaul, but that Gaul had been transplanted into Greece.

[1] XLIII, 4.

Such contact as this with a new civilisation, such evidence of the understanding of its customs, is a very different thing from the second-hand borrowing of fashions that up to 600 B.C. had been the only method whereby the prehistoric Gallic culture was modified from outside. Here we see very plainly that not only were the arts and crafts of the natives changed, but that their mental attitude must gradually have become sympathetic with the behaviour and social system of the more highly civilised people ; or if not sympathetic, at least it must have been stimulated to an understanding of their manner of life. In other terms, the barbarian morals and religion, just as much as barbarian craftsmanship, were liable to be modified by association with the Greeks.

Whether barbarian religion was so affected, we have no occasion to debate here, and it is sufficient in this chapter to emphasize the opportunity. But it will be convenient in this place to add that so far as Keltic religion is concerned, this opportunity is not likely to have existed earlier than the 4th-3rd century B.C. The purely Keltic, or La Tène, culture was, as a matter of fact, just about to become differentiated from the Hallstatt cultures of the Alpine lands at the time when the Greeks were first establishing themselves at Massilia, so that it is rather tempting to assume that the Massiliot Greeks played an important part in its formation. But we must remember that at the beginning of the La Tène period, Massilia was separated from the Keltic world by coastal Ligurian tribes, who, although they had acquired a Hallstatt culture, were directly descended from the Bronze Age inhabitants of this part of Gaul. It is quite true, of course, that these Ligurians were in constant communication with the Alpine regions ; it is true that 6th century black-figure Greek pottery has been found in Gaul as far inland from the coast as at a Hallstatt *oppidum* at Salins (Jura) ; [1] and it is true that a certain number of intruders

[1] *Rêvue Archeologique*, 4 S., XIII (1909), 193. It is rather hard to say whether this pottery came up the river valleys from Massilia, or along an Adriatic-North Italy-Switzerland route ; but I must admit I am much impressed by the arguments of M. Piroutet (*L'Anthr.*, XXIX (1918-1919), 219 ff.) in favour of a Massiliot source.

from the East, forerunners of the Kelts, had already made their way to the southern coast of Gaul. But, even so, the coastal people at this early period cannot properly be called Keltic, and it may be safely asserted that the Kelts themselves did not come into complete contact with Greek corporate life, as represented by a colony, until the time of their first expansion. Consequently, it is natural to suppose that it would not be until some time after this, as late as the 3rd century perhaps, that Greek influence, as exerted from Massilia, would be likely to have any appreciable effect upon Keltic thought.

However, we have already remarked on the slight, but unmistakable influence of Greek ornament during the evolution of La Tène art, so that it looks as though there must have been some other medium, distinct from Massilia, whereby Greek culture could reach the future Keltic world, whose nucleus lay north and east of the Alps, in the 6th and 5th centuries. But this other medium was not, I think, the trade-enterprise of the Ionic Greeks along the Danube valley, or from the head of the Adriatic across the North Italian plain ; and its nature will be better understood if we turn our attention for the moment from the Greeks themselves, and continue our narrative of the other adjacent peoples who might have influenced Gaul.

From the 7th century onwards Hellenic interest in the Western Mediterranean steadily increased, and Greek colonies were established and maintained in undiminished vigour ; but it was not long before the supremacy of the Greek fleets and the security of the Greek traders were challenged. With the first of the rival powers, Carthage, we have little to do here ; the early years of the 5th century B.C. witnessed her achievement of complete domination over the declining Phœnician colonies, and as an inevitable result of her rise to power the same period saw the beginning of a bitter struggle between the Carthaginians and the Greeks. But Massilia itself was not attacked by the Punic fleets, and there is no record of serious interference in Gallic affairs by the Carthaginians, although Justinus records [1] friction

---

[1] XLIII, v. 2.

between Massilia and Carthage on account of the capture of some fishing-boats.

The other rival was the Etruscan people. They had migrated into Italy from Asia Minor somewhere between 1000 and 800 B.C., and after two hundred years of consolidation in their new home, they were strong enough to enter the field as formidable adversaries of the Greeks. It is difficult to say how far their civilisation concerned Gaul,[1] but it has been argued that many of the Italian importations into Gaul, such as cordoned bronze buckets, black-figure Greek pottery like that from Salins just mentioned, and numerous other articles, are proof that at a very early time the Etruscans were in direct communications with the inhabitants of Gaul. And in addition to these finds of 5th and 6th century date in Gaul that might be attributed to Etruscan influence, we have to remember that at the end of the 6th century the Etruscan nation had extended its boundaries northwards from Etruria proper, and that its settlements were now established right up to the valley of the Po (Fig. 17), so that geographically their people stood at the doorway into the Gallic world ; and we can well understand the statement of Polybius [2] that close relations existed between Kelts and Etruscans in the 4th century. Moreover, as we know very well, about 390 B.C. a section of the Kelts had crossed the Po and pushed southward into Etruria itself ; while a hundred years later in the last Samnite war another section of the same people served as allies of the Etruscans in an attempt to stay the rising power of Rome. It is not surprising, therefore, that Etruscan influence should be plainly discernible in the archæology of Gaul during the 3rd and 4th centuries B.C. ; for Etruscan-Campanian wares were freely imported, and a very interesting and even more intimate sign of this connection is the discovery in the bed of the Saône at Chalons of a bundle of Etruscan currency-bars.[3]

[1] On this subject see the remarks of M. René Gadant, La Religion des Éduens, Autun, 1922, pp. 15-23.
[2] Hist., II, 17.
[3] Déchelette, La Collection Millon, Paris, 1913, p. 228.

With this and other proof before them of close relationship between Etruscans and Gauls, archæologists have
ventured further and have attributed to Etruscan influence
such important innovations as the introduction into Gaul
of the art of writing, of enamel-work, the use of defensive
armour, and the art of sculpture. Obviously it is but a
short step to proceed to the discovery in Gallic religion of

FIG. 17.—Map of Italy, showing the Etruscan settlements.

points of resemblance with the Etruscan system, an example
being the comparison of that Gaulish god who bears a
hammer, with the Etruscan *Charu* or *Charun*, who has a
similar attribute.

It may well be that the earlier Italian importations into
Gaul were not so much a sign of sudden Etruscan influence
as a natural consequence of an ancient connection between
Italy and the Rhône valley, Switzerland, and the Jura.

The Ligurian province of the Bronze Age afforded testimony of such a cultural union in the distant past, and in the succeeding centuries traffic across the Alps into Gaul, Southern Germany, and the Danube valley, had always been maintained ; indeed, in the early Iron Age Italy was the chief market for northern amber, great lumps of this material, sometimes as large as the human hand, being repeatedly used as ornaments upon the Italian brooches. If we also take into account the similarity already mentioned between the Keltic and the Latin tongues, we shall see that there is reason for regarding the majority of the signs of Italian influence in Gaul that are of a date earlier than the Keltic migration, as a natural result of the common Central European-Danubian parentage of the Kelts and most of the North Italian peoples, such as the Villanovans and the Veneti.

But this does not dispose of the Etruscans. The Kelts, Polybius said, just before the time of their first raid into Italy *associated much* with them, so one can hardly deny their possible influence upon Keltic thought in the 4th century B.C., or even earlier. And in addition to this we have to take into account the markedly Hellenic character of the Etruscan civilisation. We know very well that by the middle of the 6th century the Etruscans had begun to copy Ionian metal-work on a large scale, and to import Greek pottery in immense quantities. It is quite likely, therefore, that the traffic between them and the people north of the Alps would enable the influence of Greek art to make itself felt in the Keltic province as early as the 6th century, and to become manifest, as it certainly did, in Keltic art. At any rate, this possibility must be added to the certain source of Greek influence that existed at Massilia ; for we saw that it was doubtful whether the Massiliot Greeks in the early period of the colony had much to do with the Kelts, and we suspected that another medium would be found to explain the earlier Greek influence for which La Tène art is, to some extent, a witness.

In the 3rd century Rome became the dominating power

in the Italian peninsula, and its first decades witnessed her struggles with the Gauls for final supremacy in the North Italian plain.   The resistance of the barbarians was strenuous at first, but by 196 B.C. the remnant of them was in complete submission beneath the Roman yoke, and from that time onward Rome marched victoriously forward to her future position as a world-power, Greece, Carthage, and Spain falling before her conquering armies.   For a while Gaul itself escaped, but an attack by the barbarians on the colony of Massilia resulted in an appeal by the isolated provincial Greeks for Roman protection, and in 155 B.C. the Roman armies went to their aid, beginning the wars that ended in the foundation of the province of Transalpine Gaul.   By 120 B.C. they were masters of the lower Rhône valley, and the stage was set for the final conquest of all Gaul that was achieved by Julius Cæsar.

Of the Roman occupation of Gaul we shall subsequently have more to say.   But in this chapter it does not concern us, for the reason that before the clash of Roman and Gaul, druidism was already in existence, and there is no occasion to complicate at this stage a sketch, already over-burdened with detail, of the prehistory and early history of the lands in which druidism flourished.

To sum up, then, we noticed first of all a relatively static Bronze Age that was divisible into distinct provinces, and we witnessed the development across the eastern frontiers of Gaul of the Iron Age civilisation of Western Europe, a civilisation that contained the new element of the Urn-Field culture from Central Europe, and that, after a *Hallstatt* phase, consolidated itself into a La Tène, or Keltic, civilisation.   The Hallstatt culture, we saw, spread gradually throughout all the Bronze Age provinces, partly by means of minor movements of people, and, principally, as a result of the normal traffic ; but the La Tène civilisation was transmitted more effectively by a gigantic expansion of the Keltic-speaking peoples themselves.   And it is amongst those of the Kelts who established themselves in Gaul and Britain that we suppose druidism originated.   Of the other races concerned, we have mentioned the Ligurians and the Iberians, whom the Kelts encountered in the south of Gaul ; and the Germans, who were ever pressing upon them from the north. And finally, taking a wider survey of the ancient world, we have spoken of the opportunity afforded to the Greeks and the Etruscans to influence Keltic thought in Gaul.

One word more, and we have done. So much talk of changes in culture, and the comings and goings of people, may well obscure the undoubted continuity of the population in prehistoric times, a consideration of the utmost importance in considering so delicate a subject as the development of a religion. I have already referred to the favourable chances for the development of a native faith in Bronze Age Britain, though not with complete assurance, and I should like to give one good example of the age-long persistance of native tradition in a single district to show that the subject is really worth serious consideration.

For this purpose, I have deliberately chosen a district in the north-east of France, because this is a part of the world where, as I have already said, cultural changes of far-reaching importance took place during the two thousand years that our survey has covered. The Oise department of France, to which I am now going to refer, belonged in neolithic times to what has been very happily named the *Flint-Culture*, a province embracing North-Eastern France, Belgium, and parts of England. Its Bronze Age was little more than a direct continuation of this same culture, altered by the appearance of a few metal tools and weapons ; and the first change of importance was the introduction of the Hallstatt culture. This was followed by the Keltic invasion and the development of a peculiar local Keltic culture (the Marne-culture), which was subsequently interrupted and altered by the arrival of the Germans. After this came the Roman occupation.

It is not a district in which one would expect to come across evidence of the survival of Flint-Culture tradition, yet I think such evidence is forthcoming. In the ruins of a little Gallo-Roman temple in the Forest of Halatte near

Senlis (Oise) [1] two hundred or more ex-voto offerings were discovered, including a number of small chalk heads that varied in height from 4 to 10 inches. Some of these heads, as well as many of the other ex-votos, were clumsily cut in imitation of the Roman style of sculpture; but others of them were not in the Roman style at all, the face being schematically represented by a wedge-shaped nose hanging from a curved arcade in high relief that marks the eyebrow line (Fig. 18). Now this style, this same device for representing the face, is exactly that employed only about a hundred kilometres away in the well-known carvings (Fig. 19) at the entrance to the prehistoric burial-grottoes in the Petit-Morin valley; and though these last are certainly as old as 1500 B.C.,

FIG. 18.—Small votive-heads of chalk from temple-site, Halatte.

if they are not older, and the little heads belong to the 1st-3rd centuries A.D., I think the similarity in style is sufficiently remarkable to be taken as proof of the survival of a native artistic tradition throughout all this length of time. [2]

[1] *Congr. Archéologique de France*, LXXII (1905), Beauvais, p. 334. The finds are better illustrated by Espérandieu, *Recueil général des Bas-Reliefs de la Gaule Romaine*, V, 3864-3889.

[2] I have also been very much impressed by the rather remarkable affinities in shape between the rough pottery vessels from the grottoes and those later associated with the Marne-Culture. Twenty or more pots from the grottoes are in the de Baye collection in the St. Germain Museum, and an observer will probably notice how the later pedestal and the sharp shoulder of La Tène times are foreshadowed in the grotto-pottery; conversely, it is interesting to see how closely some of the simpler varieties of these later pots recall the earlier grotto fashions.

And such persistence of native tradition on the scene of
so much ethnological and archæological change should warn
us that where the growth of a religion is in question, we should
not only take into account foreign incursion and the influence
of strangers, but also that we must make allowance for the
genius loci, the ancient and unalterable spirit of the country-
side that can preserve as a living force the immemorial
thought and behaviour of the humble folk born of its soil.

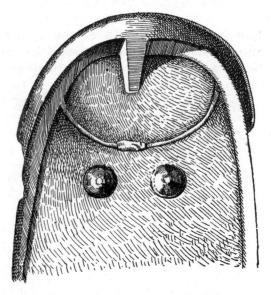

FIG. 19.—Wall-carving from prehistoric grotto-grave, Marne (*after de Baye*).

It should warn us that the spirit of the land may prevail
over all the impositions of conquering and powerful invaders,
and that a religion carried everywhere by a single people
may acquire in certain districts native characteristics that
cause it to differ notably from the same religion in its original home.   It will explain, in fact, how it comes about that
druidism may be Keltic, and yet, because it was built up of
the prehistoric faith of certain only of the provinces wherein
the Kelts intruded, not a universal Keltic faith.

CHAPTER III

HISTORY

WE derive our knowledge of the ancient druids almost entirely from the casual mention of them by the classical writers. But with a single exception, all the references to them were written after the Roman occupation of Gaul, so that only once does an allusion to the druids, and it is a very brief one, reach back to the days of the Greek colony at Massilia. This means that all our other information comes directly or indirectly from Roman sources, and it is natural enough that there should not be any very considerable stock of information available. For it is clear that first-hand knowledge would be exceptional, even among the historians and geographers of the Empire, and, consequently, we need not anticipate anything more than rather vague allusion to this single barbarian priesthood in the general literature of the Roman world.

But this insufficient store of positive knowledge, and the meagreness of the subsequent comment, is also very largely due to what, in its simplest terms, is lack of interest. Colonising Rome attempted no missionary enterprise ; outlanders may have been barbarians, that is *savages*, but primarily they were not in Roman eyes what we should now call *heathen ;* and if ultimately Jupiter, and Mars, and Mercury, and other members of the Roman pantheon were worshipped in far corners of the Empire, it was the result of the gradual fusion of native with Roman gods, due to a policy of toleration, and not to direct conversion. Doubtless such a policy was only possible because the outward observance of the barbarian cults, and the very natures of the gods worshipped, presented few radical differences from the rites and the

73

deities to which the Romans themselves were accustomed, no such apparent differences, that is to say, as separate the great religious systems of the modern world. But whatever the cause may have been, it followed that the Romans did not study nor debate over the barbarian religions they encountered, nor did they make any serious attempt to comprehend their underlying philosophies. When, therefore, we turn to them for enlightenment about the druids, we must not expect to find as the centuries pass a growing, even if purely academic, interest ; indeed, it is a fact, as we shall soon see, that the scholars of the late Empire contribute singularly little to our poor stock of information concerning the flourishing druidism of the days of their forefathers.

In this chapter I propose to recite the greater part of the classical evidence relating to druidism, and this will present us with almost the whole of the material that we have to discuss. It would not be convenient, therefore, to deal with all the separate items of information as we meet them, for that would entail a continual shifting of our interest from one aspect of druidism to another ; and I think it will be better to confine our attention at the first reading principally to the subject of the druidic authority, that is to say, the power and prestige of the order, and its decline in the face of Roman hostility. We shall then be able to deal in another chapter with its dogma and ritual.

In the extant literature the druids make their few appearances, which become increasingly rare as time passes, from about 52 B.C., when Cæsar wrote the Commentaries, to about the year A.D. 385, when Ausonius wrote his collection of odes to the professors of Bordeaux. But in the first half of the 3rd century after Christ, Diogenes Laertius tells us, in a chance remark in the preface to his *Lives of the Philosophers*, that the druids were mentioned in two lost works, a treatise on Magic, then ascribed to Aristotle but now known to be apocryphal, and a big book by a Greek, Sotion of Alexandria, that must have been written somewhere about 200 B.C. This passage from Diogenes, therefore, although out of the proper chronological order of our authors, must be the starting-point. I give a translation of the passage here ; the original Greek of this, and the Greek and Latin of the other translations quoted subsequently, is set forth in an appendix at the end of the book.

DIOGENES LAERTIUS. *Vitæ, intro.*, I

Some say that the study of philosophy was of barbarian origin. For the Persians had their *Magi*, the Babylonians or the Assyrians the *Chaldeans*, the Indians their *Gymnosophists*, while the Kelts and the Galatæ had seers called *Druids* and *Semnotheoi*,[1] or so Aristotle says in the " Magic," and Sotion in the twenty-third book of his " Succession of Philosophers."

Vitæ, intro., 5

Those who think that philosophy is an invention of the barbarians explain the systems prevailing among each people. They say that the Gymnosophists and Druids make their pronouncements by means of riddles and dark sayings, teaching that the gods must be worshipped, and no evil done, and manly behaviour maintained.

This is the allusion that reaches back, as I say, behind the period of the Roman occupation of Gaul ; and there is no doubt that it takes us back for a considerable distance beyond this point. For to have had even this much of reputation outside their own Keltic world in the second century before Christ, the druids must have been already long-established ; and by the very terms of the allusion to them it is plain that they cannot have been regarded, or indeed have boasted themselves to be, a localised sect. It seems likely, therefore, that as a generally recognised Keltic institution druidism must extend backwards in antiquity to a date, at a moderate estimate, a hundred and fifty years before Sotion wrote. And since there was a celebrated druids' grove near Massilia, well known in Roman times, and even then considered to have been of great antiquity,

---

[1] This word is not found elsewhere, and is probably corrupt ; the meaning, if any, is *reverend gods*, which makes nonsense here ; the tempting rendering *reverencers of the gods* is scarcely admissible. For the view that the word might be a distinctive name for the Galatian priests, see Jullian, *Recherches sur la réligion gauloise*, Bordeaux, 1903, p. 102.

it is tempting to add that it must have been from Marseilles that their fame was spread abroad among the Greeks. Thus we may go so far as to say that any theory of their origin which does not allow of druids in Southern Gaul as early, let us say, as 350 B.C., seems to be discountenanced by this passage.

Our next authority is Julius Cæsar, and the following extracts from the sixth book of the *Gallic War* form the mainspring of our knowledge of the early druids. It is, of course, possible that the importance of this testimony might be over-estimated, a natural result of thankfulness for any information vouchsafed by one who had actually been in prolonged contact (nine years) with the people of Gaul. For we must remember that a campaigner is not altogether fortunately situated in regard to the study of normal religious life in the theatre of his wars. It is just possible, for instance, although we have no reason to feel sure that it was so, that Cæsar may have been to some extent deliberately deceived by his informants, especially in the information given him concerning the political power of the druids ; while in the other matters of their faith and customs, and of their origin, in which he was not in all probability very keenly interested, he may have been content in recording whatever surmises were current in his army, or the ill-remembered gossip of the Gaulish chieftains.[1] But, on the other hand, I would urge very strongly that there is certainly no suggestion of such practice in the account itself ; for it is at once brief, lucid, authoritative, and, in its own scale, complete. Furthermore, as we are to see later on, the Gaulish noble most likely to have been Cæsar's chief informant on many of the details was himself a member of the druidic order, and also one whose record is sufficiently well known to enable us to feel sure that there were no intelligible motives for his telling Cæsar anything but the truth. I think, therefore, that most

---

[1] Cf. the aspersions of Asinius Pollio upon the trustworthiness of Cæsar's writings : Suetonius, *Div. Iul.*, 56, 4. But see generally on the credibility of Cæsar's narrative St. G. Stock, *De Bello Gallico*, I-VII, Oxford, 1898, p. 11, and also Rice Holmes, *Cæsar's Conquest of Gaul*, Oxford, 1911, pp. 211-256 and 527.

reasonable people will deem material considerations such as these to outweigh the purely hypothetical sources of error ; and, accordingly, I shall not waste any time in hesitation over this very important document, but shall assume that Cæsar has given us an account of the druids that, although brief, is a considered and authentic description of the order in so far as it had come within his experience.

CÆSAR. *De Bello Gallico,* VI, 13 [1]

Throughout Gaul there are two classes of persons of definite account and dignity. As for the common folk, they are treated almost as slaves, venturing naught of themselves, never taken into counsel. The more part of them, oppressed as they are either by debt, or by the heavy weight of tribute, or by the wrongdoing of the more powerful men, commit themselves in slavery to the nobles, who have, in fact, the same rights over them as masters over slaves. Of the two classes above-mentioned, one consists of Druids, the other of knights. The former are concerned with divine worship, the due performance of sacrifices, public and private, and the interpretation of ritual questions : a great number of young men gather about them for the sake of instruction and hold them in great honour. In fact, it is they who decide in almost all disputes, public and private ; and if any crime has been committed, or murder done, or there is any dispute about succession or boundaries, they also decide it, determining rewards and penalties : if any person or people does not abide by their decision, they ban such from sacrifice, which is their heaviest penalty. Those that are so banned are reckoned as impious and criminal ; all men move out of their path and shun their approach and conversation, for fear they may get some harm from their contact, and no justice is done if they seek it, no distinction falls to their share. Of all these Druids one is chief, who has the highest authority among them. At his death, either any other that is pre-eminent in position succeeds, or, if there be several of equal standing, they strive for the primacy by the vote of the Druids, or sometimes even with armed force. These Druids, at a certain time of the year, meet within the borders of the Carnutes, whose territory is reckoned as the centre of all Gaul, and sit in conclave in a consecrated spot.

[1] The translations of this and other passages from the *Gallic War* are taken unaltered from H. J. Edwards's version (*Loeb Library,* 1917).

Thither assemble from every side all that have disputes, and they obey the decisions and judgments of the Druids. It is believed that their rule of life was discovered in Britain and transferred thence to Gaul; and to-day those who would study the subject more accurately journey, as a rule, to Britain to learn it.

De Bello Gallico, VI, 14

The Druids usually hold aloof from war, and do not pay war-taxes with the rest; they are excused from military service and exempt from all liabilities. Tempted by these great rewards, many young men assemble of their own motion to receive their training; many are sent by parents and relatives. Report says that in the schools of the Druids they learn by heart a great number of verses, and therefore some persons remain twenty years under training. And they do not think it proper to commit these utterances to writing, although in almost all other matters, and in their public and private accounts, they make use of Greek letters. I believe that they have adopted the practice for two reasons—that they do not wish the rule to become common property, nor those who learn the rule to rely on writing and so neglect the cultivation of the memory; and, in fact, it does usually happen that the assistance of writing tends to relax the diligence of the student and the action of the memory. The cardinal doctrine which they seek to teach is that souls do not die, but after death pass from one to another; and this belief, as the fear of death is thereby cast aside, they hold to be the greatest incentive to valour. Besides this, they have many discussions as touching the stars and their movement, the size of the universe and of the earth, the order of nature, the strength and the powers of the immortal gods, and hand down their lore to the young men.

De Bello Gallico, VI, 16

The whole nation of the Gauls is greatly devoted to ritual observances, and for that reason those who are smitten with the more grievous maladies and who are engaged in the perils of battle either sacrifice human victims or vow so to do, employing the Druids as ministers for such sacrifices. They believe, in effect, that, unless for a man's life a man's life be paid, the majesty of the immortal gods may not be appeased; and in public, as in private, life they observe an ordinance of sacrifices of the same kind. Others use figures of immense size, whose limbs, woven out of twigs, they fill with living men and set on fire, and the men perish in a sheet of

flame. They believe that the execution of those who have been
caught in the act of theft or robbery or some crime is more pleasing
to the immortal gods ; but when the supply of such fails they resort
to the execution even of the innocent.

VI, 18, 1

The Gauls affirm that they are all descended from a common
father, Dis, and say that this is the tradition of the Druids.

VI, 21, 1

The Germans differ much from this manner of living. They
have no Druids to regulate divine worship, no zeal for sacrifices.

The immediate interest of Cæsar's description of the
druids lies in his emphasis on their political and judiciary
functions. Although they officiated at sacrifices and taught
the philosophy of their religion, they were a great deal more
than mere priests ; for instance, at their annual meeting
near Chartres, it was not to worship nor to make sacrifices
that the people came from afar, but to present their disputes
for lawful trial. And it was not only minor quarrels that
the druids decided, for another of their functions was the
investigation of criminal charges, and the determination of
the necessary punishment. To them, therefore, was due
the awe invariably paid to judges ; but, in addition to this,
larger matters of national importance, such as intertribal
quarrels, were brought to their council for adjudication.
This, together with the facts that they held national assemblies and acknowledged the single authority of an arch-
druid invested with supreme power, shows that their system
and their authority were conceived on a *national* basis and
were independent, that is to say, of *ordinary* intertribal
jealousy and dispute. And when we add to this political
advantage the enormous influence over educated public
opinion that was theirs by virtue of their position as the
chief instructors of the young, and, finally, the formidable
religious sanction behind their decrees, we feel that it is
scarcely an exaggeration to say that before the clash with
Rome the druids must have very largely controlled the
civil administration of Gaul.

Nothing could be more apposite here than the next reference to the druids that we have to record. It comes from the pen of Cicero, and it is peculiarly important in this matter of the political prestige of the druids because we happen to know something about the particular druid to whom Cicero refers.

Cicero. *De Divinatione*, I, xli, 90

Nor is the practice of divination disregarded even among uncivilised tribes, if indeed there are Druids in Gaul—and there are, for I knew one of them myself, Divitiacus,[1] the Æduan, your guest and eulogist. He claimed to have that knowledge of nature which the Greeks call " physiologia," and he used to make predictions, sometimes by means of augury and sometimes by means of conjecture.[2]

Cicero wrote the *De Divinatione* about eight years after Cæsar had published the *Commentaries*. It is in the form of a dialogue between himself and his brother, Quintus Cicero, who had served in Gaul under Cæsar, and had shared with Cæsar the friendship of Divitiacus, that noble-minded Æduan so often mentioned in the pages of *De Bello Gallico*.[3] The statement in this paragraph, therefore, is not one that Tully would be likely to venture upon with anything but complete assurance, and there can be no reasonable doubt that Divitiacus was actually a member of the order of druids. This, in conjunction with Cæsar's testimony, throws a flood of light on the conditions of service in the priesthood during the first century before Christ, and at once disposes of the quite natural idea that all its members were secluded and mysterious ancients, holding aloof from the common world in a gloomy atmosphere of esoteric ritual and priestly taboos. For Divitiacus was a man of affairs, acknowledged ruler of the Ædui, and a politician and diplomatist of established reputation throughout the whole of Gaul ; it was, in fact,

---

[1] The correct spelling of this name is probably *Diviciacus*.

[2] The translation is from Judge Falconer's version (*Loeb Library*, London, 1922).

[3] I, 3, 5 ; 19, 2 ; 20, 2 ; 31, 9 ; 41, 4 ; etc. Divitiacus is still a popular figure ; there is a life-sized bronze statue of him in the Promenade des Marbres, Autun.

an important diplomatic mission that took him to Rome on
the occasion when he was the guest of Quintus Cicero and
discussed divination with Tully. Moreover, he was, as no
druid of our accustomed picturing could be, a warm sym-
pathiser with Roman ideals and an unswerving adherent to
the cause of the conquerors in Gaul. Cæsar's own account [1]
describes a trusted Keltic nobleman, sagacious in strategy
and eloquent in debate, who was incessantly occupied in the
difficult domestic problems of Gaul ; and when we add to this
picture Cicero's testimony as to his religious calling and to his
knowledge of druidic lore and methods of augury, we seem
to find ourselves confronted in this man with a forerunner
of the great political priests of history. At any rate, we are
compelled to enlarge our ideas of the druidic functions, so as
to include the practical administration of government with
the necessary complete liberty of movement and freedom
from priestly duties.

But once the Romans came to Gaul, the political significance of the druids was short-lived. Their organisation, as
I have said, was proof against *ordinary* intertribal dissension,
yet it was not long before a situation arose in the face of
which it was impossible to maintain cohesion in the order.
In 52 B.C. took place the famous rebellion of Vercingetorix,
and throughout a whole year Cæsar was engaged in a long
and difficult struggle, while Gaul, led by the brilliant, tragic
young Arvernian, made its last resistance against the Roman
power. The disaffected tribes were chiefly those situated in
central Gaul between the Seine and the Garonne, so that a
very large part of the country was involved in war with the
Romans ; but at no time were the rebels able to command
the one essential for success, namely, that all Gaul should
respond to their call to arms. Despite the best endeavours
of Vercingetorix to rouse the whole country, large sections
of the populace took no part in the struggle, while some tribes,
who had experienced the advantages of friendship with the

---

[1] Cæsar himself does not say that Divitiacus was a druid ; it has
been suggested therefore that Cicero is misleading us, and that he
was really only a layman who had been educated by druids. But
see Rice Holmes, *Conquest of Gaul*, p. 526 n.

Romans, definitely declared themselves against him and entered the field as allies of Cæsar. Corporate druidism was therefore helpless; the order was divided against itself; united action was impossible.

The blow to their prestige was irreparable. Plainly the national gods cannot take both sides in a struggle fraught with such significance, and the division of their priests into hostile camps spelt ruin. The authority of the archdruid was at an end; the national assembly could no longer meet, and there was nothing left for the druids to do but to give such local encouragement or advice as opportunity afforded. But their power was gone; and this disruption of corporate druidism is beyond all doubt the turning-point in their story. It was a disaster from which their authority as a national clergy never recovered, and henceforward their political significance was at an end. That is why, when we turn to our next author, Diodorus Siculus, who wrote somewhere about 8 B.C., we see at once that their influence was over, and that by this time they were simply regarded in the eyes of the outside world as seers.

Diodorus Siculus. *Histories*, V, 28, 6

The Pythagorean doctrine prevails among them (the Gauls), teaching that the souls of men are immortal and live again for a fixed number of years inhabited in another body.

Histories, V, 31, 2-5

And there are among them (the Gauls) composers of verses whom they call Bards; these singing to instruments similar to a lyre, applaud some, while they vituperate others.

They have philosophers and theologians who are held in much honour and are called Druids; they have sooth-sayers too of great renown who tell the future by watching the flights of birds and by observation of the entrails of victims; and every one waits upon their word. When they attempt divination upon important matters they practice a strange and incredible custom, for they kill a man by a knife-stab in the region above the midriff, and after his fall they foretell the future by the convulsions of his limbs and the pouring of his blood, a form of divination in which they have full confidence, as it is of old tradition. It is a custom of the Gauls that no one performs a sacrifice without the assistance of a philosopher, for they say that offerings to the gods ought only to be made through the mediation of these men, who are learned in the divine nature and, so to speak, familiar with it, and it is through their agency that the blessings of the gods should properly be sought. It is not only in times of peace, but in war also, that these seers have authority, and the incantations of the bards have effect on friends and foes alike. Often when the combatants are ranged face to face, and swords are drawn and spears bristling, these men come between the armies and stay the battle, just as wild beasts are sometimes held spellbound. Thus even among the most savage barbarians anger yields to wisdom, and Mars is shamed before the Muses.

This so very closely resembles the contemporary testimony of Strabo that the germane passages from the *Geographica* must follow immediately.

STRABO. *Geographica*, IV, 4, c. 197, 4 [1]

Among all the Gallic peoples, generally speaking, there are three sets of men who are held in exceptional honour : the Bards, the Vates, and the Druids. The Bards are singers and poets ; the Vates, diviners and natural philosophers ; while the Druids, in addition to natural philosophy, study also moral philosophy. The Druids are considered the most just of men, and on this account they are entrusted with the decision, not only of the private disputes, but of the public disputes as well ; so that, in former times, they even arbitrated cases of war and made the opponents stop when they were about to line up for battle, and the murder cases in particular, had been turned over to them for decision. Further, when there is a big yield (of criminals for sacrifice) from these cases, there is forthcoming a big yield from the land too, as they think. However, not only the Druids, but others as well, say that men's souls, and also the universe, are indestructible, although both fire and water will at some time or other prevail over them.

Geographica, IV, 4, c. 198, 5

But the Romans put a stop to these customs, as well as to all those connected with the sacrifices and divinations that are opposed to our usages. They used to strike a human being, whom they had

---

[1] The translations are from the version by H. L. Jones (*Loeb Library*, 1917).

devoted to death, in the back with a sabre, and then divine from his death-struggle. But they would not sacrifice without the Druids. We are told of still other kinds of human sacrifices ; for example, they would shoot victims to death with arrows, or impale them in the temples, or having devised a colossus of straw and wood, throw into the colossus cattle and wild animals of all sorts and human beings, and then make a burnt offering of the whole thing.

Strabo is the first to give the name of the Vates, or diviners, but in other respects he adds little to the statement of Diodorus, although he has obviously incorporated considerable borrowings from Cæsar. Even so, we can detect the fallen estate of the druids in his reference to some of their political functions as belonging to the past, a circumstance that is partly explained by the additional information that they already come into conflict with the Romans on account of their cruel customs.

There is another item of testimony that must belong to the same period, if its author, Timagenes, is correctly identified with the rhetorician and historian who practised at Rome in the time of Pompey, and afterwards under Augustus. The following extracts from his lost account of the Gauls are given by Ammianus Marcellinus in the fourth century, A.D. :—

Ammianus Marcellinus, XV, 9, 4

According to the Druids, a part of the population (of Gaul) was indigenous, but some of the people came from outlying islands and lands beyond the Rhine, driven from their homes by repeated wars and by the inroads of the sea.

XV, 9, 8

In these regions, as the people gradually became civilised, attention to the gentler arts became commoner, a study introduced by the Bards, and the Euhages, and the Druids. It was the custom of the Bards to celebrate the brave deeds of their famous men in epic verse accompanied by the sweet strains of the lyre, while the Euhages strove to explain the high mysteries of nature. Between them came the Druids, men of greater talent, members of the intimate fellowship of the Pythagorean faith ; they were uplifted by searchings into secret and sublime things, and with grand contempt for mortal lot they professed the immortality of the soul.

This does not make much advance upon the information already given by Diodorus, and, generally, it seems clear enough that at about the beginning of the Christian era, although the outside world had at least learnt of the triple division of the order, the reputation of the Keltic priests depended on a charitable interpretation of the pre-existing notions about them, rather than upon any new and substantial witness to their increased wisdom and authority. More and more, we find the emphasis falling on single items of Cæsar's original statement, together with a certain elaboration of the details of their ritual and divinations, seemingly introduced as examples of superstitious barbarism.

There is a gap of nearly fifty years before we come to our next authority, Pomponius Mela. During that time considerable progress was made with the Romanisation of Gaul; a census of the natives was taken and the methods of local government reorganised; also the encouragement of the cult of *Divi Imperatores* and the Genius of the reigning emperor, with its official priests (*augustales*), and the institution of the annual religious assembly at Lyons around the altar of Rome, was intended to consolidate the normal Roman observances in the province at the expense of the native ritual. This would, of course, tend to weaken whatever remained of the secular and religious power of the druids, even supposing their co-operation was invited, for their former political duties would be usurped, their ceremonies supplanted, and their own annual assembly eclipsed. Moreover, the establishment of Roman schools would considerably affect their position as teachers. It was almost inevitable, therefore, that they should have resisted this Romanising process,[1] and that, as a consequence, they should have incurred official repudiation. As a matter of fact, three distinct movements against their prestige were

[1] That is to say, the followers of the anti-Roman druids in the great rebellion, who were doubtless trying to preserve their traditional dogma and ceremonies. The pro-Roman druids probably taught the official religion, and were not regarded as a hostile native clergy; it is possible that they had already ceased to call themselves druids.

made by the Romans during this period. Pliny and Suetonius are the sources of our information, and the short passage in which the last-named author refers to the subject, written somewhere about A.D. 120, may conveniently be interpolated here.

SUETONIUS. *Claudius*, 25

He (the Emperor Claudius) very thoroughly suppressed the barbarous and inhuman religion of the Druids in Gaul, which in the time of Augustus had merely been forbidden to Roman citizens.

We learn, then, that at the very beginning of the first century after Christ Roman citizens, a term that must refer here to those of the Gauls who claimed the advantages conferred by the title of citizenship, were forbidden to practise the druidic rites. This was neither suppression nor persecution, but it was an emphatic declaration that there was some element in druidism out of accord with the ideals of the Empire, and that impeded the accustomed policy of Roman toleration. Strabo has already told us that they practised rites repugnant to Latin usage, and there can be little doubt that this irreconcilable factor was human sacrifice ; for we know that in Carthage, too, the Romans set themselves to abolish this same custom. The reference to the next official action against the druids is in agreement with this hypothesis, for when Pliny tells us, in a passage quoted below (p. 90), that in the reign of Tiberius (A.D. 14-37) a decree of the senate was issued against these priests, the context of his disquisition on magic suggests, as Fustel de Coulanges observed,[1] that this severity was really inspired by the abominable practices of the order, and was not primarily directed against the druidic beliefs or doctrinal system. At any rate, we do know, on Mela's showing, that

[1] " Comment le Druidisme a disparu," in *Nouvelles Recherches sur quelques problèmes d'histoire*, Paris, 1891, p. 187. On this subject and the fall of the druids generally, see also Duruy, *C.R. de l'Academie des Sciences Morales et Politiques*, n.s. XIII (1880), p. 896 (reprinted *Revue Archeologique*, n.s. XXXIX (1880), p. 247) ; for a different view see D'Arbois de Jubainville, *Rev. Arch.*, n.s. XXXVIII (1897), p. 374.

at about this time the ritual of human sacrifice, as described by Diodorus and Strabo, was modified into a procedure in which the actual killing was omitted.

The third official movement was the suppression under Claudius (A.D. 41-54), and this time it certainly seems to have been a thorough attempt to eradicate all the druidic observances.[1] But we have no means of judging how severely it was prosecuted ; we can only note that it was not successful if it aimed at the extermination of the order, for we shall soon see that there were druids in Gaul long after this date.

Pomponius Mela wrote at about the period of the Claudian suppression, and we might therefore expect some fresh, if not particularly creditable, details concerning the druids. This makes it rather disappointing to find that his statement, except for the information about the mock sacrifice, is almost entirely based on that of Cæsar. He does, nevertheless, introduce the notion of the druids meeting in secret and remote places, and although this may easily be a mere rhetorical flourish on his part, it is interesting all the same as a possible result of the contemporary persecution.

POMPONIUS MELA. *De Situ Orbis*, III, 2, 18 and 19

There still remain traces of atrocious customs no longer practised, and although they now refrain from outright slaughter, yet they still draw blood from the victims led to the altar. They have, however, their own kind of eloquence, and teachers of wisdom called Druids. These profess to know the size and shape of the world, the movements of the heavens and of the stars, and the will of the gods. They teach many things to the nobles of Gaul in a course of instruction lasting as long as twenty years, meeting in secret either in a cave or in secluded dales. One of their dogmas has come to common knowledge, namely, that souls are eternal and that there is another life in the infernal regions, and this has been permitted manifestly because it makes the multitude readier for war. And it is for this reason too that they burn or bury with their dead, things appropriate to them in life, and that in times

---

[1] Compare the 4th century testimony of Victor Aurelius, *De Cæsaribus*, IV, 2 : " Denique bonis auctoribus compressa per eum vitia ac per Galliam Drysadarum famosæ superstitiones."

past they even used to defer the completion of business and the payment of debts until their arrival in another world. Indeed, there were some of them who flung themselves willingly on the funeral piles of their relatives in order to share the new life with them.

A few years later, during the reign of Nero (A.D. 54-68), we find this same picture drawn with the grand emphasis of Lucan's verse; and, incidentally, probably as a sort of poetical flourish, we have the groves mentioned for the first time as the haunts of the druids.

LUCAN. Pharsalia, I, 450-8

And you, O Druids, now that the clash of battle is stilled, once more have you returned to your barbarous ceremonies and to the savage usage of your holy rites. To you alone it is given to know the truth about the gods and deities of the sky, or else you alone are ignorant of this truth.[1] The innermost groves of far-off forests are your abodes. And it is you who say that the shades of the dead seek not the silent land of Erebus and the pale halls of Pluto ; rather, you tell us that the same spirit has a body again elsewhere, and that death, if what you sing is true, is but the mid-point of long life.

We depart, however, from this traditional account of the druids when we come to the *Natural History* of the elder Pliny, published about A.D. 77, for this work includes a generous parcel of new information as to the ritual and superstitions of the order. But the salient item of his testimony is that at this period the druids had degenerated into rather disreputable magicians, still retaining certain priestly functions perhaps, yet apparently without any vestige of the civil authority they had enjoyed in the time of Cæsar.

PLINY. Nat. Hist., XVI, 249

Here we must mention the awe felt for this plant by the Gauls. The Druids—for so their magicians are called—held nothing more sacred than the mistletoe and the tree that bears it, always supposing that tree to be the oak. But they choose groves formed of

---

[1] Lucan means that druidic teaching is so unusual that either they alone know the truth, or else they are ignorant of a truth that is the common property of the rest of mankind.

oaks for the sake of the tree alone, and they never perform any of their rites except in the presence of a branch of it ; so that it seems probable that the priests themselves may derive their name from the Greek word for that tree.   In fact, they think that everything that grows on it has been sent from heaven and is a proof that the tree was chosen by the god himself.   The mistletoe, however, is found but rarely upon the oak ; and when found, is gathered with due religious ceremony, if possible on the sixth day of the moon (for it is by the moon that they measure their months and years, and also their *ages* of thirty years).   They choose this day because the moon, though not yet in the middle of her course, has already considerable influence.   They call the mistletoe by a name meaning, in their language, the all-healing.   Having made preparation for sacrifice and a banquet beneath the trees, they bring thither two white bulls, whose horns are bound then for the first time.   Clad in a white robe, the priest ascends the tree and cuts the mistletoe with a golden sickle, and it is received by others in a white cloak. Then they kill the victims, praying that God will render this gift of his propitious to those to whom he has granted it.   They believe that the mistletoe, taken in drink, imparts fecundity to barren animals, and that it is an antidote for all poisons.   Such are the religious feelings that are entertained towards trifling things by many peoples.

Nat. Hist., XXIV, 103

Similar to savin is the plant called *selago*.   It is gathered without using iron and by passing the right hand through the left sleeve of the tunic, as though in the act of committing a theft.   The clothing must be white, the feet washed and bare, and an offering of wine and bread made before the gathering.   The Druids of Gaul say that the plant should be carried as a charm against every kind of evil, and that the smoke of it is good for diseases of the eyes.

Nat. Hist., XXIV, 104

The Druids, also, use a certain marsh-plant that they call *samolus*, this must be gathered with the left hand, when fasting, and is a charm against the diseases of cattle.   But the gatherer must not look behind him, nor lay the plant anywhere except in the drinking-troughs.

Nat. Hist., XXIX, 52

There is also another kind of egg, of much renown in the Gallic provinces, but ignored by the Greeks.   In the summer, numberless snakes entwine themselves into a ball, held together by a secretion from their bodies and by their spittle. This is called *anguinum*. The Druids say that hissing serpents throw this up into the air, and that it must be caught in a cloak, and not allowed to touch the ground ; and that one must instantly take to flight on horseback, as the serpents will pursue until some stream cuts them off. It may be tested, they say, by seeing if it floats against the current of a river, even though it be set in gold. But as it is the way of magicians to cast a cunning veil about their frauds, they pretend that these eggs can only be taken on a certain day of the moon, as though it rested with mankind to make the moon and the serpents accord as to the moment of the operation. I myself, however, have seen one of these eggs ; it was round, and about as large as a smallish apple ; the shell was cartalaginous, and pocked like the arms of a polypus. The Druids esteem it highly. It is said to ensure success in law-suits and a favourable reception with princes ; but this is false, because a man of the Vocontii, who was also a Roman knight, kept one of these eggs in his bosom during a trial, and was put to death by the Emperor Claudius, as far as I can see, for that reason alone.

Nat. Hist., XXX, 13

It (magic) flourished in the Gallic provinces, too, even down to a period within our memory ; for it was in the time of the Emperor Tiberius that a decree was issued against their Druids and the whole tribe of diviners and physicians. But why mention all this about a practice that has even crossed the ocean and penetrated to the utmost parts of the earth ? At the present day, Britannia is still fascinated by magic, and performs its rites with so much ceremony that it almost seems as though it was she who had imparted the cult to the Persians. To such a degree do peoples throughout the whole world, although unlike and quite unknown to one another, agree upon this one point. Therefore we cannot too highly appreciate our debt to the Romans for having put an end to this monstrous cult, whereby to murder a man was an act of the greatest devoutness, and to eat his flesh most beneficial.

Pliny gives us the only detailed account that we have of an actual druidic office. But his picture is probably incomplete by reason of his failure to explain the underlying significance of the mistletoe rite ; for all this ceremony can hardly have been occasioned by the mere magical or medical properties of the plant, and it is probable that the performance he describes was the manifestation of some belief dependent on an ancient form of tree-worship.[1] But at the moment, however, we are not so much interested in the druidic cults as in the status of the priests themselves.

We have said that Pliny's testimony is far from flattering, but we must notice that although Roman opinion, following upon an official suppression, treated the druids simply as wizards, they must nevertheless have retained in their religious capacity a certain dignity and impressiveness ; or so, at least, the tale of the sacrificial bulls, the white robe, and the golden sickle, suggests. Moreover, this view is emphasized by Pliny's comment upon the particularly august ceremonies of the magic art in Britain.

It is interesting, therefore, to turn immediately to our next author, Tacitus, who, in the first of the two passages quoted below, supplies the only well-founded and informative statement that we possess concerning the early druids in Great Britain. The event he is describing is the raid on the Isle of Anglesey by Suetonius Paulinus in A.D. 60, and even though Tacitus was patently unsympathetic with the unfortunate defenders, it does not look as though there could have been anything very august about their druids ; indeed, so far from possessing that authority in time of battle claimed for the order by Cæsar, the Anglesey druids seem to have been little better than a pack of howling dervishes.

But this was probably the result of their wellnigh hopeless circumstances, and we are able to find some confirmation of Pliny's general estimate in our second passage from Tacitus, wherein, in reference to the burning of the Capitol in A.D. 70, we rather surprisingly come upon the suggestion that the continental druids were occasionally, even at this date, of some political importance. The explanation must be that there were partial and local revivals of the druidic activities, following upon the attempt at their suppression, wherever there was a temporary weakening of the Roman power, as, indeed, there was in Gaul at this time. We have to admit,

[1] On this point see MacCulloch, *Religion of the Ancient Celts*, p. 162.

therefore, that although the first century after Christ undoubtedly saw the rapid decline of the power of the druids in the Roman provinces, there are nevertheless unmistakable signs that they did remain an effective factor in Keltic national life. In a word, the Romanisation of the Kelts had not by any means divested druidism of all its ancient significance as a beneficent religion, even though its practice was now officially considered as antisocial and black magic.

As regards druidism in Britain, however, it is, I think significant that Tacitus does not even mention them in the Agricola, a biography that is principally concerned with the events of a seven years' administration of the island. He knew, of course, that the British faith was much the same as that of their kinsfolk on the continent,[1] and, accordingly, he may not have felt himself under any obligation to attempt a minute description of the national customs in this respect ; but it is astonishing, nevertheless, when we think of his remarkable opportunities of hearing every detail of those seven years from his father-in-law, that the druids were of such little account in the ordinary domestic and military affairs of the province that their name does not once occur in the record of a long and busy administration. It certainly looks as though there cannot have been any concerted action on their part, or any discipline within the group under a powerful arch-druid, and it is very unlikely that there were any important annual gatherings at Stonehenge or anywhere else. In fact, there is no reason to suppose that our estimate of the status of the British druids during the second half of the first century, based on the Anglesey passage, was overstated, and we must conclude that at any rate in those districts where Roman rule was established druidism was completely ineffective and moribund.

TACITUS. *Annals*, XIV, 30 [2]

On the shore stood the opposing army with its dense array of armed warriors, while between the ranks dashed women in black

[1] Cf. *Agricola*, XI, 4.
[2] From the translation by Church and Brodribb, London, 1876.

attire like the Furies, with hair dishevelled, waving brands. All around, the Druids, lifting up their hands to heaven and pouring forth dreadful imprecations, scared our soldiers by the unfamiliar sight, so that, as if their limbs were paralysed, they stood motionless and exposed to wounds. Then urged by their general's appeal and mutual encouragements not to quail before a troup of frenzied women, they bore the standards onwards, smote down all resistance, and wrapped the foe in the flames of his own brands. A force was next set over the conquered, and their groves, devoted to inhuman superstitions, were destroyed. They deemed it, indeed, a duty to cover their altars with the blood of captives and to consult their deities through human entrails.

Histories, IV, 54 [1]

The Gauls, they remembered, had captured the city in former days, but, as the abode of Jupiter was uninjured, the Empire had survived ; whereas now the Druids declared, with the prophetic utterances of an idle superstition, that this fatal conflagration (of the Capitol) was a sign of the anger of heaven, and portended universal empire for the Transalpine nations.

The evidence of Dion Chrysostom, the golden-mouthed orator, dates from about A.D. 100, and it seems to be, at first sight, in rather marked disagreement with the opinion we have just formed.

DION CHRYSOSTOM. *Orations*, XLIX (*Teub.*, 1919, pp. 123, 124)

The Persians, I think, have men called Magi . . . , the Egyptians, their priests . . . , and the Indians, their Brahmins. On the other hand, the Kelts have men called Druids, who concern themselves with divination and all branches of wisdom. And without their advice even kings dared not resolve upon nor execute any plan, so that in truth it was they who ruled, while the kings, who sat on golden thrones and fared sumptuously in their palaces, became mere ministers of the Druids' will.

But Dion had not travelled in Gaul ; and he was an orator, not an historian ; so that all this may fairly be discounted as a rhetorical elaboration of some one else's earlier statement of the former power of the druids. At any rate, that

---

[1] From the translation by Church and Brodribb, London, 1873.

is what the talk of golden thrones will suggest to most people, and it is plain that we should have had very different accounts from Tacitus and Pliny had the druids still possessed the power with which they are credited in this passage. Moreover, it may well be that all Dion's remark really means is that no civil action was undertaken without the consent of the gods, an enterprise being abandoned if the druids declared the omens unfavourable. If so, this is no more than the state of affairs obtaining in early Rome itself, and it is only the exaggerated language of the orator that suggests that the druids maintained more than the ordinary power of priests and wise men.

On the other hand, there is no need to under-estimate the possible power of individual members of the order, wherever druids survived, over those of the native princes who had still little love for the Romans, and who were able to raise these traditional councillors to temporarily important positions. We shall see that at a later period the Irish druids certainly had an authority of the kind described by Dion, and there is even an instance of something of the sort in England (p. 98). But, all things considered, I think that so far as the Roman Empire is concerned there is nothing very much in this particular passage to increase materially the prestige of the order.

The next references to the druids, following the chronological order of authors, date from the 3rd century, and are contained in the works of Clement of Alexandria and Hippolytus. The extracts, however, are solely concerned with the historical aspects of druidic belief, and their evidence may for the moment be postponed. I shall therefore pass immediately to that dubious and uncertain compilation, the *Historia Augusta*, and quote the testimony of Lampridius and of Vopiscus, writers (or one writer?) who flourished about A.D. 300, in order to set forth what little is known about the survival of druidism in Gaul after more than two centuries of Roman rule. The first passage relates to the year A.D. 235, when Alexander Severus was starting on an expedition to free Gaul from the Germans.

LAMPRIDIUS.   *Alex. Severus*, LIX, 5.

While he (Alexander Severus) was on his way, a Druidess cried out to him in the Gallic tongue, " Go forward, but hope not for victory, nor put trust in thy soldiers."

Vopiscus also refers to the prophecy of a druidess in the second half of the 3rd century.

VOPISCUS.   *Numerianus*, XIV

When Diocletian, so my grandfather told me, was sojourning in a tavern in the land of the Tongri in Gaul, at the time when he was still of humble rank in the army, and had occasion to settle the daily account for his keep with a certain druidess, this woman said to him, " You are far too greedy and far too economical, O Diocletian."   Whereto he replied, jestingly, " I will be more liberal when I am emperor," to which the druidess answered, " Laugh not, Diocletian, for when you have killed The Boar, you will indeed be emperor."

After this Diocletian coveted the purple and never missed the chance of killing a boar when out hunting ; but Aurelian, and Probus and Tacitus, and then Carus, were all emperors before him, so that he was moved to exclaim, " I kill the boars, but it is always another who reaps the reward ! "   At last, however, he killed the præfect Arrius, surnamed The Boar, and then the prophecy of the druidess was fulfilled, and he ascended to the imperial throne.

Vopiscus also relates another druidical prophecy that was made in the reign of Aurelian (A.D. 270-275).

VOPISCUS.   *Aurelianus*, XLIII, 4 and 5

He (Asclepiodotus) used to say that on a certain occasion Aurelian consulted the Gaulish druidesses to find out whether his descendants would remain in possession of the imperial crown. These women told him that no name would become more illustrious in the state annals than that of the line of Claudius.   It is true, of course, that the present Emperor Constantius is of the same stock, and I think that his descendants will assuredly attain to the glory foretold by the druidesses.

One asks, of course, whether this reference to *dryades*, or druidesses, really constitutes legitimate evidence of the survival of druids and druidism in the 3rd century. All that we know about these women is that they were fortune-tellers, such as we might find among many peoples, and it is possible that the name dryades, or some form of name like it, was bestowed on them by these two authors through a misapprehension based on an imperfect knowledge of the status and functions of the true druids. They might have represented, in fact, to the uncritical eyes of the biographers of the emperors, the remaining Keltic exponents of a known druidic practice of earlier times, that is divination ; and so might have been called druidesses, regardless of the question of their actual connection with the real druidic order.

A more serious consideration is that there is some slight evidence of the existence among the continental Kelts of priestesses in the proper sense of the word (p. 140), and these were not, to our knowledge, called druids or druidesses. We cannot assume, therefore, that anyone performing a religious rite, or practising divination, in the Keltic lands was a member of the druidic order ; in England, for example, it seems that Boadicea herself exercised certain priestly functions, and no one has yet thought of calling her a druidess. This freedom of action in the performance of religious observances by those who were not druids, increases the likelihood of the existence of an independent class of male and female soothsayers and fortune-tellers, so that we have good reason for some hesitation in the matter of the women mentioned by Lampridius and Vopiscus, before we accept the mention of them as proof of the survival of druidism in their time.

On the other hand, we do know that diviners or fortune-tellers were, in the earlier centuries, a sub-order of the druids, so that I think it must be admitted that on the whole the chances are that these women, by continuing the func-tions of the Vates, were invested with a traditional authority that entitles them to be regarded as corporate members of the old priestly system. We have heard from Tacitus of the association of women with the druids in Anglesey ; and, in addition, we know that there were female diviners in Ireland (*ban-filid* or *ban-fáthi*) who were popularly grouped with the druids, and were sometimes actually called druid-esses (*bandrui*) by the mediæval scribes.[1] There is nothing, therefore, inherently unlikely in women usurping the druidic reputation in Gaul, though the conjunction of their professional fortune-telling with an inn-keeper's life, as related in the first extract from Vopiscus, is an obvious index of the very low estate into which druidism had fallen.

That such continuity between the Vates and the women fortune-tellers is reasonable, is suggested by the fact that at the end of the 4th century we find that a pedigree reaching back to the druids themselves was still a boast of honourable ancestry. This is illustrated by two passages from Ausonius, and, although it does not by any means decide the question of the pretensions of the 3rd century diviners to the title of druids, at least it provides evidence of the continued memory of the order a hundred years later.

AUSONIUS. *Commem. professorum*, IV, 7-10

If report does not lie, you were sprung from the stock of the druids of Bayeux, and traced your hallowed line from the temple of Belenus.

X, 22-30

Nor must I leave unmentioned the old man Phœbicius, who, though keeper of Belenus's temple, got no profit thereby. Yet he, sprung, as rumour goes, from the stock of the druids of Armorica (i.e. Brittany), obtained a chair at Bordeaux by his son's help.

Finally, we have to take into account a scrap of evidence telling of the survival of Keltic wise men, or *magi*, in England in the first half of the 5th century. Their interest here is that they were obviously of the same character as the Gaulish wise women, or druidesses, that Vopiscus tells us were consulted by Aurelian. The passage is from "Nennius," a work that dates from about A.D. 800, but there is a faint possibility that in this particular extract, since it quotes

---

[1] The word is not found frequently. See the Rennes Dinnsenchas (*Revue Celtique*, XVI (1895), 34, and cf. XV (1894), 326) ; E. Windisch, *Die altirische Heldensage Táin Bó Cualgne*, Leipzig, 1905, 331 ; also the " Siege of Druim Damhghaire (*Revue Celtique*, XLIII (1926), 57, 79, 104).

Roman consul-names as authority for the dates, the source may have been a lost contemporary history of the events described.[1] The extract refers to the British king Vortigern at the time when the discovery of his incestuous marriage had brought down upon him the utmost wrath of St. Germanus.

NENNIUS. *Historia Britonum*, 40

After this, the king summoned his magicians in order that he might enquire of them what he ought to do.

An Irish version of the *Historia Britonum* was made in the 14th century, and the word *magos* was therein translated *druids*. This naturally does not prove that Vortigern's *magi* called themselves by that name, but it illustrates rather well the survival of functions and office that may have been a direct heritage from druidism in decay.

We have now reached the end of the literary evidence bearing upon ancient druidism. The outstanding fact is that only once, in the account given by Cæsar, are we vouchsafed any information about druids and druidism in the days of their power. All the succeeding references to them belong to the period when their power was gone and when their organisation was smashed.[2] And this means that we must be very much on our guard against under-estimating their earlier significance in the Keltic world.

But so far as this classical opinion is concerned, the story suggested by all these extracts is a simple one. We know that the druids had a reputation outside Gaul as early as the 2nd century B.C., and that in Cæsar's time they were an organised and powerful body having important educational, judicial, political, as well as religious, functions ; more-over, the order included various kinds of officials, priests and

[1] See Liebermann, *Essays in Mediæval History presented to T. F. Tout*, Manchester, 1925, p. 40.

[2] Unless, as Professor Rose suggests to me, the passages from Diodorus Siculus, Strabo, and Dion Chrysostom have enough in common to show that they are borrowing from an earlier account, perhaps by Poseidonius ; if so, they may refer back to the period of Gallic independence.

prophets and poets, while we gather that some of its members were free to devote themselves entirely to the duties of government and international affairs. The rebellion of Vercingetorix, however, seems to have spelt ruin for the order as a corporate society, and henceforward the preservation of traditional druidism was in the hands of a minority of individual anti-Roman members. At the beginning of the Christian era, the cruel sacrificial rites of their religion brought them into direct conflict with Rome, and this ended in their complete exclusion from recognised Gallic religion. At the end of the 1st century their status in the eyes of the outside world had sunk to that of mere magicians, though it is nevertheless possible that druidism was still to some extent a current faith and capable of occasional revival wherever Roman power was temporarily weakened. In the 2nd century there is no direct reference to druids or druidism, and after this we learn nothing more than that there were female fortune-tellers called *dryades* in Gaul in the 3rd century, and that in the 4th century there were still certain people who could boast of druidic descent.

FIG. 20. — Stone with ogam inscription, Port St. Mary, Isle of Man.

The bulk of the evidence quoted refers, of course, to Gaul in particular. We have no knowledge from these sources of the ancient druidism in Ireland, and all that we have been able to produce for the whole of Britain is one brief mention of the druids in Anglesey. So far as England is concerned, there is no reference to druids at all, and it seems obvious that in this country they were of negligible importance as an organised body after the Claudian conquest.

It is alleged, however, that the existence of druids in the Isle of Man can be proved by means of a stone found near Port St. Mary in the parish of Rushen.[1]   This was a sandstone slab (Fig. 20) nearly 4 feet high, bearing an inscription in ogam characters that has been read as

DOVAIDONA MAQI DROATA

Droata, said Sir John Rhys, is the genitive of the early Goidelic form of the word for druid ; and although *druada* was put forward as an alternative reading, it seems to have been generally accepted that druid is the meaning of the third word.   Accordingly, if Keltic scholars have made up their minds that it cannot be a proper name, and their interpretation

[THE STONE] OF DOVAIDONA, SON OF THE DRUID

be accepted, we can at least say that there were druids (in the Irish sense) in Man as late as the 5th or 6th century, for the inscription itself is not likely to be older than that. But clearly this is very little advance upon the knowledge we already possess.

At this point, it will be best to say a word about the other inscriptions and sculptures that have been thought to name or to depict the druids ; but I may remark in advance that the information to be gained from this source is negligible.

In ancient Gaul the word druid does not appear in any inscription at all, no doubt because the name had ceased to be an honourable title in the eyes of the Romanising Gauls by the time they had learnt to set up inscribed monuments of their own.   One example, however, is alleged to have existed in the Mosel country ; but the stone is now lost, and so formidable a chorus of condemnation has assailed the surviving transcriptions that we are compelled to treat them as worthless, and I do not propose to perpetuate error by a fresh notice of them.[2]

---

[1] *The Academy*, 1890, 954, p. 134 ; 955, p. 154 ; 957, p. 201. P. M. C. Kermode, *Proc. Soc. Ant. Scot.*, XLV (1911), 437.

[2] The inscription is given as SILVANO | SACR ET NYMPHIS LOCI | ARETE DRVIS | ANTISTITA SOMNO MONITA | D, by J. C. von Orelli,

FIG. 21.—FOURTH FACE (LOWER SECTION) OF STONE ALTAR, MAVILLY

Just as Gallo-Roman inscriptions ignore the druids, so do Gallo-Roman sculptures. Of course, it is tempting wherever one comes across the representation of a venerable and nameless person, to say that he may have been a druid, but I do not know a single example that can be recommended with full confidence. The ingenious suggestion of Borlase [1] that the elders on the Montmorillon sculptures were druids is ruled out because the work is really of mediæval date, and not Gallo-Roman at all; and I can only say that the most promising instance that has come to my notice is one of the reliefs on the altar of Mavilly, near Beaune (Fig. 21). The group, w ich is about 3 feet high, consists of a dignified seated personage, accompanied by a dog and a bird, behind whom stands a man holding his hands over his eyes; and the natural interpretation is that the scene represents the healing of a blind man. Now Pliny makes it clear that the druids possessed considerable medical lore, and he even mentions that they had a particular remedy for diseases of the eye; and the dignity of the figure suggests a priest; hence the supposition that the seated person is a native physician-priest, a druid in fact. It may be so; but I am not impressed. However, M. René Gadant, who has described the monument in a most instructive study,[2] points out that there is nothing typically Roman about its form, and that its inspiration is rather Greco-Asiatic than Roman; wherefore, he thinks, it may be a much more valuable document of native religion than most people suppose. But I confess I find it difficult to share this view. The monument was erected by the Ædui, the people who were proud to style themselves friends of the Romans; and, to take a single instance ready to hand, the two heads in this very group seem to me to be obviously executed in the Roman

Inscriptionum Latinarum selectarum amplissima collectio, Turici, 1828, I, 2200. For a discussion see Charles Robert, *Épigraphie gallo-rom. de la Moselle*, Paris, 1873.

[1] *Antiquities of Cornwall*, London, 1769, pp. 104 ff., and Pl. (p. 53). I do not know the altar he mentions on pp. 153, 157.

[2] René Gadant, *La Religion des Éduens et le monument de Mavilly*, Autun, 1922; Espérandieu, *Recueil général des bas-reliefs . . . de la Gaule Romaine* (22), III, 2067.

manner. I cannot see, therefore, why this priest, if he is a priest, could not have been a minister of the official Roman version of the native faith, and no more representative of original druidism than an English Protestant is representative of the Roman Church. Moreover, there is an entirely different interpretation of this sculpture in the field, for M. Salomon Reinach has argued [1] that the twelve figures on the altar represent the twelve Roman gods known as the *Dii consentes ;* and he recognises amongst them Jupiter, Neptune, Vulcan, Mars, Mercury, Apollo, Venus, Ceres, Diana, and Minerva. And when we come to this particular group we find that instead of a druid healing the blind, he discovers a seated figure of Juno with her eagle, and behind her the Roman goddess Vesta, who, as protector of the hearth, is shown shielding her eyes from the smoke.

Passing from Gaul to Ireland, we find there is one single monument (Fig. 22) deserving of mention. It is a stone in the Killeen Cormac cemetery, County Kildare,[2] that has bilingual inscriptions : one,

IVVENE DRVVIDES

and the other, in ogam characters, translated

DUFTANO SAFEI SAHATTOS

that is,

[THE STONE] OF DUFTAN, THE WISE SAGE

The Latin inscription, being highly unusual in many respects, has been under suspicion ; and Hübner, for instance, decided against it.[3] But although every one is alive to the possibility of druidic advertisement at the time when druidism became a fashionable antiquity, that is to say, after the Romantic Movement, there is a good deal to be

[1] *Cultes, Mythes, et Religions*, Paris, 1908, III, p. 191.

[2] G. Petrie and M. Stokes, *Christian Inscriptions in the Irish Language*, Dublin, 1878, II, p. 2, and Pl. I.

[3] E. Hübner, *Inscriptiones Britanniæ Christianæ*, Berlin and London, 1876, p. xviii.

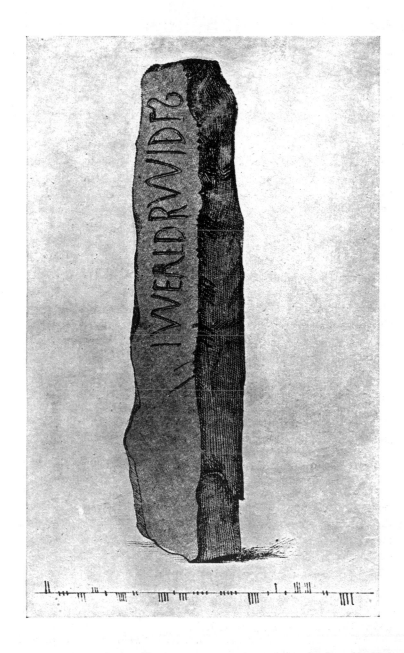

FIG. 22.—INSCRIBED STONE FROM KILLEEN CORMAC, CO. KILDARE

(AFTER PETRIE AND STOKES)

said on the other side,[1] and I think it would be unfair to ignore this stone. But elsewhere in Ireland stones do not bear the name druid, even in native characters ; and its occurrence in Latin suggests it must have been the work of some clerk who chose the word from his classical lore as homage to a learned young man, who, in his Keltic epitaph was *not* called a druid. It suggests, in fact, that the scholar's notion of a druid at the time this monument was erected, in the second half of the 1st millennium A.D., was derived from book-learning, and was not that of the Keltic druid ; him they called merely a magician, *magus*. Thus, it may be that this word here on the Killeen Cormac stone is only an ignorant and ill-cut Latinist compliment to a person who was definitely not what the Kelts themselves would call a druid.

[1] See H. Gaidoz, *Notice sur les inscriptions latines de l'Irlande, Melanges publiées par l'École des Hautes Études*, Paris, 1878, pp. 124 ff.

CHAPTER IV

RELIGION

WE pass on now to an account of druidism itself. The passages in ancient literature that have just been quoted do not give us as much information as we should like to have upon this subject, and it is natural that we should try to add to the picture by recourse to later Keltic literature and folk-lore.

But in this book I want to distinguish very clearly between our positive knowledge of the druids and of druidism, and inferences concerning them that are not based upon this knowledge; so we ought continually to keep in mind the simple proposition that because druidism was associated with certain of the Keltic-speaking peoples, it does not follow that all phenomena of ancient Keltic religion are to be taken as evidence of the nature of druidism. That is to say, as we can only *guess* how far druidism was based upon, or included, pre-Keltic belief, how far it was represented in later Keltic religion, and how far druidism corresponded with Keltic belief in the non-druidic provinces, we must be very cautious in admitting any evidence depending upon such premises. In this chapter, therefore, I intend to give only a minimum account of druidism, instead of one that is extravagantly complete.

The subject suggests itself for consideration under various headings, and I propose to treat them in serial form. Thus I shall discuss (1) the druidic doctrine of immortality; (2) druidic theology, ethics, philosophy, and lore; (3) procedure; and (4) the organisation of the order.

(1) THE DOCTRINE OF IMMORTALITY

Cæsar's statement is undoubtedly the most important contribution towards a knowledge of the druidic belief in this matter. The druids taught, he says, the immortality of the human soul, and maintained that it passed into other bodies after death.

The first thing that we have to note is that this belief, probably known to other writers only in the terms of Cæsar's report, was identified by Diodorus Siculus with the Pythagorean doctrine, according to which the souls of men proceed, after death, to fulfil expiatory existences in animal or other tenements. Such an identification was upheld, as we have seen, at the beginning of the Christian era by Timagenes, and also by Hippolytus, who wrote the following passage in the 3rd century :—

HIPPOLYTUS. *Philosophumena*, I, xxv [1]

The Keltic Druids applied themselves thoroughly to the Pythagorean philosophy, being urged to this pursuit by Zamolxis, the slave of Pythagoras, a Thracian by birth, who came to those parts after the death of Pythagoras, and gave them opportunity of studying the system. And the Kelts believe in their Druids as seers and prophets because they can foretell certain events by the Pythagorean reckoning and calculations. We will not pass over the origins of their learning in silence, since some have presumed to make distinct schools of the philosophies of these peoples. Indeed, the Druids also practice the magic arts.

Shortly before this was written, Clement of Alexandria had also made a brief reference to the subject; in this he seems to suggest that he considered druidism to be the older system.

CLEMENT OF ALEXANDRIA. *Stromata*, I, xv, 70, 1

Alexander, in his book " On the Pythagorean Symbols," relates that Pythagoras was a pupil of Nazaratus the Assyrian . . . and will have it that, in addition to these, Pythagoras was a hearer of the Galatæ and the Brahmins.

---

[1] Cf. *Philosophumena*, I, ii, 17. Origen also refers to the druids in *Contra Celsum*, I, 16, so does Cyril of Alexandria, *Contra Iulianum*, IV, 133.

Stromata, I, xv, 71, 3 [1]

Thus philosophy, a science of the highest utility, flourished in antiquity among the barbarians, shedding its light over the nations. And afterwards it came to Greece. First in its ranks were the pro- phets of the Egyptians ; and the Chaldeans among the Assyrians ; and the Druids among the Gauls ; and the Samanæans among the Bactrians ; and the philosophers of the Kelts ; and the Magi of the Persians. . . .

The same identification of the druidic belief in immortality with the Pythagorean teaching was made by Valerius Maxi- mus in the early part of the 1st century.

VALERIUS MAXIMUS, II, 6, 10

Having done with the description of the town (Marseilles), an old custom of the Gauls may now be mentioned ; for it is said that they lend to each other sums that are repayable in the next world, so firmly are they convinced that the souls of men are immortal. And I would call them foolish indeed, if it were not for the fact that what these trousered barbarians believe is the very faith of Greek Pythagoras himself.

There is a considerable conflict of opinion as to whether this identification is justifiable or not. In order to test its likelihood the first thing to be ascertained is whether it is at all probable that Pythagoras ever came into contact with the Kelts. It is true, of course, that the legends of the travels of Pythagoras are not by any means invention of his later biographers, but there is certainly a tendency to widen their extent in the more recent accounts. Thus the original tradition confined his journeys to Egypt, Chaldea, and Persia, and there is no authority of any kind for the subsequent assertions that he visited Arabia, and India, and Gaul. In so far as concerns this last country, we have only the statement of Alexander Polyhistor, cited by Clement, and it is of no historical value, being rejected as early as the 3rd century A.D. by Diogenes Laertius. Nor is the remark of Hippolytus about the rôle played by Zamolxis of any

---

[1] Cf., as probable source, the first passage from Diogenes Laertius (p. 75).

practical significance. Although the legend that Zamolxis was the slave of Pythagoras dates back at least to the 5th century B.C., we find that Herodotus, who reports it,[1] himself believed that Zamolxis belonged to a much earlier age than that of Pythagoras, and was, in fact, a Getan deity. This was the true position ; but because the Getæ were notable in the ancient world on account of their claim to immortality,[2] it is easy to understand how a fancied coincidence of ideas on this subject with the creed of the Pythagoreans suggested the tale circulated at a later date that Pythagoras and Zamolxis were really master and slave. It is equally obvious that the fable of the influence of Zamolxis as an apostle of the Pythagorean system would be expanded, as in the instance of the Gauls related by Hippolytus, wherever this supposed coincidence of religious ideas was observed.

There is accordingly no assured record of any intercourse between Pythagoras and the Kelts, and if we choose to believe, in spite of this, that a direct connection did exist, all that can be said in favour of it is that by their colonising activities, as we have seen, the Greeks had certainly rendered the requisite passage of philosophical ideas possible ; and, that as the Greek towns of Italy were the real stronghold of developed Pythagoreanism, the school was advantageously placed for propagation in the direction of Gaul.[3]

But there are one or two considerations that seem to weigh heavily against the possibility of Pythagorean influence

---

[1] *Herodotus*, IV, 96. [2] *Ibid.*, 93.

[3] It is claimed, too, that the occasional occurrence of the pentagram, which Lucian (ed. *Jacobitz*, I, 330) says was a Pythagorean symbol, on Gallic and British coins (Fig. 23) is a proof that Gaul absorbed some of the tenets of Pythagoreanism. But I am inclined to doubt this, for the copying of a symbol used by Pythagorus no more proves a knowledge of his teaching than the copying of the head of Philip of Macedon, so frequent in Gallic coinage, proves a knowledge of, or obedience to, this monarch's decrees. But see Rice Holmes, *Gaul*, p. 34.

FIG. 23.—Coin of the Suessiones, showing pentagram on reverse.

in Gaul. In the first place, I very much doubt whether
Pythagoreanism ever spread *anywhere* far afield outside a
limited world of educated Greeks ; for it was essentially
esoteric and exclusive, admission to the school only being
accorded to the privileged few ; that is to say, I do not
think it was the kind of faith likely to have been paraded
before barbarians. Moreover, as an active cult it was not
long-lived ; it arose in the 6th century, flourished in Magna
Græcia in the 5th century, and was then, rather suddenly,
suppressed. As a result of this suppression, its philosophy
enjoyed a short vogue in Hellas proper, but by the middle
of the 4th century the school had ceased to exist.

And there are two other points. Firstly, the recorded
instances of resemblances between the druidic and Pythagorean systems are not sufficiently remarkable to justify a
claim for their intimate relationship ; and secondly, in each
case the growth of the systems can be explained in local
terms without recourse to such distant borrowings.

It is at once noticeable in the testimony of Valerius
Maximus that the Gallic custom he describes, that of the
repayment of debts after death, does not really conform with
the Pythagorean doctrine. And this divergent view upon
the soul's immortality is also emphasized by Mela who told
us that the Gauls burnt or buried with their dead such things
as they would normally need in life, while sometimes the sur-
vivors were even willing to kill themselves in order to share
the new life with their beloved dead. Such practices show
that the Gauls did not by any means appreciate or profess
Pythagoras's teaching, according to which such continued
enjoyment of one's belongings, or the transaction of postponed affairs, after death was impossible. They could not
have believed, it is clear, in an instant metempsychosis, perhaps into animal as well as into other human bodies, but
rather in the survival of the identity of the deceased in its
recognisable form, apparently in the first instance in or about
the grave, and, later on, in another region.[1] Moreover, the
idea of justice, so far as we can tell, was absent from the

---

[1] The expression *orbe alio* in Lucan does not mean *in another
world*. See Reinach, *Revue Celtique*, XXII (1901), 447.

faith of the Kelts : for they do not seem to have distinguished between the fate of the good and the fate of the evil, and they are not likely, therefore, to have had any notion of an expiatory succession of lives, whereby the soul is prisoned in a chain of earthly bodies, that is the essential of the Pythagorean creed. In fact, the kernel of the simple druidic belief, as it is now known to us, seems to have been summed up by Lucan : " The same spirit has a body again elsewhere, and death is but the mid-point of long life."

The doctrine of metempsychosis was not, of course, invented by Pythagoras ; but there is, nevertheless, not the slightest reason to suppose that he founded his system upon Gaulish teaching. For a long time it was believed that he had borrowed his notions from Egypt, but the correct view is undoubtedly that his sources were the dogmas of the Orphic religion [1] that was first developed in the semi-barbarous frontiers of Thrace. It is allowable, then, that there may have been a substratum of elemental barbaric belief common to both druidism and Pythagoreanism, but this is very far from admitting that there was any actual community between the schools in their developed forms.

It is an interesting point, however, because it shows that there is also very little likelihood of druidism owing anything to Pythagoreanism, quite apart from the outstanding improbability that the Kelts would adopt such radical beliefs at foreign instigation. For, in reality, their doctrine of immortality and the reincarnation of the soul, as taught by the druids, was simply the expression of a frequently occurring savage belief with which the ethnographer is perfectly familiar ; and, accordingly, there is no need to go out of the way to attribute such a faith, when we meet it in the Keltic world, to the influence of Greek thought. Even such wild folk as the aborigines of Central Australia, for example, believe that human personality survives death in the form of a spirit that may be re-born into the world, and a large number of kindred notions held by other primitive societies

[1] For the relation of Orphism to Pythagoreanism see Cornford, *From Religion to Philosophy*, London, 1912, 198 ; and Eisler, *Weltenmantel und Himmelszelt*, Munich, 1910, 679 f.

have been recorded.[1] Perhaps a parallel creed in this respect with that of druidism is the belief of the Mandingo people of West Africa who hold, according to M. Delafosse,[2] that every living person has a soul (*niama*), or dynamic force, that is free after death to reside where it will, either in the corpse, in the home, in a sacred object, or in the body of a living being.

We conclude, therefore, that there is very little to be said in favour of the identification of druidism and Pythagoreanism suggested by the Romans ; and, in truth, the confusion of the two may properly be attributed to the accident that the doctrine of transmigration was a strange and remarkable thing in Roman eyes. To a people with their own gloomy notions of the future estate, such a theory of immortality could not fail to attract their especial notice, and consequently they would be liable to identify any two religious systems known to them in which this doctrine was taught. Therefore, I think we may be reasonably content with the view that the druidic teaching of the re-birth of the soul was part of the natural religion of a primitive society, and owed nothing to contact with the Greeks.

We must now try to formulate some statement of the real druidic belief on this subject, and, in order to do so, we must first obtain, if it is possible, a little more information than that given by the classical writers. If it was true, as we are told by them, that the certainty of immortality, in whatever terms it may have been stated, was sufficiently powerful to rob death of its terrors for the common people, then we are fully justified in searching later Keltic lore and legend for some reflection of the actual form of the belief so generally and firmly held, whether it was actual transmigration, or some other doctrine.

As a matter of fact, in Keltic literature there is very little sign of a common belief in metempsychosis, but there are

[1] In general, see Frazer, *The Belief in Immortality*, London, 1912 (for the Australians, I, p. 92 f.) ; see also article, " Transmigration " in Hastings' *Encycl. of Religion and Ethics*, and A. Bertholet, *The Transmigration of Souls*, London, 1909.

[2] *Haut-Senegal, Niger*, Paris, 1912, III, 165 f.

three or four well-known stories in the Irish sagas of the
re-birth of individual persons.[1] For example, the goddess
Etain, the wife of the chieftain Mider, was changed by a
jealous rival into an insect, and whirled hither and thither
over Ireland until finally she fell into a wine-cup in the
house of the Ulster chief Etar, where she was swallowed by
his wife and in due course re-born, retaining the same name
and identity, though no memory of her former life.   There
is also a version of the birth-story of the hero Cúchulainn,
according to which he was a reincarnation of the god Lug,
who had committed himself in the form of a child to the
care of Dechtire and had then died, and passed into her in
the guise of a little animal while she was drinking.   Both of
these stories date back to the Book of the Dun Cow, that
is the early 11th century, and, taken on their merits, they
are obviously antique legends of the primitive, i.e. pre-
Christian, Kelts.

There is also a tale in the Voyage of Bran to the effect
that the 7th century king Mongan, son of the supernatural
Manannan, was really the dead Finn, son of Cumal, " though
he would not let it be told."   Again, there is the story of
Túan Mac Cairill, one of the fabulous immigrants into Ireland from Spain, who after a long life was changed succes-
sively into a stag, a boar, a hawk, and a salmon, all the
while preserving his identity, though each metamorphosis
lasted many years ; finally, in the fish-form, he was eaten
by the wife of Cairill and then re-born.

Welsh romance gives another example of a re-birth in
the story of the famous 6th century bard Taliessin.   In
manuscript this does not approach anything like the antiquity of the Irish texts, but that does not necessarily lessen
the folklore value of its component elements, and as, in this
instance, we find an episode of re-birth after being eaten of
the same kind as that related of Etain and Cúchulainn.
there need be no serious doubt of its equal antiquity.   The

---

[1] See the essay by Alfred Nutt, " The Celtic Doctrine of Rebirth,"
appended to Kuno Meyer's edition of the *Voyage of Bran*, London,
1895-1897.   The reader will find here a full and excellent discussion
of the whole subject of druidic belief in immortality.

story goes that a woman Cerridwen was pursuing Gwion, and that the two embarked upon a transformation combat at the end of which Gwion turned himself into a grain of wheat, whereupon Cerridwen, changing into a black hen, instantly devoured him. She bore him nine months in her womb, and when she was delivered of him she could not bring herself to kill him because of his great beauty, so she exposed him to the sea ; but he was rescued and became Taliessin, the marvellous bard.

We cannot pretend that such scraps of Keltic mythology are a certain index of the content of primitive Keltic religion, but at least it can be said that the comparative rarity of these tales, and the fact that in each case they are invariably attached either to divinities or to heroes, make it plain enough that the privilege of metamorphosis and re-birth was not thought to be within the reach of ordinary mortals. Moreover, there is not, from beginning to end, even the faintest suggestion that the chain of successive lives was a method of religious or ethical purification, or that it was determined by a doctrine of moral retribution and that liberation of the soul was the ultimate hope. This is the essential of a developed creed in transmigration, and the absence of such notions in Keltic legend is a proof that the stories of re-birth are not the outcome of a religious philosophy, but are a sequel to normal primitive speculation. Thus it is likely that such simple Keltic folklore as the belief of some of the islanders in the Hebrides that the soul resides in a bird after death, or that of the Kerry peasants who will not eat hares because they think that they contain the souls of their grandmothers, is independent of any settled theory of transmigration, and is merely an example of primitive thought of a kind that can be studied in most isolated and simple societies.

We cannot claim, therefore, that the druids professed the doctrine of transmigration in its final form, that is to say, in the classical terms by which it was understood by the Greeks or by the Indians. All that the evidence seems to show is that they believed in the continued existence of the same soul in a new but recognisable body after death. This

is in accord with many stories in the Irish sagas of the return
of the dead in their familiar living form, such as the re-
appearance of Cúchulainn before St. Patrick. And it is
entirely in agreement with the custom of placing food-
offerings, and equipment for fighting or hunting or domestic
pursuits, in the grave by the side of the corpse.

(2) Druidic Theology, Ethics, Philosophy, and Lore

There is very little to be said as to the general theological system of the druids, for it is hardly possible to claim
on the strength of the available information that they professed a faith distinct from that of the ordinary Keltic
pantheism. The subject is, of course, part of a larger
question, and it will be found that the hypotheses relating
to a special druidic theology, or to druidic customs and
doctrines at variance with those generally held in the Keltic
world, are nearly all the incidental machinery of a particular theory of druidic origins. It is true that Pliny speaks
of their worshipping one single god, but the context makes
it clear that he is referring to the special deity associated
with the oak-tree cult and mistletoe ceremonies that he is
describing. At any rate, Diodorus, Mela, Lucan, and Tacitus
all speak of their revering a plurality of gods, and there is
no hint either of a selective theology or of monotheism.
Cæsar tells us that the Gauls, following the druidic teaching,
claimed descent from a particular god corresponding to Dis
in the Latin pantheon, whom they perhaps regarded as a
Supreme Being ; and in a well-known passage [1] he adds that
they worshipped Mercury, Apollo, Mars, Jupiter, and Minerva, and had much the same notions about these deities
as the rest of the world. Keltic pantheism was, in fact,
fundamentally the same as the ancient pantheism of Italy,
and Cæsar's remarks imply that there was nothing in the
druidic creed, apart from the doctrine of immortality, that
made their faith extraordinary. In short, we must be prepared to believe that druidism professed, or was in sympathy
with, all the known tenets of ancient Keltic religion, and the

[1] *De Bello Gallico*, VI, 17.

gods of the druids were the familiar and multifarious deities of the Keltic pantheon.

Similarly, there is very little to say about the ethical teaching of the druids. The little triad of instruction reported by Diogenes Laertius (p. 75) " Worship the Gods, Do no evil, Be Manly," is also a summary of an Indian system and so may not have been an actual pronouncement of the druids, though it probably describes fairly accurately their attitude on the subject of behaviour ; but it is couched in such vague terms that its translation into Greek has robbed it of nearly all its practical significance. We can only observe that the judicial functions reported by Cæsar imply a fairly well-defined code enforcing the sanctity of human life and of personal and public property, and we know that bravery was encouraged by an insistence on the doctrine of immortality. There is, as a matter of fact, very little reflection of this in early Keltic literature, but that is no reason for refusing to credit the druids with the giving of such simple moral instruction, for, after all, an ethical system such as is implied in these terms is hardly an advance on that of societies in a very low stage of organisation, and even the high-sounding judiciary activities described by Cæsar can be paralleled among very lowly folk.[1]

As philosophers the druids have enjoyed very considerable prestige, both in ancient days and in our own times, but the actual extent of their learning was by no means as great as its reputation warranted. Their boasted astronomy and geography, if it is fair to judge by the almost contemptible ignorance of these sciences betrayed by the later Kelts, was doubtless a mixture of astrology and mythical cosmogony, the crude speculation of nearly every primitive people. It is true that the very first mention we have of the druids is a reference to them as philosophers, but it belongs to a period when it was fashionable to extol the barbarians as the ultimate source of all Greek learning and probably means nothing more than that they were the local *wise* men or wizards ; at any rate, no classical writer ever

[1] See the chapter, " Law and Justice," in *Morals in Evolution*, by L. T. Hobhouse, London, 1915.

ventured to define the druidic philosophical system, and
there is no trace of its influence outside the Keltic world.
So far as the later authors are concerned, the outside reputation of the druids as philosophers was plainly a repercussion
of the wrong identification of their creed with that of Pythagoras, and we observe that the Romans, after they had had
a close acquaintance with the order, ceased to regard its
members as anything but magicians ; for example, Pliny
had evidently come to the conclusion that their vaunted
knowledge was little else than a bundle of dark superstitions.

A practical knowledge of stellar, lunar, and solar movements for the purpose of time-reckoning is possessed by
very simple societies, so that we cannot count the druids as
especially remarkable because of their studies in this direction. The lunar year is a wellnigh universal primitive
calendar ; and we are told that such folk as the Hottentots
and Bushmen have a developed star-lore, some of them even
being able to recognise the planets, while the Polynesians
understood the use of the stars for navigation purposes ;
and in another part of the world we have the Eskimos accurately observing the summer solstice. Again, we find that
there are regular astronomer-priests whose duty it is to
watch the movements of heavenly bodies in order to measure
time in places like Borneo and Java, and also in some of
the native tribes of Africa.[1] Therefore, if the druids are to
have a greater renown as astronomers, we ought to be able
to point to some additional achievement ; but it is not by
any means easy to do this. We are told that they had *ages*
of thirty years' duration, and this is certainly an advance
upon the systems of the folk mentioned above, so that there
is excuse for pushing the enquiry a little further and asking
whether the druidic calendar might not have been more
highly developed than is suggested in the remaining statements of Cæsar and Pliny to the effect that its year was
lunar and was counted by nights and not by days, a fact
that is well attested in Irish literature.[2]

It may be said at once that if there really were anything

---

[1] Nilsson, *Primitive Time-reckoning*, Lund, 1920.
[2] See Loth in *Revue Celtique*, XXV (1904), p. 115 f.

particularly ingenious about the druidic calendar, we should surely have been told something about it by so great an expert in calendrial science as the author of the Julian reform, especially as Cæsar does actually mention the subject of their time-reckoning. But we cannot dispose of the subject quite so simply, because there is an ancient calendar, usually

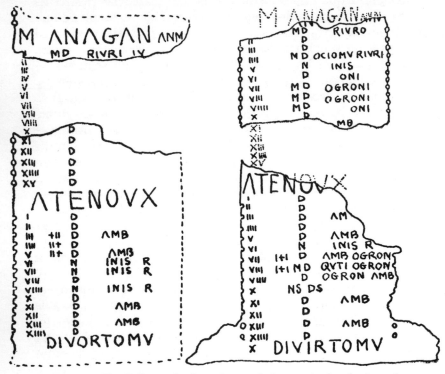

Fig. 24.—The Coligny calendar: the month Anagan (2nd and 4th year).

called Keltic, actually available for study. In 1897 the fragments of a massive bronze panel engraved with a calendrial table (Fig. 24), now in the Palais des Arts at Lyons, were found at Coligny in the Ain department, close to the Swiss frontier. The language of the calendar,[1] chiefly expressed in hitherto unknown single words and abbrevia-

[1] See Dottin, *Manuel*, Paris, 1906, p. 79 ; for the calendar itself see Seymour de Ricci, *Revue Celtique*, XXI (1900), 10 and 427 (two

tions, is still untranslatable ; but it has definitely a Keltic flavour, and there can be no doubt that it represents a system of reckoning intended for native use, so that it is proper to examine it as a possible index to the system employed by the druids.

It is drawn up in sixteen columns of months covering a period of five years, each month being divided into two blocks of days by the word ATENOUX ; in the first block are 15 days, and in the second block are either 14 or 15 days bearing a new, not a continued, enumeration. This is the regular usage of a lunar calendar in which the month is cut into two periods corresponding with the waxing and the waning of the moon ; but the important point about the Coligny calendar is that its real basis is not only lunar, but luni-solar, since an attempt had been made to square the system of lunar months with the solar year. The lunar year of the calendar had only 355 days, and the annual loss of 10 days from the true solar year of 365 days was restored by the insertion of an intercalary month of 30 days, occupying a double mensual space in the column, once in every $2\frac{1}{2}$ years. This gives a total of 1835 days at the end of the 5 years, so that the table ends in excess of solar time, which should be just over 1826 days ; but it is none the less a very creditable scheme, and if it were the work of the druids we should certainly have to allow them much more credit as calendar-makers than we have suggested is their due. For scientific intercalation of this nature is quite beyond the scope of those primitive methods of measuring time with which we have compared the druidic calendrial system as described by Cæsar and Pliny.

But is the Coligny calendar druidic ? It was written in Roman characters, and it was found close to a Roman road, together with fragments, separately smashed, of a bronze statue of Apollo [1] that is thought to date from the 1st century A.D. And the calendar itself is cognate with the Roman system in use before the Julian reform whereby

plates with Ésperandieu's reconstruction) ; Rhys, *Proc. Brit. Acad.*, 1909-10, 207 ; 1911-12, 339 ; also Prof. Eoin MacNeill, *Érin*, X, Pt. I, 1.

[1] The statue is now labelled *Mars*.

biennial intercalation adjusted a lunar year of 355 days.[1] Moreover, its arrangement is very like that of the Roman calendrial tables, and although the days are indicated by a number sequence only, instead of a letter sequence with or without a number sequence, they are followed by *notæ* that one suspects must be of much the same character as those explaining the nature of the days on the Fasti ; thus we find NSDS on the Coligny calendar which looks as though it must signify a *nefastus dies* of the Romans, a day during which it was wrong to transact legal business.[2]

Considerations of this kind suggest a comparison between the calendar and Roman inscriptions on bronze that were intended for Romanised natives, such as the military diplomas. In respect of the technical achievement in the work and of the style of the lettering there is a rather marked agreement, and one is accordingly tempted to assume that the calendar, like the diplomas, is a product of local metal-workers who were following Roman instructions. In fact, the calendar is an achievement of metal-work no less remarkable than the huge and celebrated table containing a decree of Claudius that was found in Lyon in 1528, and that measures about 4½ feet in height, and whose two plates are together about 6 feet broad.[3] But in this instance the local founders were inscribing not a Roman text, but a modified version of the Roman calendar, omitting the difficulties of the Roman system, such as the backward count from the Calends and the Nones and the Ides, and ignoring the complications of Cæsar's reform, the whole scheme being forced into a conformity with the native system and expressed in the native idiom by means of Latin letters. The conjunction of the tablet with a statue of Apollo suggests, though it

---

[1] See A. Philip, *The Calendar*, Cambs., 1921, pp. 10-11.

[2] But see Thurneysen in *Zeitschrift f. Celtische Philologie*, Halle, 1899, II, p. 528 ; for the latinity of the calendar, see Nicholson, *Sequanian*, London, 1898. Prof. MacNeill, on the other hand, claims that the *mechanical* apparatus of the calendar is borrowed from Greek culture (see his interesting note on the peg-holes against the date numerals, *loc. cit.* p. 62, and cf. *Proc. Brit. Acad.*, 1911-12, p. 355).

[3] *Musée de Lyon. Inscriptions antiques :* Allmer et Dissard, I (1888), 58 f.

is far from proving, that the find was made on a temple-site, and that the purpose of the calendar was primarily religious ; if this was really the case, it may well have represented a part of the deliberate Romanisation of native religion attempted by Augustus, a consolidation of the system of native festivals and of unlucky days into an organised cult of the Roman pantheon. It is clear enough that such speculation brings us no nearer to the end of the discussion of the origin and purpose of the calendar, but at least it demonstrates that it would be improper to accept it un-hesitatingly as the direct offspring of druidic time-reckoning, or to use it as evidence of their astronomical and mathe-matical ability.

We must also remember that there is no evidence that the druids had sufficient skill to tabulate the results of their enquiries in calendar form ; certainly, no other inscriptions hitherto discovered hints that the natives were capable of a sustained effort of this kind. It is reported by Cæsar that some of the druids knew how to use the Greek alphabet, and there are enough Keltic inscriptions in Latin characters to show that after the Conquest the Roman alphabet was also fairly general ; but this is very far from proving the druids capable of a complicated composition, particularly as we are told that it was not their custom to commit their lore to writing.[1] The rather improbable nature of the alleged reasons why they refrained from writing down their verses and spells might almost be taken as an additional proof that they were in fact unable to do so ; for a dread of an unrestricted publication of their tenets is hardly a plausible excuse, seeing that few outside the number of their chosen pupils could have read a word of their writings ; and it is also quite incredible that they were really swayed by the consideration that the use of manuscripts would lessen their students' powers of application, as though they had

---

[1] It is true that there is a legend in the *Tripartite Life of St. Patrick* (Whitley Stokes ed., II, 284) suggesting that the Irish druids had books, but this rather dubious hint does not materially affect the question of the scholastic attainments of the earlier members of the order in Gaul.

actually experimented with written records and then abandoned them. It seems very likely that both these reasons
are charitable fictions either invented by Cæsar or suggested
to him by Divitiacus, and that in reality the druids were
compelled to depend on purely oral teaching simply because
they were unable to make written records of the necessary
extent. Even if they were possessed of an alphabet, as
Cæsar says, and knew how to keep tallies and accounts,
they may not have advanced beyond the most laborious
methods of writing on wood and stone ; and, accordingly,
the production of anything in the nature of a book or a fully
annotated calendar may well have been altogether outside
their power.

But although they may have been limited in this direction, there is no doubt that as teachers the druids had a real
importance, and, at any rate until the Romans attempted
the establishment of schools in Gaul, they must have exercised considerable influence on all phases of native thought.
That the actual learning imparted may not have been of
much account does not affect their possible power in this
respect, for it was not only neophytes of the order who
attended for instruction, but also, according to Mela, the
high-born Gauls. Thus, later on in Ireland, as well as
teaching *druidecht*, the lore of druidism, to large classes, we
find that there are also stories of the druids instructing royal
ladies, and even great heroes like Cúchulainn ; [1] and we may
imagine that newcomers to the Keltic lands trying to introduce altered manners would be confronted by an organised
hostile opinion. This is probably the real secret of the early
respect shown by the classical world for the druids, their
reputation resting not on their creed, nor on their philosophy
nor general lore, but on their ability to control the popular
mind by concerted action as a teaching body. Such a state
of affairs no doubt soon came to an end in Gaul after the
arrival of the Romans, while the corporate nature of the
instruction seems to have been of little or no significance in
Ireland ; but, taken in conjunction with the early judicial

[1] Cf. *Tripart. Life*, 103.

powers of the druids, it must, nevertheless, be regarded as the most impressive basis that we can find for a statement of their worth in Keltic life.

(3) PROCEDURE

As diviners there is no need to rate the druids over highly. All the records of the omens that impressed the Kelts, such as the flight of birds and the course of the clouds, are no more than the elementary superstitions of simple folk ; even the divining rod and the wheel of the Irish druids, though they are more specialised methods of telling the future, are in no way remarkable. Haruspicy or hieromancy are also methods employed in very primitive societies, and peoples like the Nagas of Assam and the natives of Borneo are accustomed to divine by the observation of the death-struggles of a fowl ; but, on the other hand, the druidic use of a human victim for this purpose, anthropomancy, attested by Strabo and Tacitus, is a very unusual procedure, and could only occur in highly organised religion.

This is also true to a certain extent of human sacrifice itself. Here we have to choose between the standard of the peoples of Polynesia, such as the inhabitants of Tahiti and the Marquesas or the Maori of New Zealand, who only offered human beings to the gods on occasions of extreme urgency or of the greatest importance, or that of certain higher civilisations in which human sacrifice had been raised to a systematised routine of continued slaughter. If we judge the druids by the standards of the Roman writers, who had learnt to detest a rite practised by their own fore-bears, we are compelled to assume that the Kelts, too, had made human sacrifice a regular and reckless affair of the last-mentioned kind, and we find ourselves thinking of it in the terms of the wholesale slaughters of ancient Mexico, or of the Phœnicians and Carthaginians. It is certainly very difficult to minimise the revolting nature of the holocausts in the wicker cages, or of such episodes as the cruel slaughter of her female captives by Boadicea, in honour of Adraste ; [1]

---

[1] Dion Cassius, *Hist. Rom.*, LXII, 7.

but we must remember Diodorus hints that the victims of the wicker cages were malefactors,[1] and that most of the other tales of wholesale offerings of human beings refer to prisoners of war, so we must admit the possibility that these Keltic sacrifices were to some extent governed by the factor of economic expedience,[2] and were not entirely matters of religious observance. It is significant that there is very little indication in the Irish texts that human sacrifice was a widespread and frequent practice, and this is a notable thing in a Keltic land that had not experienced the Roman suppression of this barbarism, particularly as the Christian writers would not be likely to have glossed over any survivals of, or even memories of, so favourable a count against paganism. It is a curious thing, however, that it is only in Irish literature that we come across a reference to a form of human sacrifice among the Kelts that was anti-social and therefore a purely religious institution, namely, the ritual killing of the first-born. This is to be found in the 12th century *Book of Leinster*, where it is said that the Irish used to offer the first-born of their children to the great stone idol, Mag Slecht ; but as it is the only legend relating to this form of sacrifice, and is of so late a date, it is permissible to doubt its worth as a testimony of original druidic practice.[3] Cæsar's remark [4] that in Gaul fathers did not see their children until they were grown up has been taken as evidence of this same custom in ancient times, on the grounds that the mothers must have hidden their children for fear lest they should be sacrificed ; but the custom may also be read as a survival of primitive taboo, so it does not seem necessary on this account to go out of our way to charge the druids with a regularised slaughter of children, and on the whole we may incline to the view that their share in

---

[1] Diodorus Siculus, *Hist.*, V, 32.

[2] See article, " Sacrifice (Celtic)," by Sir E. Anwyl, in Hastings' *Encycl. of Religion and Ethics*.

[3] This is not the view of Alfred Nutt. See *The Voyage of Bran*, II, 147 f. ; on the subject of human sacrifice in Ireland see also F. N. Robinson, *Anniversary Papers—G. L. Kittredge*, Boston, 1913, pp. 185 ff.

[4] *De Bello Gallico*, VI, 18.

the human sacrifices of the Kelts was rather by way of being assistance in occasional national purging [1] than the result of the special inspiration of their own particular creed. It is certainly true that the classical writers emphasize the occasional nature of the human offerings made by the druids, suggesting that they took place only in times of a great danger or when for any reason the emotions of the people were deeply stirred, and, accordingly, we have no need to assume that they formed part of the regular routine of druidism. On the other hand, it is not fair to claim that Keltic sacrifice was in all its aspects non-religious ; in Strabo's account, as also in the Irish story of the rites at Mag Slecht, we are told that the purpose of the sacrifice was to ensure a generous measure of the earth's bounty, and, if that be so, it cannot be denied that the druids administered the ritual killing as a definite function of their creed. The only point that can be justly made is that there is no evidence that they were directly responsible for all the wholesale slaughter of which the continental Kelts were guilty, and nothing to justify us in ranking druidism among the particularly bloodthirsty religions of which we have record.

The one druidical ritual that has been described for us in some detail is the ceremonial gathering of the mistletoe. This is a remarkable plant, both because of the appearance of its downward-turned and evergreen leaves, and because of the parasitical nature of its growth, so that it is not surprising that it has attracted the attention of simple superstitious folk outside as well as inside the Keltic lands, even as far away as the Torres Straits, or among the Ainos of Japan ; [2] and if we knew nothing more than that the druids respected it on account of its magical and medical properties there would be very little reason for comment. But we know, not only from Pliny's account, but also on the express testimony of the Greek rhetorician Maximus of Tyre, [3] that the oak was a sacred tree to the Kelts, and it is

---

[1] Cf. Frazer, *Golden Bough*, XI, 41.
[2] *Ibid.*, 79. [3] *Dissertations*, VIII, 8.

clear, therefore, that the culling of the mistletoe was a definite function of the druidic religion, and not merely the collecting of a potent charm. Not only did the druids choose their groves of oak trees and insist that a branch of the sacred tree should be present at all the ceremonies they performed, but they identified the tree itself with a god, so that its cult was undoubtedly a very important factor in their religious observances.

It is probable that this was also true of the druids outside Gaul. We do not know definitely that the Irish druids performed their rites in oak-groves, but it has been argued that this may be inferred from the fact that on the introduction of Christianity churches and monasteries were sometimes built in oak-groves or near solitary oaks, as though the choice of the site was determined by the immemorial sanctity of the tree.[1] And it is a curious thing that there is evidence that the oak, and perhaps the mistletoe too, was of peculiar significance in England at a very early period, for in a tumulus at Gristhorpe, near Scarborough, excavated in 1834,[2] there was found an oak coffin, *covered with oak branches*, in which was an old man's skeleton, accompanied by a bronze dagger and flint implements, together with a large quantity of vegetable material that was then identified as mistletoe.[3] This, if the identification

---

[1] *Golden Bough*, II, 242 and 363.

[2] *Gents. Mag.*, 1834, II, 632 f.

[3] The mistletoe identification was repeated as late as 1865 by Davis and Thurnam, *Crania Britannica*. It was originally due to Professor W. C. Williamson (see a pamphlet, *The Discovery of a Tumulus . . . at Gristhorpe*, Scarborough, 1834, and 2nd ed., 1836) ; but the professor was then a very young man, and I am obliged to my friend, Mr. Elgee, of the Dorman Memorial Museum, Middlesbrough, for pointing out to me that in a much later (1872) and completely revised edition of this pamphlet Professor Williamson, at that time an honoured and distinguished botanist, omits all mention of mistletoe in connection with the vegetable matter in the coffin ; and I note that he also refrains from naming the mistletoe in the *Reminiscences of a Yorkshire Naturalist*, London, 1896, p. 44 f., where he refers once more to the Gristhorpe find. This certainly looks as though the Professor had come to the conclusion that the substance was not really mistletoe, but it is strange that he does not expressly say so.

of the mistletoe is correct, is a very interesting discovery, as the burial dates from the Bronze Age. Something of the same sort is also recorded in Brittany, where in many of the megalithic tombs the funeral deposits were laid on a bedding of oak leaves.

The most usual habitat of the mistletoe is on apple-trees, poplars, and willows, and it is only rarely that it is found on the oak. Its occasional occurrence on the sacred tree, therefore, would obviously encourage the belief, as Pliny suggests, that the tree was marked with the sign of an especial favour of the god, so that the gathered shrub would, of course, be invested with peculiar sanctity. Perhaps its evergreen character constituted it as a symbol of immortality, or, since Maximus says that the oak was worshipped by the Kelts as a symbol of Zeus, that is to say, a god of the heavens or thunder-god, it may have been accepted as an embodiment of the lightning fallen from the sky, or it may even have been thought to have contained the life, or divine essence, of the tree. After a consideration of all the evidence, Sir James Frazer has suggested [1] a link, in addition to that of language, between the Kelts and the early inhabitants of Italy; for he observes that the white steers sacrificed on the Alban Mount and in the Capitol at Rome invite comparison with the white bulls that the druids sacrificed under the holy oak when they cut the mistletoe; and this comparison is rendered the closer since evidence can be adduced that the Latins themselves originally worshipped Jupiter in oak-groves. Such a coincidence of language and of religious ideas must either betoken a common inheritance or a direct intrusion of peoples, and we must return to the subject again when we deal with the question of the origin of druidism.

The ritual performance in securing the *serpents'-egg*, described for us by Pliny, is based on an elementary and widespread faith in talismans and charms; and we cannot even say with certainty that this particular form of the superstition was the especial property of the druids, as an example

---

[1] *Golden Bough*, II, 189.

of a somewhat similar belief in the potency of so-called snake-stones has been found in Ceylon.[1] Nevertheless, it is in the Keltic lands that the folklorist has discovered the most remarkable instances of its survival,[2] and we find that a version of the druidic account of the formation of the eggs from the saliva of serpents was still repeated in recent times by the peasant folk in our own island, while the old faith in its marvellous medical properties exists in almost unabated strength.

Naturally there has been considerable speculation as to the real nature of this mysterious *egg* that Pliny said he himself had actually handled. Probably many different objects have been known as snake-stones in the course of time,[3] and amongst them are prehistoric beads of blue and green glass of a kind that are sometimes embellished with

FIG. 25.—Glass beads of the Iron Age from England and Ireland.

protruding bosses and with streaks and bands of white paste (Fig. 25). Such beads were called snake-stones in Cornwall and Wales and Scotland, and it is said that in Wales and in Ireland they were also sometimes called " Druids' Glass," [4] so that it is not surprising that many writers have assumed that they must have been the original *serpents'-eggs* of the druids. This was not the view of Edward Lhuyd,[5] who was the first to call attention to the

---

[1] *Journ. R. Anthrop. Inst.*, XXXVIII (1908), 188 and 200.

[2] See Skeat in *Folklore*, XXIII (1912), 45 f., and *Golden Bough*, X, 15 f.

[3] See, for instance, Mary Trevelyan, *Folklore and Folkstories of Wales*, London, 1909, p. 170. On this subject generally, see W. R. Halliday, *Folklore Studies, Ancient and Modern*, London, 1924, p. 146 ff.

[4] *Golden Bough*, X, 16. Cf. N. Owen, *Hist. of Anglesey*, London, 1775, p. 45.

[5] Rowlands, *Mona Antiqua Restaurata*, London, 1766, p. 318 ; and Camden, *Britannia* (Gough, 1789, II, 571).

glass talismans of this type, but the identification was adopted by Borlase [1] in the 18th century and by Thomas Pennant, [2] who gives an illustration of three such snake-stones from his own collection, and, more recently, by Sir James Frazer. However, many of these beads date from the first two or three centuries before the Christian era, [3] and the druids must have been perfectly familiar with them in necklaces, even if they were not actually aware of the secrets of their manufacture ; it is hardly likely, there-fore, that they could have imagined them to be natural formations, nor even that they could have pretended that they thought so, seeing that the Kelts were craftsmen of considerable ability in enamel-work, and could scarcely have been deceived by a simple glass ornament of this kind. Still less is it likely that Pliny would have been deluded ; in fact, he makes it almost certain that the original *serpents'-egg* was not a glass bead, by telling us that the object he examined was about the size of an apple, and that its shell was cartilaginous and covered with little cavities.

The only possible alternative to the beads is a fossil, for as we have to discount the absurd story of how the egg was obtained, we can also overlook the state-ment that it could float in water. Edward Lhuyd thought that the fossil in question must be an echinus ; but the ammonite is a rival choice, since it is commonly called a snake-stone by peasants, who sometimes add to it a clumsily carved serpent's head in order to increase the likeness of the fossil to a coiled serpent. [4] It is, notwithstanding, rather improbable that in their simple form these fossils would have deceived Pliny [5] any more than the glass beads, and it may be that the object he actually examined was something more complicated and less common, perhaps a conglomeration of

[1] *Antiquities of Cornwall*, London, 1769, p. 142.

[2] *British Zoology*, 1812, III, Pl. 42.

[3] Those figured by Pennant, for example. On the other hand, the Anglesey beads described by Owen (*loc. cit.*) sound as though they might be Saxon or Viking.

[4] Sowerby, *Mineral Conchology*, II, Pl. 107, 2, and p. 10.

[5] Cf. Conybeare, *Roman Britain*, London, 1911, p. 70.

tiny ammonites, one of the echinoidea with spines attached, or even a coral formation. But no doubt the simple fossils would easily have satisfied the Kelts as a product of the summer assemblies of the snakes ; and we have ample proof of an interest taken in such objects in early times, witness the remarkable burial on Dunstable Downs where a ring of more than two hundred fossil echini surrounded the skeletons of a woman and child.[1]

The survival until modern times of the fabulous story of the formation of this *egg*, repeated in almost the very words of Pliny, and the continued belief in its magico-medical potency, encourages some further enquiry in this matter of existing folk-custom as a reflection of ancient druidic practice. We have already seen that the lore of the *serpents'-egg* is not an isolated instance of such a survival of primitive ideas ; faith in the medical efficacy of the mistletoe is still strong in many parts of Europe, and we even hear of the persistence of details of the ancient gathering-ceremony, as in the instance of those Swiss peasants who always take care to catch the falling bough in the left hand.[2] Of more interest to our special search is the strange fact that the druidic holocausts in the wicker cages were represented in France not very long ago by the burning of wickerwork giants, or, more vividly, by the actual burning of live animals in wickerwork frames.[3] Even in England there may be traces of the persistent practice of ancient sacrifices, for there are records of the burnt-offerings of calves conducted surreptitiously by country-folk who were anxious to avert a cattle plague.[4]

But there will be little profit in searching those lands alone where we know that there once were druids for any survival of special lore or ritual that we could attribute to the influence of these priests, and we must be content with a procedure on broader lines, trying merely to enlarge our ideas of the actual druidic faith by demonstrating its community in the larger Keltic religion. For we cannot hope to satisfy ourselves with any particular instance of an actual

---

[1] W. G. Smith, *Man the Primeval Savage*, London, 1894, p. 337 f.
[2] *Golden Bough*, XI, 82.   [3] *Ibid.*, 38.   [4] *Ibid.*, X, 300.

folk-memory of the druids, and we must be very careful to distinguish between, on the one hand, such localised traditions vouched for by modern, or comparatively modern, historians, and, on the other hand, the general and incontestible evidence of the survival of ancient beliefs and customs over wide areas. This last constitutes a scientific basis for the reconstruction of pagan religious ideas, while, contrarily, the local traditions as to the sites of druidic worship or to druidic customs have little more than a cumulative value as confirmatory material and invite a critical examination in each instance. This is a caution especially necessary where druid-associations are concerned, for our studies are complicated by the extraordinary revival of interest in these priests in the 18th and 19th centuries, a revival that brought in its wake so many imaginary attributions to them, both of sanctuaries and of ceremonies, that we are compelled to deal very warily with traditions that were not set down in writing before the revival began.

An agreement between druidic observances and widespread Keltic customs is suggested by an examination of the pagan festival days that are still, or were until recently, celebrated in France and Great Britain by the lighting of bonfires and kindred demonstrations. This is a task already accomplished, for in the *Golden Bough* we shall find all the relevant matter set forth in systematic array and interpreted by a master in the modern study of folklore ; from Sir James Frazer's survey it becomes clear that both within the area of druidic influence and outside it, the Kelts observed two principal festivals, one on May Day or the evening before it, called Beltane, and another on 1st November, or on the evening before (the modern Hallowe'en), that was called in Ireland, Samhain.[1] There is ample evidence of the observance of these two festivals in France, England, Wales, Scotland, and Ireland, and it is exceedingly interesting to find that in Scotland and in Ireland there are also instances of a very ancient tradition that the ceremonial fires were lit

---

[1] For a study of the Keltic festivals see also MacCulloch, *Religion of the Ancient Celts*, Edinburgh, 1911, 256 f.

on ground associated with the druids, or actually by the druids themselves. Thus the Irish historian, Dr. Geoffrey Keating,[1] who was born in the 16th century, speaks of druidic sacrifice on the occasion of the Samhain bonfire, and in *Cormac's Glossary*,[2] a 9th century compilation preserved in 14th century and later texts, we read that on Beltane the druids used to make two fires, accompanying the preparations with solemn incantation, and that they used to drive cattle between the two fires as a safeguard against diseases ; while in Scotland we are told by an 18th century writer [3] that Beltane fires were lit on an artificial mound, surrounded by a low circular wall and surmounted by an upright stone, that was traditionally a site of druidic worship, and that was afterwards chosen as a place for holding courts of justice.

The interest of this primary division of the year into two halves, beginning on 1st May and 1st November, is that it does not in any way depend on the principal events of the solar calendar, that is to say, the solstices and the equinoxes. Nor does it correspond with the ordinary divisions of the agricultural year, the times of sowing and of reaping, but rather, as Sir James Frazer observes, with the behaviour of a pastoral people originally governed by the necessity of moving herds to and from their summer feeding-grounds. A similar division of the year can be traced in Central Europe, so that it is evident that we are here in touch with the primitive Keltic system of reckoning time, and it is a very important consideration, as we shall see later on, that we are thus able to say that the druids in these outlying corners of the Keltic world were its ministers.

Of course, side by side with the Beltane and Samhain celebrations we find, as was the case throughout Europe generally, that there was a festival coincident with the principal event of the solar year, Midsummer Day. But

---

[1] *History of Ireland*, ed. Irish Text Soc., II, 246.
[2] Trans. by O'Donovan and ed. by W. Stokes, Calcutta, 1868, s.v. Belltaine.
[3] *Scotland and Scotsmen in the 18th Century*. MSS. of John Ramsay of Ochtertyre, ed. by A. Allardyce, London and Edinburgh, 1888, II, 444.

here we are dealing with an almost universal stage in cultural progress that is characteristic of many different peoples who have learnt to depend upon agriculture for a livelihood. For, apart from such celebrations of the summer solstice throughout the whole extent of Europe, we find that this date was ceremoniously observed in distant parts of the world, as, for example, among the Incas of Peru, or the Zuñi Indians of New Mexico.[1]   It is not to be expected, then, that the Kelts should have been throughout all their history different in this respect from their Continental neighbours, and the evidence of the observance of the midsummer festival, slight, indeed, in comparison with that betokening the observance of Beltane and Samhain, in no wise detracts from the significance that has been attributed to these major events in the Keltic world.   It is a reasonable conjecture, in fact, that the adoption of agricultural pursuits following upon the extensive migrations of the Kelts is a sufficient explanation of the inclusion of the midsummer festival in the rota of annual observances.

(4) ORGANISATION

We are vouchsafed some information upon the subject of the organisation of the druidic order, but it is, nevertheless, far from easy to present any confident statement of its original character.   In Gaul there is said to have been an arch-druid as the single and all-powerful head of a corporate body, a sign that there was a more highly developed sense of nationality among the Kelts than other evidence would incline us to suspect.   We cannot reasonably doubt Cæsar's assertion, for he goes on to describe the manner of the arch-druid's election, and it is obvious that the existence of such a supreme authority was within the powers of any body capable of organising annual national assemblies like those held by the druids.   It is, in fact, additional proof of the achievement that we have said most of all entitles them to our respect, namely, a capacity for controlled and systematised behaviour.

We do not, however, find much evidence of an equal

[1] *Golden Bough*, X, 132.

organisation of the druids in Ireland, for there are very few signs here of concerted action on their part, or that any one druid was supreme over the others. But in all questions affecting the status of Irish druids, we must bear in mind that our information relates principally to druidism in the period of its decline and disintegration following upon the introduction of Christianity. When we recall the fact that there most certainly were important assemblies held in Ireland,[1] taking place at fixed intervals and attended by delegates from distant parts, it will be seen that we cannot fairly assume that Irish druidism lacked that co-ordination of its members such as obtained in Gaul. Moreover, we hear once of a " chief poet of the Gael,"[2] so that we cannot ignore the possibility that formerly there may also have been a chief druid.

From Mela's testimony, and from our knowledge of the life of the druid Divitiacus, we can conclude that in Gaul the order was mainly recruited from the high-born Kelts, and that members of the order were in nowise excluded from the possession of wealth, or from marrying, or from a political life. They were, it is true, exempt from military service, but this did not mean that they were prohibited from accompanying or controlling armies, or from warfare itself, and we know that bravery in battle was one of the main points of their teaching. Although we have less positive information at our disposal, all this seems to have been true of the Irish druids as well, who certainly fought,[3] and also married, so that in matters of general conduct there are no marked distinctions to be drawn, and, taking everything into consideration that we have mentioned with regard to belief, behaviour, and organisation, it seems safe to say that there are no good reasons for disputing the essential sameness of druidism as represented in Gaul and in Ireland.

---

[1] Joyce, *Social History*, II, 436 ; see also T. J. Westropp in *Proc. R. Irish Acad.*, XXXV, 363.

[2] *Book of Rights*, Dublin, 1847, p. 33 ; but cf. *Rev. Celtique*, XLIII, 299, where *two* chief druids are mentioned ; this suggests " chief " merely means " locally pre-eminent ".

[3] See, for instance, *Rev. Celtique*, XLIII, 25, 39.

In addition to fulfilling the offices of sacrifice and of the dispensation of justice, the Gallic druids had also to act both as prophets and as poets ; that is to say, they practised the art of divination, and were also employed in the composition of epics and spells.   So much is clear from Cæsar, and it seems certain that those who were especially concerned with these secondary functions, and were distinguished by the later writers as *vates* (in Greek οὐάτεις), or *bards*, were all members of the corporate druidic order.   It is very likely, in spite of the testimony of Diodorus, Strabo, and Timagenes, that these names were originally synonymous and referred to a single class of person, a druid whose priestly and political functions were allowed to lapse in favour of the duties of divining or of composing verses ; for, from the first, natural talent would inevitably lead to specialisation in these directions, and it is more probable that the prophets and the poets would develop into separate officials from within the priestly body than that they should be a subsidiary and specially recruited non-priestly class.   No doubt as the political and religious power of the druids declined, as it did very rapidly, the secondary functions would assume an increasing importance ; and we can readily understand the attempt of writers after Cæsar's time to rank those druids distinguished for their gift of divination or versification as a distinct class of Keltic official, only vaguely connected with the native religious life.   But the truth is that whatever distinction time may have brought about, the classical writers did not understand it, and it is of little avail to try to remedy matters now ; for it will be seen from the extracts we have quoted that the functions of druid, diviner, and bard, are inextricably mixed.[1]   Thus, while Cæsar suggests that it was the druids who performed all the various functions, Strabo distinguishes three orders, druids, diviners, and bards, but he admits at the same time that druids and diviners were both concerned with natural philosophy ; moreover, he adds that the druids conducted the sacrifices,

---

[1] See MacCulloch, *Religion of the Ancient Celts*, Edinburgh, 1911, p. 299.

whereas Diodorus suggests it was the diviners who sacrificed. Divitiacus, according to Cicero, was both a druid and a diviner, and Tacitus also describes the druids as prophets. Lucan only apostrophises bards and druids, but in addressing the bards [1] he uses the word *vates*, which is the equivalent of Strabo's name for the diviners, and can mean prophet as well as poet. Finally, we see that Pliny altogether ignores the bards when he condemns the druids as a band of wizards and physicians.

But if we cannot deduce from this confusion of officials and their functions an original and systematic organisation, we can at least say that its existence confirms the supposition that the three classes of functionary mentioned in the classical references to druidism represented one corporate body. And we may proceed to the reasonable claim that from the subsequent wreck of druidism the bards would be likely to survive with honour in their capacity of recorders of the prowess of the Keltic peoples, while the diviners would be equally likely to persist in obscurity as surreptitious purveyors of native wizardry.

This opinion that the bards and diviners were druids must, to some extent, however, be qualified by the admission that the Kelts may also have employed secular bards who were *not* members of the order. This seems to be warranted by the early testimony of Poseidonios, who speaks of professional poets in the service of Keltic princelings accompanying armies during a campaign,[2] and also of a poet being rewarded for his eloquence by a bag of gold thrown to him by one of these chieftains.[3] In addition to this, there is a story in the History of Rome by Appian [4] about a musician who accompanied an envoy in order to extol the prowess of his countryfolk to the Romans ; and in all these instances it is implied that the persons concerned were men of inferior

---

[1] *Pharsalia*, I, 447-449, three lines preceding the passage quoted above, p. 88.

[2] *Athenæus*, VI, 49. In the latter part of the passage Poseidonios refers to bards by name, but I cannot read that he distinguishes them from the company of the parasitical musicians.

[3] *Athenæus*, IV, 37.   [4] *Keltika*, 12.

rank attached to the households of the great, and that they
were not invested with the dignity of the priestly calling.
It is obvious that the existence of secular bards of this kind
need occasion no surprise, since it must have been the wellnigh inevitable outcome of the Keltic talent in this
direction, and it need not lead to any alteration of our view
concerning the bards mentioned by Strabo and others ; for
this must not be taken to mean that the druids either
invented versification and declamation, or monopolised
their employment.

Very much the same state of affairs seems to have obtained among the ancient Irish. We hear of three classes
of officials corresponding with those named by Strabo, that
is to say, druids, prophets (*fáthi*), and poets (*filid*), and we
find traces of the same confusion of their functions, and
signs that the various offices, in particular those of the
druids and the prophets, were occasionally administered by
single individuals. And side by side with the Filid, or
learned poets who composed according to strict rules and
were possessed of a profound and special lore, there existed
rhymsters of inferior status like the itinerant or sycophantic
poetasters of Gaul.

The difficult problem of the origin of druidism would
be easier of approach if we could determine whether it
monopolised the religious activities of the Kelts in Gaul,
or whether it existed side by side with the remnants of a
pre-druidic organisation. Unfortunately, our present knowledge does not justify any confident answer to this question,
and the most that we can say is that there was one class of
priest seemingly distinguished by name from the druids, and
that there were also certain religious confraternities altogether unconnected with the druidic system.

The priests were called *gutuatri*.[1] As we only hear of
them in four inscriptions and in a passage from the eighth
Book of the Gallic War, by Hirtius, it will be possible to
define the extent of our information with some precision.

---

[1] The latinised form of the singular is *gutuater*. For the etymology, see Loth, *Revue Celtique*, XXVIII (1907), 119 ; and Holder,
Alt-celtischer Sprachshatz, s.v. *gutuatros*.

Two of the inscriptions, one a tiny Roman altar (Fig. 26), and the other a marble slab, are at Autun,[1] and were set up respectively by Narboneius Thallus and Gaius Secondius Vitalis Appa,[2] each of whom is described as a gutuater, in honour of Augustus and of a local god Anvallus. Another inscription, now lost, was set up at Mâcon [3] and commemorated Gaius Sulpicius Gallus, a magistrate and flamen augustalis, who was also the priest of a god Moltinus and a gutuater of Mars.[4] The fourth is at Le Puy,[5] and was erected by a præfect of the colony, apparently an official of the iron-mines, who likewise describes himself as gutuater.

In all these inscriptions, both as regards the names of the holder of the office and the other functions that he performed, the gutuater appears as a very much Romanised person whose services to the emperor-god and to the empire took precedence over his duties as the priest of a local divinity. Since the druids, at any rate in their priestly capacity, resisted Romanisation, even to the length of incurring deliberate suppression, it looks as though the gutuater of the 1st and 2nd centuries A.D. were not druids, and we may imagine that their office was largely a Roman institution, based, of course, upon existing native practice, but definitely intended to assist the fusion of the Gallic religion with that of the conquerors. These minor priests were only the servants of local shrines, so that there is nothing unreasonable in suggesting that they were a class apart from the druids ; but, nevertheless, to affirm that the two kinds of priest were *never* originally connected is a good deal more than the evidence warrants. Moreover, we must take into account the fact that the druids, before the coming of the

---

[1] *Mem. Soc. éduenne*, N.S., XXVIII (1900), 353.

[2] In the paper referred to above it is suggested that the word Appa is an abbreviation for *apparator*, or magistrate, and not a fourth name ; but see Jullian, *Revue des Études Anciennes*, II (1900), 411.

[3] *Corpus Inscriptionum Latinarum*, XIII, 2585.

[4] One reading is " six times gutuater of Mars," but probably MART(IS) VI is really MART(IS) VL, i.e. ult(oris), as suggested by Hirschfeld, or MART(IS) VI[C(TORIS)] as suggested by Reiner.

[5] *C.I.L.*, XIII, 1577.

FIG. 26.—MINIATURE VOTIVE-ALTAR FROM AUTUN, DEDICATED
TO ANVALLUS (½)

Romans, were extraordinarily powerful in Gaul, so that it is difficult to conceive of them as tolerating another and distinct body of religious officials who were sufficiently firmly established to persist where they themselves failed. The only scrap of direct evidence upon this point is the passage where Ausonius describes the keeper of the temple of Belenus, who was doubtless a gutuater (or his 4th century equivalent), as coming of druidic stock ; but, unfortunately, this testimony is of much too late a date to have practical value.

There is some additional information available that would be very precious, since it refers to the actual period of the Roman conquest, if only it did not depend on a rather obscure question of textual criticism. This concerns a passage wherein Aulus Hirtius,[1] who wrote the eighth Book of the *Commentaries*, gives Gutuatrus [2] as the proper name of a Gaul put to death by Cæsar, doubtless the rebel Cotuatus.[3] It is usually held that his use of the word was mistaken, and that he merely intended to convey that Cotuatus held the sacerdotal title of gutuater.[4] If this view is correct, it is interesting to recall that Cotuatus was a turbulent member of the Carnutes, presumably a person of some local standing, who was one of the ringleaders of the massacre of the Romans at Cenabum. Cæsar, not unnaturally, calls him a desperado, and the fact that he was later hunted down and delivered to Roman justice by his own people shows that whatever office he formerly held was not sufficient to invest him with lifelong sanctity. This last consideration does not mean very much, but it seems to be a fair inference that the man was not a druid ; for though we can easily understand that neither Cæsar nor Hirtius knew precisely what a gutuater was, they certainly knew a good deal about druids ; yet the rebel is not called a druid, nor even *sacerdos*. If, then,

---

[1] *B.G.*, VIII, 38.

[2] There are many variants in the MSS., such as *gutruatrus*, and even *maturatus*.

[3] *B.G.*, VII, 3, 1.

[4] Naturally the whole subject is controversial. See Rice Holmes, *Cæsar's Conquest of Gaul*, Oxford, 1911, p. 831.

he really was a gutuater, we must admit that even in the
1st century B.C. these priests were apparently distinct from
the druidic priesthood, and that the office was, in its sacerdotal aspect, of so lowly a character that it was not important
enough for Cæsar's notice. If only we could be quite sure
that Hirtius meant to imply that the man was a *gutuater*,
we might proceed to argue that this insignificance of the
office explains the difficulty that has just been raised of the
druidic toleration of its existence, and that it might, after
all, be a pre-druidic priesthood that only received a revived
respect under later Roman encouragement, and simultane-
ously with the decline of the druids. This is an attractive
hypothesis, and a useful one, but it is obvious that it depends
on little better than a bundle of guesses.

On two or three other occasions the classical writers
mention Keltic priests who, though they are not named as
gutuatri, seem to be local officials of the same kind.   Lucan,[1]
for example, speaks of the priest (sacerdos) of the sacred
forest near Marseilles ; similarly, Livy [2] describes the
antistites templi of the Boii in Cisalpine Gaul, whom he distinguishes from the ordinary sacerdotal brotherhood ; and
Ausonius [3] salutes Phœbicius, the keeper of the temple of
Belenus.   There is also an inscription of 1st century date
at Agen [4] in which an *antistes* records his gift of a marble
basin to the Genius Loci, but as his name was Silvinus, son
of Scipio, it may be that his office was not a Keltic one.

The possibility of the independence of the gutuatri and
antistites from the druidic organisation is measurably increased by the consideration that there certainly were non-
druidic religious organisations in Gaul. Foremost among
these is that of the famous nine virgins of the Isle of Sein,
off Pont du Raz on the western coast of Brittany.   These

---

[1] *Pharsalia*, III, 424.   [2] XXIII, 24, 12.
[3] See above, p. 97.
[4] *C.I.L.*, XIII, 919.   I take it that the priests (*sacerdotes*) mentioned by Cæsar (*B.G.*, VII, 33, 3) were probably druids ; at least,
there is no reason to suppose that they were not.   See generally on
this subject of non-druidic religious functionaries, Jullian, *Recherches
sur la religion gauloise*, Bordeaux, 1903, p. 99 f.

women, described by Mela,[1] were possessed of marvellous
magical powers, and might be approached by those who
set sail especially to consult them. There was also another
community of women, devoted to orgiastic cults, established
on an island near the mouth of the Loire [2] whereon no man
was allowed to set foot. The historicity of these stories of
Mela and Strabo has been questioned,[3] but although it is
quite possible the authors were tempted to interpret the
reputed existence of Keltic island-communities in the terms
of classical mythology, with its tales of the Isle of Circe and
so on, yet, since there is abundant evidence that the Gauls,
like many other ancient peoples, felt that some peculiar
holiness was attached to lonely islands, it is an almost
inevitable consequence that the quality of sacredness should
be translated to those who lived upon them. Thus we are
expressly told in one of Plutarch's essays [4] that some of the
small and desolate islands near Britain were called Isles of
Demons or of Demi-Gods, and that when one of these islands
was visited, it was found that its inhabitants were few in
number, but all regarded as sacred and inviolate. Then
there was also an island near Britain where sacrifices were
conducted that Poseidonios explains resembled those offered
to Demeter and Persephone at Samothrace.[5] The Germans,
too, had a holy grove on an island,[6] and perhaps we can
detect an inherent respect for their sanctity in the choice of
small islands, such as Alderney and Herm in the Channel
Islands, or of Er Lanic in the Morbihan Gulf, as important
cemeteries of prehistoric folk, thus making them veritable
Isles of the Departed. This last is rather an interesting
point in that the graves take us back to pre-Keltic peoples
and, therefore, encourage the belief that the island-cults
represented a deeply rooted faith of the indigenous folk and

---

[1] *Chorogr.*, III, 6, 48.

[2] Strabo, IV, 4, 6. M. Jullian suggests the island was Le Croisic
(*Hist. de la Gaule*, I, 145).

[3] S. Reinach in *Revue Celtique*, 1897, 1 ; and *Cultes, Mythes,
Religions*, Paris, 1905, I, 195.

[4] *Moralia : De defectu oraculorum*, XVIII.

[5] Strabo, IV, 4, 6.   [6] Tacitus, *Germania*, XL.

were not necessarily of Keltic origin. Indeed, if we accept
the stories of these communities of women, we can scarcely
avoid admitting at the same time that they probably
existed in addition to, and not as part of, the druidic religious
system, and thus must have continued the observances of a
pre-druidic faith.

Apart from the instances of the island-communities, the
existence of holy women in early Europe is well attested,
and is in accord with our general knowledge of women in
the barbarian lands. Among the Galatæ we know that the
wife of Sinatos was a priestess,[1] while in Gaul an inscription
at Antibes [2] records a *flaminica sacerdos* of the goddess
Thucolis, and two other inscriptions at Arles [3] commem-
orate women described respectively as *antistita deæ* and
antistis. In our own country Boadicea exercised priestly
functions ; [4] and perhaps the behaviour of the black-clothed
women of Anglesey before the battle with the Romans may
be taken as suggesting their influence in spiritual matters.[5]
In Ireland, moreover, there were *ban-fáthi* or divineresses ;
and it is just possible that we can detect a relic of former
communities of women-devotees of a pagan cult, just like
those of Gaul, in the custom of the nuns of St. Brigit, who
tended a perpetual holy fire at Kildare right up to the time
of the suppression of the monasteries under Henry VIII ; [6]
the same custom of tending a holy fire in Britain being
mentioned as far back as the 3rd century by Solinus,[7] who
says that one was kept up in honour of a goddess identified
with Minerva. Thus we see that there is nothing improbable in the stories of the islands with the holy women dwelling
upon them ; and, furthermore, that there is a good deal to
be said in favour of the hypothesis that these women might
have continued to practice, altogether independently of
druids and druidism, the immemorial religious rites of the
land.

The question whether there ever were druidesses is quite

[1] Plutarch, *Moralia : Virtutes Mulierum*, XX.
[2] *C.I.L.*, XII, 5724, and p. 862.   [3] *C.I.L.*, XII, 703 and 708.
[4] Dion Cassius, LXII, 6 and 7.   [5] Tacitus, see above, p. 93.
[6] Frazer, *Golden Bough*, II, 240.   [7] XXII, 10.

another matter, and I have already said something on this subject (p. 96). It is plain that in the 1st century B.C., when druidism was flourishing, there is no reason to believe that women were admitted into the order. But, as we have seen, in the 3rd century A.D. both Lampridius and Vopiscus describe female fortune-tellers in Gaul as *dryades*, a term which it is naturally assumed denotes druidesses ; and this might be read as a hint that some of the priestesses just mentioned were also members of the corporate druidic system. We must remember, however, that these authors were not talking about religion or religious functions at all, and that at the time when they wrote Gallic druidism was discredited and moribund ; so that it is probable that the word druidess was applied to wise women, without any other significance than that the women were native prophetesses who performed functions included amongst those once attributed to a priestly order whose fame and whose name was well known by reason of the earlier writings of Cæsar and others. In the same way, it would be difficult to prove that the occasional use of the word *bandrui* in late Irish literature adds anything to our knowledge of original druidic organisation.

I observed at the beginning of this chapter that I intended to give only a minimum account of druidic religion, an intention that I hope will explain the disjointed and incomplete nature of the series of remarks that followed. I very much wish it were possible to give a more adequate summary of druidism, and I should like to persuade myself that it is fair to make Keltic literature, especially the usual material of mediæval bardic rigmarole and Christian invective, responsible for a fuller account of this special pagan faith. But I am far from convinced of the validity of such evidence, and since in these chapters I am trying to present nothing but the basic facts about the druids, I shall avoid a fanciful embroidery of the few certainties, even at the risk of depriving my subject of much of its superficial interest.

What, then, can I add ? I see no reason to suppose that the druids had developed a special sun-worship, or a monotheistic religion. I do not see much evidence that they possessed any remarkable learning, astronomical or otherwise.

But we naturally ask ourselves whom they worshipped ; and if we take a general survey of the manifestations of Keltic religion as a whole we shall quickly find the most probable answer. In the eyes of the ancient Kelt the land was peopled with spirits. Doubtless many of them were of primitive and pre-Keltic origin ; but the Kelt was himself a primitive, and the native spirits of the trees and the wells and the fountains and the streams were familiar to him in whatever land he trod. He had passed, however, beyond this stage of simple animism, and in addition to these homely spirits inhabiting the well-known features of the surrounding landscape, had learnt to worship the great natural forces that controlled his world, the moon, the sun, the sea, and the wind. Of these by far the most important was the moon,[1] while the sun, so often supposed to be the focus of druidic worship, was demonstrably of less account ; thus, the Keltic year was lunar, time-reckoning was lunar, festivals began with the rising of the moon, on what we should now call their *eve*, and many agricultural operations were controlled by its wax and wane. But the Kelt had likewise passed beyond the stage of mere nature-worship, and he had come to believe in the existence of higher deities, the local tutelary gods of his townlet and his tribe, and, above these, a whole pantheon of divinities presiding over his various interests ; such were the gods of agriculture and of commerce, of healing and of speech, gods of war, gods of the Earth and the Under-Earth, and goddesses of fertility and of plenty. These dwelt in Elysium, a blessed region of the world ; and because of their intimate correspondence with the deities of the Greek and Latin pantheons, which were both conceived on the same primitive system, they were very easily identified, after the Roman conquest, with the Roman gods ; and Cæsar was able to write that the Gauls worshipped Mercury, Apollo, Mars, Jupiter, and the rest.

[1]See MacCulloch, *Religion of the Ancient Celts*, Edinburgh, 1911, pp. 175 ff.

I think it is hardly possible to doubt that the druids were the special servants of this higher Keltic pantheon, emphasising, perhaps, the *divinity* of its members at the expense of the local spirits of the trees and the fountains and other natural phenomena ; for this is the tendency of development in religion, to proceed from the awe of the merely *supernatural* to the service and placation of the *divine*. I do not see that there are any valid arguments to support the contention that druidism had lagged behind in a stage either of animism or of nature-worship. Such primitive beliefs had survived into their day, they were still a part of practical Keltic faith, and long remained so ; but that they constituted the major creed of druidism is unthinkable. Indeed, it is in direct conflict with Cæsar's statement that the druids claimed the Gauls were descended from Dis, the god of the Under-Earth ; and we can state positively that the druids were abreast with, nay leaders of, developed Keltic theology.

They served the ordinary Keltic pantheon, then ; and they believed in the immortality of the soul. To this I can only add that they doubtless conceived the future estate as continued and similar existence in the Under-Earth. But there is nothing to show that they had any notion of moral retribution in the after-life, that the good were happier than the wicked. Had that notion existed we should have to credit them with something higher than a simple and primitive philosophy.

It remains to say a word as to whether these gods were worshipped directly, or through the medium of idols. Cæsar said of the Gauls that they revered especially the god Mercury *huius sunt plurima simulacra*, of whom there are many images ; [1] and Lucan also says that there were *simulacra* in the famous druidic grove near Marseilles. [2] The existence of effigies of gods and goddesses would be in no way remarkable at the Keltic stage of religious development ; for, to take an example from a parallel culture of those early days, it will be recalled that Tacitus described how the

---

[1] *De Bello Gallico*, VI, 17.   [2] *Pharsalia*, III, 412.

worship of the Earth-Mother among some of the northern German tribes included a festival in which the goddess, that is to say, an effigy of her, was carried around in honour among the people.[1] There are, moreover, so many references to idols and images in early Irish literature [2] that we cannot discount them all as Christian invention ; and, on the whole, there seems to be a strong probability that the Kelts believed that the divine essence of their gods was focussed in or resident in certain objects, which were therefore revered as idols.

I take it that the statements of Cæsar and Lucan are sufficient to show that the Gallic druids did not dissociate themselves from this worship of idols. But the question arises as to what these *simulacra* really were. At a first glance, one supposes that a Roman author would not use this word except for recognisable anthropomorphic effigies ; but it will be seen that Lucan has made it clear that even in such a context as the passage in Cæsar it might have a very different significance. In the druidic grove, he says,

> simulacraque maesta deorum
> Arte carent caesisque extant informia truncis.

Roughly carved tree-trunk images must have been idols of the crudest kind ; and the legends of the Irish idols, suggesting stones or posts ornamented with metal plates (p. 191), confirm the general suspicion that the visible divinities of the druids were natural objects, either left in their original form or distinguished only by some simple shaping or ornament. The Kelts, said Maximus Tyrius, worshipped Zeus in the form of a tall oak,[3] and I daresay that all their idols were survivals of the primitive notion that a divinity often selects some familiar object, a stone, or tree, or what not, as his abode.

However, I do not think that *as a class* simple menhirs, that is to say artificially erected standing stones, were likely to have been idols of the druids, though no doubt one or two

---

[1] *Germania*, 40.
[2] Cf. *Cormac's Glossary*, p. 95, s.v. idol.
[3] *Philosophumena*, II, 8.

of them may have been so. It is sometimes argued that as a statuette of Mercury was found under one,[1] and as Mercury is one of the four deities carved upon another,[2] it looks as though the exceedingly numerous menhirs must be the *plurima simulacra* of which Cæsar speaks. But, for myself, I do not consider it even probable that any one would bury a statuette of the god under the very stone that was his idol, nor carve the presentiments of three other deities thereon. Moreover, if, as seems likely, many of these stones were boundary-marks, then in Roman days they would have needed the special protection of Mercury, and this seems to me to be a much better explanation of the presence of the statuette and the carving.

Contact with Greece and Rome introduced Gaul as a whole to naturalistic sculpture, and it was not long before there was a large output of native anthropomorphic carvings of many kinds. Some of these were frankly imitations of the altars and other accessories of Greek and Roman cults, but it is always possible that a few of the uncouth single figures may have served as idols for native worship. However, I myself am inclined to believe M. Reinach is right in imagining that the large body of conservative druidism that stood aloof from Roman innovations was definitely hostile to anthropomorphism ;[3] and, as a working rule, I think it is safe to assume that naturalistic carving, however crude, represents the Romanisation of Gallic religion.[4]

[1] Near Péronne, Somme (*Revue Celtique*, XII (1891), p. 484).

[2] Formerly at Kernuz, Finistère (*Revue Arch.*, N.S., I (1879), pp. 104, 129, and Pl. III-V).

[3] For M. Reinach's celebrated paper on this subject, see *Revue Celtique*, XIII 1892), 189, and cf. XI, 224.

[4] An exception is, perhaps, the St. Martin's statue-menhir in Guernsey ; but I shall deal with this remarkable carving in my forthcoming book on Channel Island archæology.

CHAPTER V

TEMPLES

IT seems to be a general rule that the building of elaborate places of worship is not characteristic of primitive people whose religion is in about the same stage of development as druidism. For such folk the ritual of worship is itself sufficient to lend adequate sanctity to whatever spot is chosen ; and, although tradition very often demands the choice of the same spot, it is rare to find that its suitability is controlled, or rendered permanent, by building.

It is true that many exceedingly simple savage folk reserve a portion of the large communal living-huts as repositories for their idols, so that these shut-off spaces become, in a sense, sanctuaries. But mere store-rooms for gods are not temples according to the meaning of the word I am using in this chapter, that is to say, artificially constructed places of public worship ; and to find these we have to turn to more highly civilised folk, like certain of the Polynesians who built truncated pyramids of stone as platforms on which to conduct their religious rites, or like the natives of Bali, who assembled for worship in a temple consisting of three open courts that were bounded by low walls.

The Maori of New Zealand afford a rather interesting example here. They are as fully civilised as their ancestors, the pyramid builders of Eastern Polynesia, and their religion is in every respect as advanced as druidism. Thus their notion of immortality closely resembled that of the ancient Kelts ; they believed in Io, a supreme being from whom all things originated, and who seems to correspond, therefore, with the druidic notion about Dis Pater ; and they wor-

shipped a similar system of tutelary and tribal gods.   But
the Maori never erected anything in the form of a temple,[1]
his places of worship were little clearings in the bush, generally in some secluded district, which were either left
unmarked, or distinguished by one or more unworked
standing-stones, or perhaps a wooden post.   Occasionally
a small platform was set up to receive offerings, but there
was no other attempt to add impressiveness to the place by
ornament or building of any kind.

It cannot be maintained, therefore, that druidism was a
religion so developed that its priests *must* have worshipped
in temples made by hands.   And it is a fact that there is
plenty of evidence to show that the druids were likewise
content with the opportunities afforded by nature, and that
the forests, especially the oak-groves, were the favourite
scene of their ritual.   Lucan plainly said that groves were
their haunts,[2] and in a famous passage he described a particular grove near Massilia.[3]   It was Pliny who added that
the druids preferred the oak-forests above all others.[4]   Dion
Cassius tells of sacrifices and orgies in the grove of Andate
that followed the initial successes of the rebels under Boadicea ; [5] and Tacitus mentioned [6] the woods of Anglesey
that were devoted to cruel superstitions.

Nor are there wanting tokens of the long survival of the
memory of the sacred grove.   The expression *fid-nemed*
(sacred grove) occurs in the Senchus Mor, an ancient code
of Irish law ; [7] and in the 8th century *Capitulatio de partibus
Saxonie* a fine is threatened against those who still honour
fountains, trees, or groves.[8]   It is a small wonder, then, that
the scholiast on Lucan,[9] and others down to Schedius in the
17th century, should have asserted unanimously that the
druids worshipped in groves ;   indeed, until Aubrey's time
(p. 8), it never occurred to anyone to suppose that they
worshipped elsewhere.

---

[1] Elsdon Best, *The Maori*, Wellington, N.Z.; 1924, I, 2888.
[2] P. 88, above.   [3] *Pharsalia*, III, 399 ff.
[4] P. 89, above.   [5] LXII, 7.   [6] P. 93, above.
[7] *Ancient Laws of Ireland*, Dublin, 1865, I, 164.
[8] Cited by Holder, *Altceltische Sprachschatz*, II, 712, s.v. nemeton.
[9] Teubner Series, I, 451.

On the other hand, we have to remember in this question of temples that when the Kelts had been for some time in contact with the Greek and Roman world, the religious practices of those who were nearest to the new influence would be profoundly affected.   They would be introduced to the grand temples built to the gods of the classical pantheon, and it is natural that once they had learnt to build for themselves, certain of them should desire to erect more dignified places of worship, temples that would be recognised as such by their neighbours.   Thus, in the 3rd century B.C., the Boii, according to Livy,[1] had a temple in which the spoils of war were stored ; and the Insubres, so Polybius says,[2] had a temple dedicated to Athena.   I see no reason to suppose that these temples were not built of stone and according to the classical model ; and I imagine that not only in Italy, but in Gaul also were such holy places erected. Cæsar, it is true, speaks simply of *consecrated places* in Gaul ; but Diodorus Siculus [3] refers both to sacred places and to temples, and Plutarch mentions the temple of the Arverni.[4]

It is probable, however, that in Gaul the temples built of stone were entirely a Roman innovation, and that, at the outset, they were only erected by the pro-Roman tribes. Nothing suggests that druidism, as a distinct native faith, ever abandoned the groves for artificial places of worship ; in fact, I feel sure that the first building of these temples was coincident with the collapse of organised druidism, and that afterwards, its remaining adherents nursed their resentment away from Roman eyes in the seclusion of their ancient forest-haunts.

At any rate, archæology has afforded singularly little evidence of artificial places of native worship that were not built exactly on the Roman model.   But there is one good example that I have seen that I should like to mention. In the little Altbach valley at Trier (Trèves), which lies just across the railway line opposite the celebrated Kaiserthermen, Professor Loeschcke has recently excavated an ancient

---

[1] XXIII, 24.   [2] *Hist.*, II, 32, 6.   [3] V, 27.
[4] *Cæsar*, 26. Generally, on this subject, see Jacob Grimm, *Teutonic Mythology*, London, 1880, I, ch. iv.

FIG. 27.—FOUNDATION OF CIRCULAR BUILDING BENEATH A RECTANGULAR TEMPLE TO MERCURY, TRIER

holy-ground on which lay the foundations of no less than
nine temples and chapels. One of these was a tiny square
building dedicated to Mercury, and under this was the circular floor (Fig. 27) of an older building, roughly about
16 feet in diameter ; it was bounded by the foot of a substantial wall in which are sunk the sockets that held the
pillars of what must have been an imposing superstructure.[1]
This is very reasonably assumed to be an example of the
native architecture of the Treveri ; [2] and since its circular
plan distinguishes it absolutely from the superimposed and
adjacent rectangular Roman buildings,[3] it can be claimed
that this must be the indigenous temple-form translated
into stone.

Of course, Trier (which, like Autun, was a town founded
by Augustus) did not come into existence until 16 or 13
B.C. ; and it is commonly held that until they were brought
down into the new city by the Romans, the natives dwelt
on the highlands on the opposite side of the Mosel, just as
the Gauls lived upon Mont Beuvray before they moved into
Augustodunum in the plain. And as the holy-ground, or
temple-area, in the Altbach valley is within the town walls
of Trier, there is an obvious probability that all the buildings on this site, being in the compass of the town, must date
from the time of the Roman occupation.

But it is not a certainty that the sacredness of the site
is of such recent date. For, although it is said that nothing

[1] I have to thank Professor Loeschcke for the photo that I reproduce here, and also for much information about this site. The excavations are not yet complete, but the following publications have
appeared : *Jahrbuch des Deutschen Arch. Inst.*, 1925, Anzeiger, 375 ;
Hannoverscher Kurier, 23 June, 1926, and 25 Nov., 1926 ; *Leipziger
Illustrierte Zeitung*, 4241, 24 June, 1926 ; and Loeschcke and Koehler,
Trier und Umgebung, p. 64. An illustrated guide is in preparation.

[2] It is uncertain whether the Treveri were, strictly speaking,
Kelts, and some believe that they were a semi-German (Belgic) folk.
See Rice Holmes, *Cæsar's Conquest of Gaul*, 394.

[3] A *circular* temple is, nevertheless, common in Roman architecture, and it is supposed that the form was derived from a primitive
Italian hut. Professor Loeschcke tells me that two other circular
foundations have been found in the Altbach temple area, one 35 feet,
and the second 9 feet, in diameter.

pre-Roman is found on the site of the town, and that before
the coming of the Romans the Treveri lived on the other
side of the river, it happens that a polished stone axe was
discovered in the temple-area itself. Its presence may,
of course, be due to accident ; but, on the other hand, it
betokens the visits of early man to this spot, so that we
cannot altogether dismiss the notion that the place may
have been a pre-Roman religious centre. And this means
that there is a possibility that the little round temple, which
was doubtless erected after the first contact with the Romans,
represents an attempt to give Roman dignity to an accustomed place of worship, an attempt, in fact, to erect an
artificial grove.

Perhaps the pillars, whose sockets still remain, stood in
place of the tree-trunks. It is a conjecture that is not
entirely fantastic, because there has recently been discovered in England the foundations of a structure that I
cannot help believing must have been an artificial grove of
the days of druidism in Britain. At present the site has
not been completely excavated, and it is rash to begin
guessing before the work has been completed ; but the place
is so interesting that I feel I must call attention to the
description already given by Mrs. Cunnington in the first
number of *Antiquity*. The site, which is close to Amesbury
in Wiltshire, has been given the name Woodhenge, because
the structure that once stood upon it seems to have been a
kind of wooden version of its famous neighbour Stonehenge.

It consists of a wide circular ditch enclosing an area of
about 250 feet in diameter, within which were six roughly
concentric rings of holes that once held wooden posts (or
tree-trunks, says Mrs. Cunnington) varying from one foot
to three feet in diameter. A wooden structure of this kind
can never have been expected to have had an immeasurably
long life, and therefore fails in the first requirement of
a memorial, so that I do not think it is likely that it was
erected to mark a grave-place ; indeed, its appearance, if
we reconstruct it in our minds, is against such a supposition.
Of course, the ground upon which it stood may have been
the scene of occasional burials, the site may even have been

hallowed by ancient tradition through the former existence
of a stone circle, barrow, or what not ; but this will not
make me believe the wooden jungle itself was a funeral
monument, nor will any analogy that has so far been
adduced ; and, that being so, I can think of no other
way to explain Woodhenge than as a druidic *grove* of the
La Tène period.

I am going to discuss megalithic monuments presently,

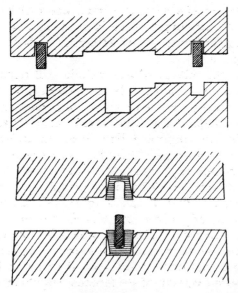

FIG. 28.—Diagram illustrating types of tenon-and-mortice lock employed
in classical building.

the so-called " Druids' Temples " and " Druids' Altars "
with which every one is familiar.   But before I begin a list
of various antiquities that were certainly *not* places of
druidical worship, I must take this opportunity of stating
my conviction that there is one building that may very
fairly be called a temple of druidism, and that is Stonehenge
itself.

The place (Fig. 29), of course, had been a famous circle-
site ever since the beginning of the Bronze Age, the time

when, I imagine, the temple began its existence as a rough
sarsen circle, or system of concentric circles, surrounded at
a distance by a ditch and a bank ; that is to say, the time
when it was probably a humble version of the giant rings
at Avebury.　But, during the Bronze Age, and not very
long after its erection, it was altered by the introduction of
an outer circle of about sixty foreign stones, chiefly dolerites
from the Prescelly mountains in Pembrokeshire.[1]　As the

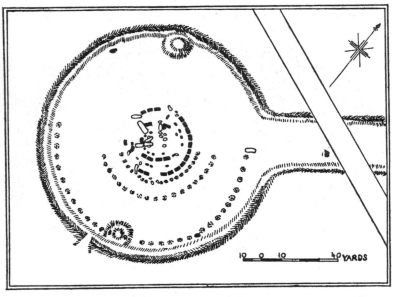

Fig. 29.—Stonehenge : diagram illustrating position of sockets of (?) earlier
circles.

eastern portion of these mountains, the source of the stone,
is a notable megalithic area, where the remains of stone
circles are still very numerous, it is clear that the laborious
transport of material from there to Stonehenge was a direct
contribution of part of the traditional sanctity of the Welsh
area ;　and so the Wiltshire site thenceforward became a
place of worship invested not only with tribal, but with
national, significance.　Such significance it never lost ;　and

though the people who thronged its area changed, the sacred
character of the site remained a fixed point in the prehistoric
religion of the island. A surprising amount of British and
Romano-British pottery has been collected from the excavations made within its compass,[1] and I do not think it is
possible to doubt the continued visits of people to the site
right up to the time of, and during, the Roman occupation ;
thus, it is obvious that it must have been frequented by
those professing the druidic religion.

Now, if we consider the existing monument, leaving

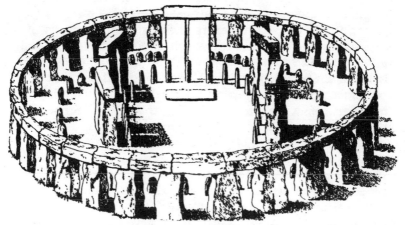

FIG. 30.—Stonehenge : the inner temple restored (*after Browne*).

aside the antique foreign stones that have been included in
the plan as inner rings to the circle and horseshoe of trilithons, we cannot fail to observe that this grand structure
(Fig. 30) is about as different from an ordinary stone circle
as a modern mansion is different from a prehistoric beehive
hut. It is true that the construction of some of the larger
megalithic chambers represent engineering problems as
formidable as that successfully solved upon Salisbury Plain,
but nevertheless we have, in the present version of Stonehenge, an architectural achievement that is completely

---

[1] See Colonel Hawley's reports of the recent excavations, *Ant.
Journ., passim.*

beyond anything hitherto attempted in the ordinary megalithic tradition ; indeed, the only other structure that was in the least like it, was a temple (Fig. 7) now destroyed, on the Odilienberg in Alsace.[1] The spirit of the work is different ; the rugged and lumbering boulder-masses are succeeded by a severe precision of outline ; clumsy weight is transformed into balanced stateliness ; the area of the enclosure is sacrificed to increase the height and dignity of the pillars ; a novel horseshoe plan was invented for the central court. But apart from the careful dressing of the stone, the builders employed a new device unknown in the megalithic architecture of Europe ; for the cross-pieces of the trilithons are secured on to the uprights by means of a peg-and-socket lock, a trick which I think they could only have learnt at second-hand from those who had some knowledge of the temple-masonry of Greece and Rome. It is, in principle, the ordinary classical method of assembling the members of a column (Fig. 28), though at Stonehenge the tenon is only a stone projection on the top of the uprights. The builders, of course, had not mastered the trick of a double socket and a movable metal tenon, but the shift they adopted is easy to understand, for it is clearly an economy of labour in the special circumstances, since it is far easier to carve out two stumps fairly close together on a short length of stone, than it is to carve them at a greater distance apart on the longer cross-pieces. And here I think it is interesting to add that the temple on the Odilienberg (Fig. 7) stood in a remarkable temple-area, whose major importance dates from the La Tène period, and which happens to be the very area wherein, as I have said, a curious Greek building-trick was detected (p. 62). I know that stone and bronze implements were also found in the neighbourhood, but this, I think, does not lessen the significance of the fact that in both of the only monuments of this kind in Europe, we find ourselves thinking of the influence of classical building.

A " fool's bolt " is soon shot at Stonehenge ; and usually

---

[1] R. Forrer, *Reallexikon*, s.v. Odilienberg.

misses its noble target! I very properly feel, therefore, that in the face of the vast literature dealing with the age of the monument, and the mass of modern expert opinion, it is almost an impertinence to aim anew. But since archæology, and also astronomy, have failed to provide any significant information concerning the date of the erection of the existing monument, I cannot help thinking we are still at liberty to make the most of such considerations that occur to us. I repeat, therefore, that the mortice and tenon betray the indirect influence of classical architecture, and bring the date of the monument down to the La Tène period.

And here is another point. If Stonehenge was not a temple of druidism, then it must have been a disused ruin in the La Tène period when druidism was the religion of the land. But does all the British and Romano-British pottery, and the actual burial of a La Tène man within its area,[1] really suggest the visit of trippers to look at a ruin? I think not. And I would ask what was the religion of this La Tène man, this early Briton who was buried there, if it was not druidism? And if it was druidism, is it not more likely that a believer would be laid to rest in the temple-precincts of his own faith than in the ruined sanctuary of a forgotten religion?

My view, then, is that the Kelticised population of Wessex took advantage of the ancient *national* sanctity of the old circle-site on Salisbury Plain to construct thereon a temple for their faith that should serve as a rallying-point, and more than that—a stimulus, for druidism after the beginning of the failure of the order in Gaul, that is to say, in the 1st century B.C. And in the final effort to assert the national faith in the face of the distant rumours of Roman aggression, the Britains tried to build for themselves, though preserving the ancient circle- and grove-tradition, as grand

---

[1] *Antiquaries' Journal*, V, 31. It might be argued that there is also mediæval, as well as British and Romano-British, material at Stonehenge. But if I am asked whether the mediæval folk were worshippers or trippers, the answer is trippers. For, so far as I can find out, the mediæval material is relatively negligible.

a temple as those the refugee druids from Gaul had seen
erected by the Greeks and the Romans.

The so-called " Druids' Altars " and " Druids' Temples "
of our islands are very primitive kinds of monuments,
being simply chambers, circles, alignments, and so forth,
built of massive blocks of stone, that are sometimes wholly
or partially " faced," but more often mere unhewn boulders.

The name *rough stone monuments* provides, on the whole,
a perfectly accurate description of these remains, and we
can think of them as displaying in a material of very large
slabs of stone the exceedingly simple kinds of architecture
we employ in building with a pack of cards.   For, in essence,
megalithic construction is nothing more than the erection
either of lines of stones, or of stone *boxes* roofed by one or
more horizontal slabs.   It is, of course, a fact that now and
again a wall of little stones, and sometimes even a cor-
belled roof of quite small slabs, may occur in a particular
structure, together with the large blocks ; but it is, nevertheless, clear enough that the real and original megalithic
architecture of our area depends, as the name implies, upon
the use of enormous and massive stones as the building-
unit.

In these remarks I am naturally thinking principally of
the megalithic structures of the druid-area, that is to say,
the north-western corner of Europe.   But it is very important
to remember that megalith-building is a custom of almost
world-wide distribution.   In fact, the first and the most
obvious objection to the theory of the druidic origin of these
remains (a point which never seems to have entered anyone's
head until well on in the last century) is that similar *temples*
and *altars* occur in many countries where quite obviously
there never could have been any druids at all.   We cannot
perhaps expect Stukeley and his followers to have been fully
acquainted with the actual distribution of these monuments
throughout the old world from Sweden to Japan, but it was
not very long after his day that their wide range was noted.
Quite apart, therefore, from questions of relative chronology, and without emphasising the fact that some Asiatic
folk are still building such structures for humble and entirely

non-druidic purposes of their own, it follows at once from the mere fact of the distribution that the theory that our own megalithic monuments were the work of the druids posits an origin for the *minority* that could not possibly be true for the *majority*.

I cannot find, however, that the early writers saw the point of this objection, although one or two attempted curiously unreasonable explanations of the existence of megaliths in far distant lands. Thus, in 1805, Cambry suggests [1] that most of these monuments outside the druid-area were simply imitations, by other races and made at various times, of the temples set up by the druids ; and he tried to prove this by a study of comparative religions, which he hoped would demonstrate that our northern druidism was a system of tremendous and far-reaching importance, a really extraordinary claim considering that there is nowhere any direct evidence suggesting that the druids had any considerable reputation outside of their own little corner of Europe.

However, because megaliths in India and in the Pacific and in Japan cannot be druidic, it does not result that ours in England are not. It will be worth while, therefore, to consider our own monuments in some detail ; and to make the enquiry simpler, I am going to treat first of the " altars " and to deal with the " temples " separately, or, to put this in more exact language, for the moment I am going to distinguish the stone chambers from the stone circles. Of course, the popular terms *altar* and *temple* are bestowed with considerable freedom, and most people may think that they are more or less interchangeable ; this is, indeed, a fact, and I must hasten to admit that there are many instances where a chamber, or the remains of one, is surrounded by a stone circle, so that together they make up a single monument. But I am going to include structures of this kind in the " altar " class, and all that my distinction really means is that I am reserving my remarks

---

[1] Cambry, *Monumens Celtiques*, Paris, 1805, p. 271, and cf. p. 281 (bottom).

upon the stone circles without central chambers, that is to
say, circles that are monuments in themselves, and not
merely an adjunct to another structure, until I have finished
with the *chamber* group.

Although I daresay they may be sometimes called
" temples," these chambers are as a general rule called
" altars " because they have the appearance, especially if
they are partly ruined, of being a primitive sort of table.
In reality they were little *rooms*, walled and roofed with
stone slabs, and I do not think anyone is likely to dispute
the statement that they were used as *tombs*,[1] and that many
of them are far, far, older than the druidic system of the
Early Britons or the Gauls in the form in which it was
known to Cæsar. I do not feel that there is any need for
me to *prove* their sepulchral nature, for no one who has any
knowledge at all of archæological record can possibly doubt
it. In North-Western Europe, to say nothing of other parts
of the world, literally hundreds of megalithic chambers have
been excavated, and in every instance where the contents
could be recovered they have turned out to be funeral
deposits of human bones or ashes with accompanying grave-
furniture. Naturally, when we say that *all* such chambers
were graves we depend on analogy, for, in our country
especially, many of them were despoiled of their contents
long before the archæologists came to investigate them ;
but the analogy is one of overwhelming strength, and the
continental evidence is strong enough to permit us to cite
for every empty English chamber a score or more of similar
structures elsewhere that have been proved to be tombs.

There should not be any need to labour this point, but
I notice that some of the modern adherents to the druidic
theory of their origin seem to be quite unaware of archæological discovery in this respect, so that it may not be amiss
to give one or two instances of the nature of the finds

---

[1] Probably there are one or two exceptions. For example, if
Mr. Hadrian Allcroft's theory is correct, as I am inclined to believe,
the peculiar " chamber " at Arradet in the mainland of Shetland is
simply the focus-point of the ceremonies (βοθρός) in a Danish
" Ting." See *Arch. Journ.*, LXXVIII, p. 352.

made in these megalithic chambers. I have chosen my
first examples from the stone monuments of the Channel
Islands, because I happen to know this group of remains
best of all ; but it would be perfectly easy to demonstrate
in any other district the sepulchral use of this kind of
structure. I think, however, that Le Trépied on the Catioroc,
a flat-topped hillock close to the northern coast-line of
Guernsey, is an excellent example of the so-called " Druids'
Altars " (Fig. 31), and it will serve to show the kind of archæological data that are available. But first of all I must point
out that this little monument provides another illustration
wherein the popular belief attached to a megalithic structure shows no recognition of druidic origin ; for Le Trépied
has long been of great renown in the folklore of the island,
but only as a notorious meeting-place for Guernsey witches,

Fig. 31.—Le Trépied on the Catioroc, Guernsey.

their " sabbats " at this spot, according to local legend,
being sufficiently important to be attended by the Devil
himself ; whereas there is nothing at all to be heard of the
druids until we come across the name " Druids' Altar " on
a 19th-century map.

Le Trépied is a small, straight-sided chamber about
18 feet long (Fig. 32) ; it was excavated in 1840 after it had
been lying for centuries exposed and partly in ruins, and it
was not to be expected, therefore, that any undisturbed
deposits should be found therein ; in fact, all that came to
light were some scraps of pottery, a few human bones, two
flint arrowheads and some flint flakes, distributed at random
in the earthen floor. There was nothing, then, to be learnt
from the manner of their arrangement as to their sepulchral
nature, and if we had no comparative material to help us
form an opinion it might perfectly well be supposed that

these little bits of pottery, bone, and stone represented the debris of some heathen sacrifice perhaps dating from druidic times. But archæological studies are sufficiently advanced to make us quite certain that in reality they were nothing of the sort ; for the potsherds are for the most part easily recognisable fragments of vessels of a well-known ceramic type called " beakers " that were a special and not very long-lived pottery fashion in vogue right at the beginning

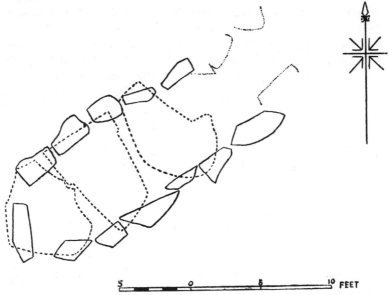

FIG. 32.—Plan of Le Trépied on the Catioroc, Guernsey.

of the Metal Era, roughly about 2500 to 2000 B.C. And the archæologist knows that these beakers were usually made to accompany funeral deposits, and on this point he speaks with proper authority, for he is acquainted with great numbers of them that have been found in single graves, as well as the large series of them that has come from bigger structures of the " altar " kind. There is an example close at hand. Across the island of Guernsey in the Vale parish, at the big *passage-grave* called Le Déhus, (Fig. 33) we find the beakers again in company with remains

that were not so seriously disturbed, and here is the account
of the excavation which was made in 1837.[1]

After removing the superficial rubbish covering the
contents of the main chamber " we arrived at an enormous
heap of limpet shells ; after clearing away several bushels
of these shells, human bones were turned up. These were
unburnt and lay mixed with the shells. In the centre . . .
two skeletons were found, one of an adult, the other of a
child ; a third skeleton was found under the third (cap-)
stone. . . . On sinking a spade or two deeper through a
bed of nothing but limpet shells, human bones again appeared in abundance, lying irregularly, some embedded in
limpet shells only, though some had a little mould around

FIG. 33.—Plan of Le Déhus, Guernsey (*after Carey Curtis*).

them." In this layer and accompanying the bones were
fragments of beakers and other vessels, " the whole resting
upon the alluvial soil of this part of the coast."

I think it would be rather difficult to argue that these
bones are simply the relics of often-repeated sacrifice, but
I will give another and more decisive example of the contents
of these great stone chambers, also from Guernsey. And I
want to mention this because it happens to be the very
monument that first suggested to Mr. F. C. Lukis, the
Guernsey archæologist who excavated it, that these structures were really sepulchres and not " altars," as he had
originally supposed. When he started his excavations as
a young man in the thirties of the last century, he was

[1] Lukis MSS., Guernsey.

naturally impressed with the altar notion, for it was at that time undisputed ; but the examination of this and a few other megalithic remains quickly changed his opinion and led to the publication of a famous paper proclaiming the re-discovery of their sepulchral nature.[1]

The monument in question is known as La Varde, from the hillock on which it stands, and it is a very fine example of a bottle-shaped passage grave (Fig. 34), being about 40 feet long and still roofed by nearly all its capstones.

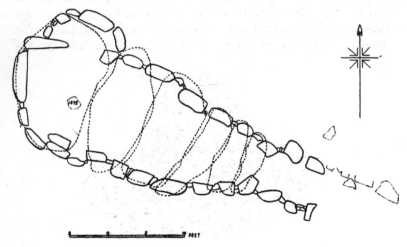

FIG. 34.—Plan of passage-grave on La Varde, Guernsey.

He found that the contents were distributed in the following order, starting from the top and working downwards :—

I　　Black soil, 6 inches thick.
H　　Loose white sand, 2 feet thick.
G　　Compact brown sand, $2\frac{1}{2}$ to 3 feet thick.
F　　Animal bones and stone rubbish.
E　　Dark earth containing limpet shells, unburnt human bones, pottery, stone implements, and burnt animal bones.

[1] *Journ. Brit. Arch. Assoc.*, IV (1849), 323. Cf. *Arch. Journ.*, I (1844), 142 and 222, and *Journ. Brit. Arch. Assoc.*, III (1848), 342.

D Pavement of granite flags.

C Yellow clay containing urns, burnt and unburnt
   human bones, stone implements, and pebbles.

B Pavement of granite flags.

A Natural earthen floor.

In the stratum C the human remains were very curiously arranged. Most of the bones were grouped together in small heaps, generally accompanied by an urn and surrounded by a ring of smooth flat pebbles (Fig. 35); over thirty such heaps were found in the eastern part of the chamber alone, and there were traces of many others elsewhere. This left no doubt in Mr. Lukis' mind that he had

FIG. 35.—Grave-group from passage-grave, La Varde, Guernsey.

found not the debris of sacrificial ceremonies, but formal funeral deposits; and I do not see how anyone can suppose him wrong. For in this instance, it must be remembered, the structure is not one that could conceivably have served as a *table* for sacrifices (although it has, of course, been called a Druids' Altar), but is simply a very large subterranean stone chamber that must have been built for the reception of deposits in the interior, and not for exterior ritual.

Before I leave the Channel Islands I must return to the monument Le Déhus, because we find there, attached to the larger chamber, four small cells built against its outer walls.

In works on the druids I have seen all sorts of fanciful uses ascribed to these side-chambers, so it may be worth while to describe the excavation of one of them in order to show that they are simply little supplementary tombs. For my example I take the side-chamber D on the plan ; it is a small cell 4 feet 6 inches deep and just under 5 feet in width and breadth ; it was excavated carefully, and the following is an abridged version of the original account of the proceedings. Passing first of all through a mixture of dry earth and limpet shells to a depth of 2½ feet, several distinct heaps of bones were found lying on a pavement of flat slabs of granite ; under this pavement were more limpet shells and earth covering a fresh series of human bones placed in heaps as in the layer above. These rested on a second pavement 1 foot below the first. On taking up these slabs and digging lower it was found that there was another 2 feet of limpet shells and earth piled upon the original gravel floor of the chamber ; on this floor in the south-east corner was a skeleton buried in a crouching position, and on the western side of the chamber was another. At the base of one of the props on the north side there was a pottery bowl resting in an inverted position on three narrow pieces of stone placed in a triangular fashion and covering a few fragments of bone (Fig. 36).

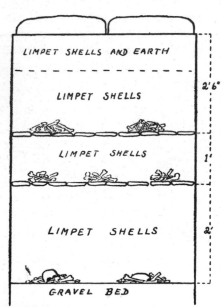

FIG. 36.—Section of contents, side-chamber D, Le Déhus, Guernsey.

I cannot leave this subject without saying a word or two about the English " altars." It is quite true that many of

them, particularly some of the best known, have long ago
been rifled of their contents, so that we can only prove that
they were tombs by means of analogy ; but, for all that,
there is plenty of direct evidence of the sepulchral nature of
this kind of monument in our own island. Take, for instance,
the chambers that were originally encased in those great
mounds called *long barrows*, for quite often these are fairly
simple cells (Fig. 37), and in the instances where the surrounding tumulus have been partially levelled we are left
with splendid examples of the " altar " class of megalithic
remains. Twenty-eight of these chambered long barrows,
clustered in Wiltshire, Gloucestershire, and Somerset, were

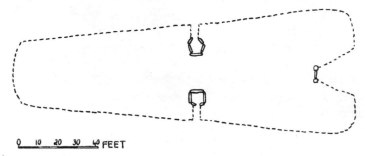

0   10   20   30   40 FEET

FIG. 37.—Diagram illustrating arrangement of chambers and dummy portal in
a British long barrow.

examined in the middle of the last century by the celebrated antiquary Dr. Thurnam, and in his report he tells
us that while in the chambers of ten of them nothing at
all was found, as their contents had long since been dis-
persed, in all the other eighteen human bones were found,
in some the skeletons of as many as fifteen, twenty-five, or
even thirty individuals. I will just give one example, and
that is the Belas Knap long barrow in Gloucestershire, where
there are two small chambers, only about 6 feet square, set
one in either side of the mound. These contained respectively fourteen and twelve human skeletons placed in a
squatting position against the walls, so that for whatever
purpose some people may *suppose* these cells to have been
used, we do at least *know* that they were once filled with

corpses, filled so completely that at that period they could not possibly have been anything else than burial-places.

I have no intention of wasting any further space upon this matter, and my few instances, chosen at random, must suffice for the hundreds and hundreds that are known ; indeed, I rather run the risk of weakening my case by giving particular examples, so I must repeat that the sepulchral usage of these stone chambers is a commonplace fact of archæology that needs no debate at all. All I have tried to do is to show the kind of evidence that, by being multiplied, as can easily be done, enables us to be quite sure, when we

FIG. 38.—Kit's Coty House, near Maidstone, Kent.

are pointed out a ruined and free-standing stone chamber, now called an " altar," that it was once a grave partly or wholly covered in a funeral mound.

I ought, however, to say that in addition to the contents, the morphology of the monuments also helps us to link isolated ruins with the great group of acknowledged burial-places. Thus the shape and character of the covering mound, if it survives, often furnishes a sure indication ; or structural details, such as the occasional window or porthole-entrance, the curving revetment of dry-walling at the door-way, may betray the makers just as plainly as a bone or a potsherd or a flint implement. There is a good example of this use of form, where excavation itself can tell us nothing, at Kit's Coty House in Kent. This, as I have said, has been claimed for the druids as a temple-cell or what not, and in its present state it certainly looks as though the Coty had once been part of some box-like structure (Fig. 39). But, as a matter of fact, old plans of the site [1] show that the remaining stones of this supposed chamber once stood at the head of a long mound, and their arrange- ment makes it quite plain, as I think Mr. O. G. S. Craw- ford was the first to point out, that they represent a feature still to be observed in a few of our west-country long barrows, namely, a sort of dummy entrance to the mound. This is a curious architectural survival that was doubt- less intended by the builders to sug- gest the door of the principal gangway into the mound ; for this was an im- portant element in the construction of earlier kinds of long barrows wherein the funeral chambers were made, not as in these later instances just within

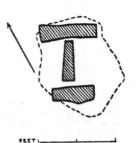

FIG. 39.—Plan of Kit's Coty House.

the sides of the tumulus, but in its very heart. Therefore, if the archæological case is sound, and I do not think it can seriously be contested, in Kit's Coty House the druids are claiming for their temple-purposes what was originally a mere external and functionless accessory of an ancient funeral barrow of pretty much the same age as those others of their " altars " that can be proved, as at Belas Knap (where there was also a dummy entrance), to have been the tombs of a pre-druidic folk.

Even so, we have not disposed entirely of these " altars," and there are still two further, and perfectly legitimate, questions to be considered. In the first place, it may be urged that although these monuments may be the tombs of

[1] See *Ordnance Survey, Professional Papers*, N.S., 8, Pt. 2 (Sheet 12).

an early prehistoric people, yet they may also have been utilised subsequently as sacred places by the druids ; and, secondly, it may have been noticed that I have been careful only to say that *most* of them are of high antiquity, so that I shall naturally be asked whether *all* are really as old as I have suggested.   Might not some, in effect, be the tombs of people of druidic days ?

To the first query I cannot give any satisfactory answer. I can only say that there is no evidence at all that the druids cared for, or worshipped at, these graves.   We do know that some later people were interested in them ; the Romans, for example, seem actually to have excavated one or two of these funeral piles, and now and then they even used the chambers therein for the burial of their own dead.   But there is no recognisable sign that the druids performed any ceremonies there.

Of course, the " altar " idea is sometimes encouraged by the discovery of naturally produced cups and channels on the top of the roof-stone that are supposed to have held the blood of the wretched creatures sacrificed thereon, but these do not merit any attention.   On the other hand, as is well known, we do also occasionally find artificially made cup-marks and other queer symbols carved upon these stone chambers.   To my mind, however, these do not in any way attest the druidic use of the tombs ; for, first of all, the markings are nearly always on the walls and the underside of the roof-stones, where they could not possibly have functioned as a gutter or collecting-place for blood (at the moment I can only think of two instances where cup-marks occur on the *top* of the roof) ; and, secondly, it is obviously impossible to prove the carvings are the work of the druids.   Whatever their purpose may have been, it is certain that markings of the same kind were made over a very wide area, including many non-druidic lands, at many different times, while in our own area it is equally certain that some of them date back to the earliest period of the building of megaliths.   Indeed, we know that the idea is older even than this, for examples have been found in France that belong to the Mousterian division of the palæolithic Cave Period.

When we come to the second question concerning the possible continued use of the megalithic chambers in the days of the druids, I must readily admit that I do not believe that all these great stone burial-places had altogether passed from living memory by the time the druidic system was established. It may be that they were thus forgotten in certain regions, in Britain it is at the best doubtful, but in France I think it may be taken for granted that many of the tombs were still known and occasionally used right up to the time of the Roman occupation. There is abundant evidence of this in Brittany ; in fact, I have found out for myself that some of the Breton tombs contain such a medley of the remains of all the different cultures succeeding that of the original builders, that it seems obvious that the later interments could not be due to a merely haphazard utilisation of ancient burial-places (although they are thickly enough distributed in the Morbihan to make this a reasonable hypothesis), but to a deliberate prolongation of their existence as sacred and honourable graves. Indeed, I will admit that in this region it seems to me that the very building of these great chambers may have been continued until within reach of druidic times, although in general much smaller and humbler single graves superseded them as the centuries passed.

The point very clearly affects the whole subject of the connection of the druids with the rough stone monuments, so I must show with rather more detail the kind of thing I have in mind. As a beginning I may point out that in Brittany there is so much pottery that is likely to be of druidic date in the megalithic tombs, that it has been seriously argued by M. Edouard Fourdrignier [1] that some of the structures must have been built during the Gaulish period, and that it is only because taboos enforced what was more or less a Stone Age ritual that we do not find in them an abundance of iron implements and other datable furniture of this advanced epoch. As a single example of the many discoveries of this kind, I will cite a small handful of

---

[1] *Congrès Préhist. de France*, Vannes, 1906, pp. 304 ff.

pottery fragments, now in the British Museum, from a large
megalithic grave in the Mendon commune of the Morbihan.
These sherds represent at least three pots of a fabric with a
brilliant black surface produced by the application of graphite
or black lead, a ceramic fashion that certainly does not
belong to the early megalithic period two thousand years or
so before our era, but that dates from the first few centuries
before Christ.

I will next give an example of a rather different kind
from North-Eastern France.   Near Breuil,[1] in the Seine-et-
Oise Département, there is a large rectangular stone chamber
over 40 feet long (Fig. 40) that was obviously built at an
early date and contained two layers of human bones sepa-

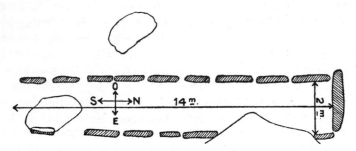

FIG. 40.—Plan of cist at Breuil, Mantes, Seine-et-Oise (*after
A. de Mortillet*).

rated by a stone pavement, the normal contents of these
cists in the Paris neighbourhood.   But in the excavation of
this great tomb, it was found that lying upon the top layer
of bones there was a hearth of the Gaulish period containing
pottery fragments and a coin, and above this there was
another hearth in which were Roman potsherds and coins ;
so that it seems to be quite clear that this particular structure was known to the common people right up to historic
times.

I must digress for a moment to point out that this cist
at Breuil had acquired the name of *Autel des Druides*,
apparently because a part of it, seemingly separated from

[1] *L'Homme Préhistorique*, Paris, 1911, p. 77, and cf. 1927, p. 49.

the rest, occupied the centre of a circle about 30 feet in diameter formed by a ring of lime trees. But although archæology agrees in this instance that the druids may very well have had knowledge of this structure, the excavators observe that the circle of trees, that probably suggested the name, cannot be more than a hundred years old, while it is known that the structure was also called by the ancient and more familiar popular names of the French megaliths whereby they are connected in folklore with the fairies, that is *Grotte, Cave*, or *Maison, des Fées.*

Not only were some megalithic structures retained in use throughout the early Iron Age, but, as I have already said, a few may even have been built in druid times. I find it rather hard to give an example of this unmistakably late construction in Northern Europe, but I will mention what I myself think to be an instance of the sort that I know of in the Channel Islands. This is La Hougue Boëte, in the north of the island of Jersey, a magnificent earthen tumulus over 30 feet in height and probably originally about 100 feet in diameter ; it was excavated in 1911 and found to contain a rectangular stone chamber, about 7 feet long and 4 feet in height, that was closed on all sides and without any approaching passage from the outside of the mound. Within this chamber were human bones, presumed to belong to a single skeleton, horse teeth, and pottery fragments ; and judging by this accompanying pottery I feel certain that the whole represents an interment of the Gaulish period just about or before the time of the Roman occupation ; and, because the tomb is sealed, and admitted no approach for secondary burial, I conclude that it was purposely built for that one interment.[1]

Brittany supplies also an example of the erection of a megalithic monument at a late date, although it is not an " altar " that I have in mind, but merely a standing-stone

---

[1] Although it was in principle just a rectangular stone box, it was really rather a complicated structure with double walls and other unusual features. This, perhaps, accords with the date I have suggested, but I ought, perhaps, to add that with the Gaulish pottery were a few scraps of rough, badly fired, and very gritty ware.

or *menhir*. This is La Blanche Pierre, near Guérande, in the Loire-Inférieure,[1] an upright block of quartz over 6 feet in height, at the foot of which rests a flat granite slab. I will not describe the excavation under these stones in detail, but it proved clearly enough that they belonged to two different epochs ; the recumbent slab, which had cup-markings upon it, was evidently a relic of the ancient mega-lithic period, but the quartz menhir (a most unusual material for a monument in this granite district) was resting upon, and steadied by, pieces of Roman brick, while in the ground immediately behind it were many fragments of Roman tile ; on the other hand, under the slab there was nothing but the dark earth and flint chips that are so well known under the older megalithic remains.   This is, I think, an undoubted instance of the erection of a stone monument as late as the time of the Roman occupation of Brittany, and, though I should not like to have to guess for what purpose it was set up, it lends force to my remarks upon the long survival of this primitive style of architecture.

But even if this be granted it does not to any very great extent invalidate our claim that the majority of the " altars " are the tombs of a much earlier civilisation than that of the druids.   For so far as these stone chambers are concerned, it is only from France and the Channel Islands that we produce this evidence of their prolonged use, and we are without any grounds for supposing that the same state of affairs obtained in England, Wales, or Ireland.   Therefore, it may be said generally of this whole class of megalithic monuments in the druidic area that they undoubtedly re-present the work of a pre-druidic folk ; and as additional warrant for such opinion we must take into account the significant fact that we are able to point out the less pre-tentious burial-places of the succeeding people,—the humbler round barrows of the Bronze Age, for example, covering little stone coffers or pit-graves for single interments, or the crowded cemeteries of the Early Iron Age.   It is clear enough, then, that the Cæsarean druids are separated from

---

[1] *Bull. Soc. Arch. de Nantes*, T. 39 (1898), 1° sem., p. 46.

the main period of the building of almost all the great tombs by the duration of one, if not more, distinct civilisations, wherein the erection of such tombs were no longer the fashion, and wherein the druids, so far as we can tell, were as yet unheard of; this is a gap that, even if represented by the Bronze Age alone, must mean an hiatus of at least a thousand years. All the evidence I have adduced apparently running counter to this assertion shows nothing more than that in one particular area of the druidic lands, namely Northern France, many of these big tombs were still known to the people in the druid period; and I repeat that, even so, there is not a scrap of information to suggest that these priests themselves were in any way connected with their alleged " altars."

Although it has not been difficult to show that the *altars* are really tombs, in most instances of a very early date, one cannot adopt quite the same measure of assurance in dealing with the *temples*, or stone circles.

Some of these, it is true, we can fairly dismiss as having been originally the encircling rings of the tumuli covering the stone burial-chambers, and, therefore, simple accessories of these graves and of equal date. Small circles of this sort are very common, and two plans (Fig. 41) of Devonshire structures will show the kind of monument I have in mind.[1] When the covering stone of the cist remains, we are left with what seems to be a *table* inside the circle ; and this, of course, immediately suggests druidic sacrifice to those who do not take the trouble to find out that this central table was really a little grave. One of the best examples of the bigger stone circles that seem to have been of this nature stands on Mynydd Carn Llecharth in the Gower peninsula of Wales, a ring of stones 60 feet in diameter still surrounding a central cist (Fig 42).[2] The component stones of this circle are

---

[1] *Trans. Devon Assoc.*, 1917, XLIX, p. 79 ; 1921, LIII, p. 84. I have to thank Mr. R. Hansford Worth for much information concerning the Devonshire circles ; both the plans reproduced here are surveys made by him.

[2] R. E. M. Wheeler, *Prehistoric and Roman Wales*, Oxford, 1925, p. 105.

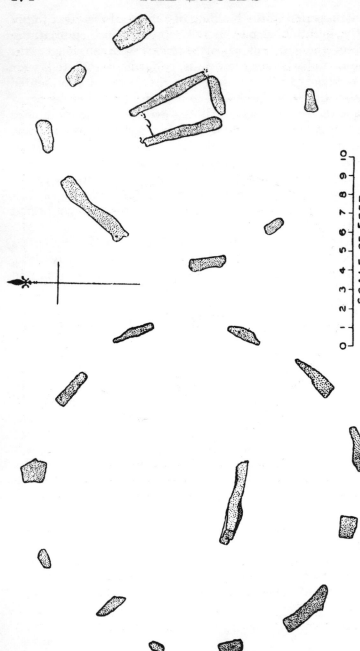

SCALE OF FEET.

FIG. 41.—Plan of stone circles, Burford Down and Erme Valley, Devon.

flat slabs set upright ; but in places they overlap one another, and they are occasionally somewhat pressed outwards, as though forced from the perpendicular by the weight of an earthen mound, or a cairn of smaller stones, since dis-

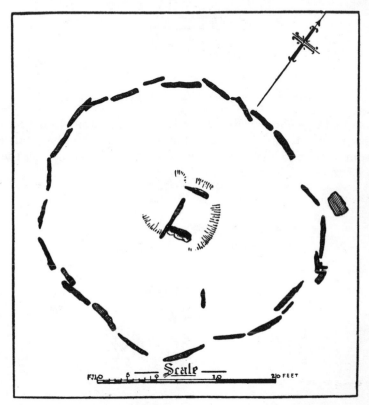

Fig. 42.—Stone circle, Carn Llecharth, Gower (*after W. Ll. Morgan*).

appeared, for which they must have acted as a retaining wall.

The section (Fig. 43) of a barrow at Ford in Northumberland better demonstrates the original function of this type of stone ring, and it will be seen how it is possible, when through various accidents the grave itself and the mound have vanished, that a stone boundary, or revetment, may finally appear as an independent and free-standing circle. This is not so unlikely as it might at first sight seem, because of the occasional custom (as in

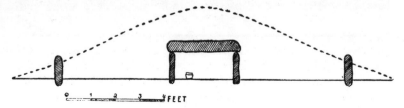

FIG. 43.—Section of barrow, Ford, Northumberland.

this instance) of allowing the edge of the mound to overlap the stones of the circle, so that they are actually hidden from view and may escape notice when the stones of the

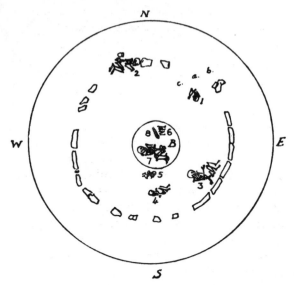

FIG. 44.—Plan of barrow 55, Hanging Grimston, East Yorks
(*after Mortimer*).

chamber are taken, as so often happens, for building purposes. As another example of this feature in barrow-building, I give the plan (Fig. 44) of barrow 55 at Hanging Grimston, in the East Riding of Yorkshire, where the circle, which enclosed eight interments, was completely covered over by the mound.[1]

In addition to those circles that were simply adjuncts of funeral mounds, a good many that were not part of mound-structures may also have been sepulchral in the sense that they were the boundaries of an area containing a grave or graves. They may be monuments, in a word, constructed on a plan like that of the Wiltshire *disc-barrows* that consist of a low earthen ring circumscribing an area in which an interment has been placed (Fig. 45). There was once a very good example of a transitional stage between the stone circle and the earthen ring to be seen on Danby Rigg in Eskdale, in the North Riding,[2] though now only a single

FIG. 45.—A Wiltshire disc-barrow.

isolated stone, about 6 feet in height (of course, called a " Druid " stone) remains. Originally this monument was a circular wall about 40 feet in diameter, and between 3 and 4 feet in height, built of earth and rubble, and incorporating at least four large upright boulders such as are typical of numbers of stone circles elsewhere ; and in the centre of the enclosed area were two pottery vases placed in an inverted position over a burial after cremation. There are scores of small funerary barrows of the Bronze Age in the immediate neighbourhood, so that there is nothing sur-prising in the fact that the two vessels (now in the British Museum), just like the urns found in disc-barrows, are of a

---

[1] J. R. Mortimer, *Forty Years' Researches*, London, 1905, p. 100. For an example in another part of the country, see *Trans. Cumberland and Westmorland Ant. and Arch. Soc.*, N.S., I (1900-1901), p. 295.

[2] *Gents. Mag.*, May, 1861, p. 506 ; April, 1863, p. 440.

late Bronze Age type known as *cinerary urns ;* thus we are
in a position to prove that in this instance a single upright
boulder, now popularly dubbed a " Druid " stone, was
really part of a funeral ring built probably somewhere about
1000 B.C.

It is quite likely, therefore, that other stone circles may
be kindred monuments, especially the smaller rings.　In the
same district, in fact, there is another stone circle [1] with a
diameter of 21 feet in which fragments of urns were found,
and yet another [2] that seems to have enclosed a central
cist.

FIG. 46.—Druidic victim awaiting sacrifice (*after Knox*).

But it is not only the small circles that may have functioned as grave-boundaries.　The Eskdale Moor circle in
Cumberland,[3] an irregular oval about 100 feet across, en-
closes five distinct funeral barrows (Fig. 47), each with its
own protecting stone circle around its circumference ; and

[1] At Cloughton, Newlands, near Scarborough.　See Robert Knox,
Descriptions in Eastern Yorkshire, London, 1855, p. 160.　According
to Knox, some mysterious clay objects, perhaps *hand-bricks*, were
also found in the area of this circle.

[2] On Standing Stone Rigg, N.R., Yorks (Knox, *ibid.*, p. 168).　I
have to thank Mr. Frank Elgee of the Dorman Memorial Museum,
Middlesbrough, for calling my attention to these two circles.

[3] *Journ. Brit. Arch. Assoc.*, XXXIV (1878), p. 35.

it is said that there were four other circles on the same moor likewise enclosing tumuli. We have no means of declaring the date of these barrows with certainty, for all that we are told in the account of their excavation [1] is that they covered interments after cremation, accompanied by some animal bones; but the analogy with the disc-barrow system of

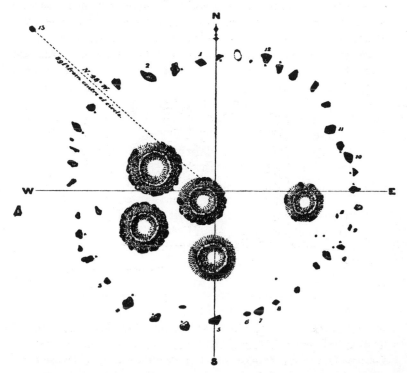

FIG. 47.—Stone circle enclosing tumuli, Eskdale Moor, Cumberland.

burial is strong enough to suggest that we have here the work of much the same period, that is to say, funeral monuments well out of the reach of druid times. Another circle in the same county, the Keswick Circle,[2] seems to be a similar funeral place, for within the stone ring, which was

[1] *Proc. Soc. Ant.*, London, 1st S., III, p. 225.
[2] *Journ. Brit. Arch. Assoc.*, XXXIV (1878), p. 33.

about the same size as the big circle on Eskdale, there was a rectangular enclosure of stones on the eastern side, and also a shallow cup-shaped depression, 13 feet in diameter, that was very likely the site of a barrow. The stone enclosure may likewise have been the peristalith of a tumulus, and the results of its excavation, though providing no definite information, are at least in accord with this supposition.

As another and very important instance of the same kind of burial ring in this district, I may mention that both Camden [1] and Dugdale [2] vouch for the existence in their day of two rubble tumuli within the area of that famous circle near Penrith, which, with the adjacent menhir or standing-stone, is known as Long Meg and Her Daughters. Yet another good example is a funerary circle on Leacet Hill, near Clifton, Westmorland. This was 37 feet in diameter, and in its centre at a depth of 3 feet was found a mass of charcoal interspersed with fragments of calcined bones and burnt stone, presumably the remains of a pyre ; and in addition to this four pottery cinerary urns, a food-vessel, and an incense-cup were found with cremated bones at the bases of various stones of the circle.[3]

In Scotland there are abundant indications of the sepulchral nature of many of the stone circles, and, better still, there is evidence of the date when they were set up. From a wealth of examples I select three to show the kind of archæological information that is available. The first is one of a group of several similar monuments on Manchrie Moor, in the Island of Arran,[4] and is a little circle 21 feet in diameter. In the centre was a stone cist 3 feet long that was buried deep in the ground, and which was found to contain

---

[1] *Britannia* (Gough, 1806), III, p. 426. But note that Gibson, in his edition (1772, II, 176), dismisses these as mere dumps of stones from the arable land around.

[2] Quoted by Aubrey, *Monumenta Britannica MS.*, Pt. 1. Stukeley seems to have noticed the sites of these cairns (*Itinerarium Curiosum*, 1776, Cent. II, p. 47).

[3] *Trans. Cumberland and Westmorland Ant. and Art. Soc.*, V (1880-81), p. 76.

[4] J. Anderson, *Scotland in Pagan Times*, Edinburgh, 1886 ; *Bronze and Stone Ages*, p. 97.

a Bronze Age food-vessel, some bone fragments, and a small bronze awl. There was no sign that there had ever been a cairn or mound piled up on the surface, either here or in the other adjacent monuments, so that the circle was simply the boundary of a grave-place and nothing else. The second is at Tuack, near Kintore,[1] in Aberdeenshire ; here there were seven interments within the area of a circle 24 feet in diameter. Four of these were simply deposits of incinerated human bones in small pits arranged around the central point of the circle, while the other three, placed near its perimeter, were similar deposits covered by inverted cinerary urns of Bronze Age, one of them including a small fragment of bronze with the bones. The third example is at Crichie,[2]

Fig. 48.—Section of stone circle at Crichie, Aberdeenshire
(*after Anderson*).

in the same neighbourhood ; here, within a broad encompassing ditch, was a stone circle 35 feet in diameter, and in the centre of this, its position marked by an upright stone, was a deep pit with a cist at the bottom (Fig. 48) ; the cist contained an unburnt skeleton and also some calcined bones under an inverted cinerary urn. At the base of a second stone was a similar burial, and near this last was a simple deposit of burnt bones ; between the two was found a polished stone axe-hammer of the Bronze Age. Several other funeral deposits were discovered in different parts of the circle.

There is no need for me to cite any other instances of circles that were probably sepulchral, and we may take it as established that many of these monuments may well be Bronze Age burial-places. But while I am dealing with

---

[1] Anderson, *loc. cit.*, p. 101.   [2] *Ibid.*, p. 104.

those of the circles that were evidently *not* built as temples, I ought, perhaps, to mention yet a third possibility concerning these rings ; for in addition to being the surroundings of funeral barrows, or funeral places in themselves, it is just possible that some of them may be the ruins of the outer walls of habitation sites. As an example of a circle incorporated in the structure of a dwelling-place, I reproduce a plan (Fig. 49) of one of the Foales Arrishes huts [1] on Blackslade Common in Devonshire ; the ring forming the wall of this hut is 30 feet in diameter, so that it is big enough to

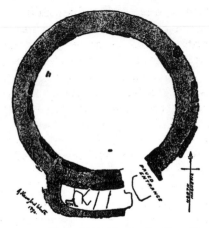

FIG. 49.—Plan of hut, Foales Arrishes, Devon.

make it quite likely that other circles of respectable size may also have been features of domestic architecture.

But even if we keep these three possibilities in mind, there remain a great many stone circles that I am quite sure cannot be accounted for under any of these headings ; and their number and size compel us to accord them rather more respect than was paid to those ransacked megalithic chambers that yielded no clue as to their original purpose. For the examples we have adduced of sepulchral and other circles cannot be said to form a convincing analogy for all the

[1] *Trans. Devon. Assoc.*, **XXIX** (1897), and *V.C.H.*, *Devon*, I, 354.

monuments of the circle class ; and this time, it must be remembered, we cannot fall back upon that convincing mass of continental evidence that encouraged us to assert that all the chambers were burial-places.

The " Stripple Stones " on the Bodmin Moors in Cornwall form a circle of just over 146 feet in diameter, surrounded by a vallum and a fosse, and having in the centre of the ring a tall upright stone. But there is no evidence that any burial was made within its area ; and after a careful excavation it was definitely decided that sepulture was not the object of the circle.[1] And there are many other large circles that, when examined, give similar results. Probably one of the earliest to be tested was the ring of the famous Rollright Stones, that was searched in vain for relics in the 17th century.[2] Accordingly, we find ourselves confronted with a series of stone rings, generally very big ones, about which we have no positive information at all, and we must now turn our attention to the very difficult problem these unexplained circles present.

As to their date, there is little to be said, for it remains one of the outstanding uncertainties of prehistory in Great Britain. Nevertheless, there are a few hints that may serve to guide our opinion ; and, as a beginning, we may note that one or two of these circles seem to be connected with tumuli that, as a result of excavation, or by inference, are believed to be of the Bronze Age. In Cornwall, for example, the " Nine Maidens " of Boskeduan,[3] in the Gulval Parish, is a stone circle just under 70 feet in diameter, whose circumference is interrupted by the edge of a cairn containing a little stone cist, and the arrangement suggests that the circle was built first. The cist had been rifled, but when the cairn, which is exactly like the scores of other Bronze Age cairns in the same county, was excavated, fragments of a Bronze Age cinerary urn were found about

---

[1] *Archæologia*, LXI, 24.

[2] Plot, *Nat. Hist., Oxfordshire*, 1677, p. 338.

[3] Lukis, *Prehistoric Stone Monuments, Cornwall*, London, 1885, Pl. IV ; for the excavation of the cairn, see Borlase, *Nænia Cornubiæ*, London, 1872, p. 281.

4 feet away from the cist ; so that all together there is a
strong probability that the circle is at least as old as the
Bronze Age. A better example is the circle at Arbor Low
in Derbyshire, where there is a tumulus, I think unmistakably of the Bronze Age,[1] adjoining the outer face of the
surrounding vallum, and partly resting upon it.   It is natural
to suppose that the circle, vallum, and fosse, were constructed
at a single operation, and if this be so, it follows that the
circle must have been built before or during the Bronze
Age ; and this conclusion is confirmed by the discovery at
the bottom of the fosse of a tanged and barbed flint arrowhead [2] of a type now generally recognised as belonging to
that Age.   Moreover, low down against the wall of the fosse
was found a second arrowhead of the earlier leaf-shaped
variety, so that it is indisputable that this ditch had already
been dug right at the very beginning of the Metal Era.

There is some general evidence, too, on this head.   In
several instances where these circles of unknown age occur, it
is found that they tend to be associated with groups of tumuli ;
and this suggests, though perhaps rather vaguely, that the
circles belong to the barrow-period.   Since we cannot as
yet speak too confidently of the factors governing the distribution of prehistoric populations, I do not want to over-
emphasize this point ; but I will mention one instance that
seems to me to be instructive.   I have said that excavation
yielded no information as to the date of the well-known
Rollright circle ; yet if we examine a map of the prehistoric
remains on the Cotswolds, we shall be struck by the fact
that this circle is set among a small group of barrows (the
Whispering Knights is a chamber of one of these) in a very
small and quite isolated area at the end of a chain of barrows
extending across Gloucestershire.   We must ask ourselves,
therefore, whether it is not more likely that all the remains

---

[1] The barrow was excavated by Bateman ; it covered a cist
containing cremated bones, bone pins, pyrites and flint, and two
pottery vessels now in the Sheffield Museum.   For an illustration of
these last, see Bateman, *Vestiges of the Antiquities of Derbyshire*,
London, 1848, p. 64 ; and (better) *Archæologia*, LVIII, 467.'

[2] *Ibid.*, 471.

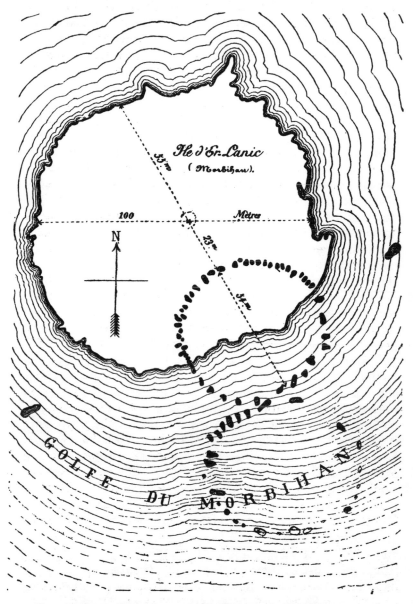

Fig. 50.—Plan of stone circles, Île d'Er Lanic, Brittany.

in this tiny stretch of land, less than half a mile in length, are the work of one civilisation at more or less the same time, than that druidic circle-builders, many centuries later, should happen to choose out this particular little piece of ground.

Such general argument as to the date of the big circles does not, I know, amount to very much, though it deserves mention because of its possible cumulative value. Unfortunately, there is not very much left for me to add in the way of precise archæological information. We know something, however, about the age of Avebury, the largest and the grandest circle in Britain ; but the value of the evidence depends on what is, after all, the perfectly natural assumption that the giant stone circle is as old as the great fosse surrounding it. This ditch was originally as much as 30 feet deep, and when it was excavated [1] it was found that the filling contained here and there, in descending order, mediæval, Romano-British, and Bronze Age pottery (including *beaker* fragments) and the so-called *Neolithic* ware ; the beaker and neolithic sherds occurred for the most part about half-way down in the accumulated silting, a circumstance very definitely suggesting that this circle, like Arbor Low, must be at least as old as the early Bronze Age.

There are several circles in Gaul that I ought to mention because of the information that is available about their chronology, but I shall content myself with a brief reference to a single and very interesting instance. This is the circle on the tiny Île d'Er Lanic in the Morbihan Gulf (Fig. 50) ; it is quite large, being about 180 feet in diameter, and was originally one of a pair of circles, but the second, as well as half of the first, is now submerged. The extraordinary thing about it is that its area, or rather the half of its area, that now remains on dry land, instead of being barren like our English circles, was crowded with a pell-mell mass of archæological material. Pots, axes, hammer-stones, flints, and even great stone hand-mills, had been piled upon the site ; and most of them, including the toughest of the axes, had been *ritually* broken, while a great many pieces of these

[1] See St. G. Gray, *Brit. Assoc. Reports*, 1908, 1909, 1911, 1922 ; especially 1909, p. 283 ; 1911, p. 150 ; 1922, p. 330.

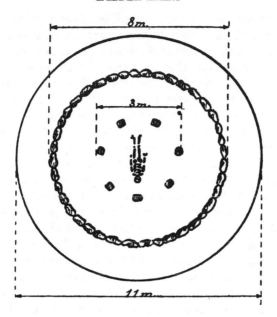

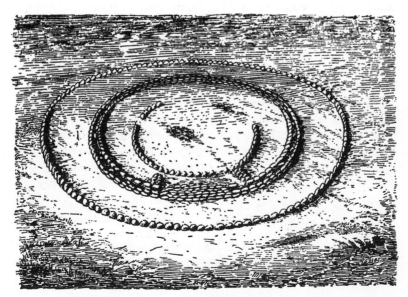

FIG. 51.—Stone circles surrounding burials of the Early Iron Age, Burgundy and Pyrenees (*after Déchelette*).

smashed stones and pots showed signs of burning as well. Although there were few human remains, my own belief is that all this debris represents funeral rites after the cremation of the dead ; but that is not the immediately important point, for what I want to observe is that the finds made it quite clear that the period when the circle was in use was the beginning of the Bronze Age. No doubt it may have remained in use for a good many centuries, but there is no certain evidence of Iron Age occupation,[1] and none whatever of visits from Gallo-Roman folk.[2] The circle on Er Lanic, therefore, was not a druidic temple.

The building of stone circles was, however, common in Gaul in Hallstatt times ; but such Iron Age circles were nearly all the appanage of places of burial. Of this kind are the exceedingly numerous rings surrounding Hallstatt graves in southern and central France (Fig. 51) ; but in Britain I do not think that I know any circle that can be proved to be of so late a date. And, even when we have made allowance for the Hallstatt burial-circles of France, the general probability is plainly that the bulk of the stone circles in the druid area were erected many hundreds of years before the druids themselves were heard of. But this does not by any means dispose of the subject, and we must not suggest without further reflection that these priests had nothing whatever to do with their so-called temples.

First as to function. We have said that some circles may be burial-places, but we have not been able to claim that all the larger circles were so employed ; indeed, it seems reasonably certain that they were not. Arbor Low, it is true, contained a central interment in a ruined cist or dolmen ;[3] but in the " Stripple Stones " there was only a

---

[1] A few of the sherds would probably be dated as Hallstatt in England, but in Brittany I think it is more likely that they belong to the Bronze Age.

[2] In all this bulk of material the only intruder that is later than the Bronze Age is a single sherd of about the 4th-5th century A.D. This, with a very interesting series from the circle, is now in the British Museum.

[3] It is usually dismissed, I admit it seems to me without adequate reason, as a secondary burial. See *Archæologia*, LVIII, 481.

single upright stone in the centre without any trace of a
burial beneath or near it, and the excavators were convinced that sepulture was not the object of the circle.   The
Rollright circle was searched in vain for funeral remains, no
interments have been found in the Avebury rings, and the
same is true of many other of the principal British circles.
We have to ask ourselves, therefore, whether it is not possible
that in spite of their great antiquity some of these circles
may have survived as places of druidic worship.

Two modern views seem to run counter to this.   For it
has been argued, first of all, that the circles were Keltic
folk-moots, that is, ceremonial places of debate, and,
secondly, that they were observatory posts for determining
by the movements of heavenly bodies the more important
dates in the year's cycle.   On general grounds, I think both
these views are reasonable ;   modern primitive man certainly uses stone circles for solemn conference, so that
there is nothing unlikely in the supposition that some of the
ancient circles were so employed.   Again, the obvious importance of the turn of the seasons to an agricultural people
makes it quite possible that exceedingly elaborate measures
should be taken to ascertain the exact time of the solstices
and so forth, such as arranging stone circles as the foci of
sight-lines.   But neither of these views, as we have surely
seen, admit of universal application, and they are commonly
pressed to absurdity.[1]   The folk-moot theory, for instance,

[1] I once made a survey of the megalithic monuments in the
Channel Islands, and I was told that, whether I believed or not all
the remains represented observatories, I ought at least to provide
adequate data concerning their celestial orientation.   Accordingly
I received instruction in method, and equipped myself with the necessary instruments.   Nothing could have been more auspicious than
my beginnings, but presently doubts arose.   One magnificent observatory, perched on a headland, had a duplicate, set in low shelving
ground surrounded by hills, that miserably failed to observe anything ;
and presently I came to another set absolutely at the foot of a hill
and *observing directly into the hillside.*   After this I contented myself
with recording the usual vague orientation to which the archæologist
is well accustomed.   These Channel Island monuments, I ought to
say, were not circles ; however, I have also tried my luck in one

cannot be applied to a big circle like that at Keswick, whose area contained several tumuli ; nor is it easy to believe that this same circle was an observatory.   And on this last score, I would observe that there is no ethnographical warrant that primitive man of the culture-level represented by the circles was capable of elaborate astronomical measurements of this kind ; and this seems to me to be an objection of some force against the supposition that the circles provided an accurate record of the movements of celestial bodies, in as much as I have not yet found any other operation of primitive man in Europe that is not also a practice of his modern representatives.   But as a more pertinent comment, I shall merely repeat Dr. Mortimer Wheeler's opinion [1] that no Welsh circle is adapted precisely for any convincing astronomical observation.

I do not intend to discuss these theories, even though there may be a modicum of truth in both, for I do not believe that they can explain all the stone circles ; and my present purpose is simply to see whether the druids can have had anything to do with them.

I remarked in the first chapter of this book that there was no ground for supposing that the country-people were exerting, either consciously or unconsciously, their *folk-memory*, when they called the stone circles *Druids' Temples ;* there was, we saw, another and a better explanation why this name appears so frequently.   But though folk-memory be set aside, it is not fair to ignore any isolated instances of legend that bear expressly upon this subject of the connection between druids and stone circles, and I must now say a word upon that aspect of the problem.

There is, as might be expected, very little material worth considering.   The most important story that I can think of is to be found in the *Tripartite Life of St. Patrick*,[2] which is thought to be a 9th century compilation preserved in an

or two English circles, and I am equally impressed by the superb ease in finding celestial orientations, and the immense difficulty in crediting primitive man with having created them intentionally.

[1] *Prehistoric and Roman Wales*, p. 106.

[2] Whitley Stokes, *Trip. Life*, London, 1887, p. 91.

11th century MS.; and it concerns an event said to have
taken place about A.D. 435, when the Saint arrived in the
Plain of Slecht, near the modern Ballymagauran, in County
Cavan.[1] It was the place in which stood the chief idol of
Ireland, known as Cromm Cruaich, something, whatever it
was, that was richly adorned with gold and silver, and
around which stood twelve other idols covered with bronze
ornaments. These smaller idols in a ring, and Cromm
Cruaich in the centre, suggest that, stripped of their metal
adornments, this Irish holy of holies was subsequently
thought to have been nothing other than a stone circle
with a central monolith, of the same type as the " Stripple
Stones " in Cornwall. In early mediæval times, therefore,
this circle-site was described as a scene of pagan worship ;
and, according to the legend, it was the scene of a mighty
conflict between the Saint and heathendom ; for, on his
arrival, Patrick threatened the main idol so effectively that
it was permanently branded with the mark of his stave,
and at the same time he caused the twelve lesser idols to be
swallowed up in the earth as far as their heads, in which
position they remained ever afterwards as a token of the
miracle.

The Reverend Dr. Healy thought the actual boulders
could be recognised at Edentinny, between Fenagh and
Ballinamore ;[2] but whether this identification be right or
wrong, I think it can hardly be doubted that the story of
the ring of idols whose heads alone were showing is an
ætiological myth to account for an ordinary stone circle.
And it is clear, therefore, that in the 9th century it was
believed by some that these remains were connected with
pagan worship, and, moreover, with the magicians or *druids*,
who were the chief opponents of Patrick's mission.

This is the only instance I know where there seems to be
any legendary contact between the druids and the stone
circles, and I do not want to lay undue emphasis upon it,

[1] See J. P. Dalton in *Proc. R. Irish Acad.*, XXXVI (1921-24),
C. 23.
[2] Healy, *Life and Writings of St. Patrick*, Dublin, 1905, p. 184.

because, of course, it may have been completely an invention on the part of the compiler of the *Life*. But I would point out that it is not only in Ireland that there is some evidence of a tradition of former worship at these places. Professor Garden of Aberdeen, who made, in 1692, a study of the famous and peculiar group of circles in his neighbourhood, reported [1] that the general tradition throughout Scotland concerning such monuments was that they were temples for worship and sacrifice in heathen times. He adds, however, that he cannot trace any connection with druidical worship, unless (he adds) the name of the priests survived in two place-names that he cites ; but we cannot rule out the possibility that the worship remembered in the tradition was Keltic worship, and so was administered by the druids. And it is worth noting that these same circles, with their principal peculiarity accurately described, are attributed by Hector Boece [2] in 1526-27 to a legendary pre-Roman king called Mainus, who built them in order that the worship of the gods might be stimulated by the performance of new ceremonies in new places ; so that a druidic connection does seem to be inferred. I am not prepared to debate whether this last story is or is not a wholesale invention of the ingenious 16th century scholar, but it is at least in Boece's favour that he seems to have had an intimate knowledge of the monuments themselves.

So far as this enquiry has gone, it has been shown that the temples of the druids were natural groves, except in the occasional instances where either a lack of an adequate natural site, or the gradual influence of Roman civilisation, prompted them to translate the groves into buildings. Stonehenge has been named as the most notable example of their achievements as temple-architects, but I do not know that there is any reason to suppose that the druids ever built a stone circle of the ordinary kind. In fact, so far as megaliths are in question, the position is that the so-called *altars* are really tombs, nearly all the work of a

---

[1] *Archæologia*, I, 339.
[2] Hector Boethius, *Scotorum Historiæ*, Paris, 1526, Lib. II, fol. xvi.

much earlier civilisation ; while some of the stone circles, or *temples*, were also burial-places of the same people, or structures seemingly erected by them for purposes now unknown to us.

Notwithstanding, we have seen that it is almost certain that *some* of the megalithic graves and *some* of the circles were known to the druids because of their continued use by the native population right into the Iron Age. And if that is so, there is a reasonable chance that the druids themselves may have appropriated certain circles for their own ceremonies. This, I think, is the utmost that can be said in support of the popular notion about our megalithic remains. I shall not, however, discuss the significance of this conclusion here, for it will be better understood in the course of the next and last chapter.

CHAPTER VI

ORIGIN

A CONSIDERABLE preparation, five chapters long, has fitted us for the final enquiry as to the origin of the druids and of druidism. But though we are packed for the journey, I confess I am tempted to delay the start. For, to begin with, it is clear that we are discussing a very elusive substance, and are not likely to make much headway unless we define our objective with some precision.

Many centuries of antiquarian interest and popular renown have invested the word *druidism* with an undeserved significance, and it is important to remember that in reality it denotes a very ordinary primitive faith, and not one that is remarkable either for an advanced philosophy or an unusual theology. Indeed, it is plain, as M. Camille Jullian has observed,[1] that if it were not for the chance that its priests had a special name, the prestige of their religion would be sensibly diminished, and (I would add) a whole library of books discussing its origin would never have been written. For if the classical authors had referred to *priests* only, and if druidism had escaped its present renown, I cannot see that it would be possible to imagine anything else than that these priests represented a purely Keltic organisation developed principally by the Gaelic, British, and perhaps Italian Kelts after the period of their wanderings. Reread, for instance, Cæsar's testimony, substituting the word *priest* for *druid*, and consider whether it is conceivable that the all-powerful caste he describes, dominant spiritually and

[1] *Histoire de la Gaule* (5me ed., 1924), p. 87.

194

politically, could have consisted of any but the Kelts themselves. And as for the opinion that their religion was derived from Britain, would it not be assumed that their faith had both naturally and intentionally come to include so much of the autochthonous religious tradition, that ultimately its origin was obscured, and was attributed to a region where that native faith was known to persist in its least altered state ?

For my part, I want to make it clear that when I talk of the origin of druidism I divest the word of all its later significance, and refer to the only expression of early druidism of which we have any definite knowledge, that is the clergy and faith of the Gauls in the 1st century B.C. Accordingly, druidism in Britain and Ireland must be explained incidentally in the terms of whatever solution we arrive at for the main problem ; and I defend this attitude on the grounds that in these last countries druidism is too nebulous and uncertain a thing to allow a reasonable basis for discussion.

The kernel of the matter is this. How can we reconcile the ascendancy of this priesthood and the religion among the ruling Keltic-speaking folk in Gaul with the belief, mentioned by Cæsar, that it originated in a country into which the Kelts only penetrated after their arrival in Gaul ? Normally, one expects to trace a religion back to the ancient home of its devotees ; but, here, it is said to have originated in a remote outpost of the Keltic world.

Let us deal with the reported origin first. Cæsar said of druidism that its discipline, by which he meant either its doctrine or its constitution, or both,[1] *is believed* to have been discovered in Britain and imported thence into Gaul. What he recorded, then, was not a statement of fact, but an opinion ; yet it was far from being an idle guess, because it was added that those who wanted to study its principles closely went to Britain for instruction.

---

[1] The context suggests Cæsar referred to druidic organisation, but I think he meant doctrine. Druidism was well organised in Gaul, and there would be little need for British instruction. And surely the one thing of which Cæsar might ask the origin would be the druidic doctrine of immortality.

I do not think that the subsequent remark of Pliny [1] has any bearing here. Magic, he said (and by magic he meant druidism in this instance) was practised in Gaul and had penetrated even to so remote a spot as Britain, where it was invested with such august ceremonies that one might almost suppose that it was from this far-off isle that the cult had spread to the Persians. This means simply that Pliny, who was generalising on the subject of magic, wished to point out that a form of it, well known in Gaul, also flourished to an extraordinary degree in Britain ; but he no more suggests as his considered opinion that British magic was derived from Gaul, than he seriously asserts that there were direct relations between Persia and Britain. The passage, therefore, in no wise detracts from the significance of the opinion recorded by Cæsar. [2]

The implications of this are important. Obviously, in order that druidism should have this reputation of a British origin, it must have been established in Britain for a long time before Cæsar wrote. But the Gallic druids were already known to the outside world by about 200 B.C. ; in all probability, therefore, they were established in Gaul for a century or so before that date, and British druidism (but not British druids) accordingly must be of an even higher antiquity. That is to say, if we accept the statement of Cæsar's informant as an expression of a genuine belief, it is difficult to resist the conclusion that at the beginning of the La Tène period, at the time of the first Keltic traffic with England, there existed in our country some novel religious element that after the Keltic invasion was grafted upon Keltic faith and spread throughout Gaul, giving rise to what thenceforward was termed druidism.

Is it possible, however, to name this British element in druidism ? Was it the priesthood itself, or was it druidic theology or dogma ?

[1] *N.H.*, XXX, 1, 4 (p. 90, above) ; the phrase *ut dedisse Persis videri posse* might be turned so as to suggest the possibility that Britain had learnt its magic directly *from* the Persians ; but I cannot accept this reading.

[2] The best destructive criticism of this passage in Cæsar is by Mr. W. F. Tamblyn, *American Historical Review*, XV (1909-10), p. 23.

Prima facie it is not likely to have been the first, for when we remember how thoroughly this clergy dominated life in Gaul in every one of its most important aspects, it seems inconceivable that such a complete reorganisation of Keltic religion, involving the absolute subjugation of the Kelts beneath the priestly caste, should have been achieved by the priests of the defeated natives in an outlying and lately conquered province. We might, of course, pretend that the Kelts had no priests, and so impressed a few of them into their service, whereupon these opportunists eventually founded a Keltic corporation of druids. But this would be a very unsatisfactory explanation, if there were nothing else to be adduced in favour of the notion that the druidic priesthood was a British innovation.

There is, as a matter of fact, something more to be said ; because it is sometimes argued that priests of the druidic type are not characteristic of the indogermanic folk, and so could not have been originally Keltic. On this view, the Kelts, like the Greeks and the Latins of old, and the Germans, were ruled by kings and princes invested with a spiritual as well as a temporal authority, and who performed the ordinary functions of the priest such as sacrifice and communion with the gods. If one believes that the Kelts did not differ in any remarkable way from the indogermanic neighbours, especially those on much the same cultural level, it would follow that in this early period of their expansion they did not have an organised clergy, and thus the druids as a priesthood would be of non-Keltic origin. Keltic legend in Ireland certainly reflects an ancient belief in the divinity of kings, so that there is justification for the notion that when the Kelts reached Ireland their religious affairs were managed by their chieftains. And here we are appositely reminded that Brennus, the leader of the Kelts who sacked Delphi, had no priests nor augurs with his band.[1]

---

[1] *Pausanias*, X, 21, 1. If the passage really *does* imply this. The historian records that the over-confident and vain-glorious chieftain had no Greek soothsayers with him and consulted no sacrificial omens ; and he goes on to express a doubt whether the Kelts knew the art of divination. That is to say, the statement is to

But none the less, we must not accept without further questioning the implication that the druids themselves were originally strangers who intruded into Keltic life and usurped the priestly functions of the Keltic kings. It is, I am sure, an overstatement to say that because the Kelts belonged to the indogermanic linguistic family, they were therefore unlikely to have had priests of their own. After all, the notion of the divine king represents only one stage in moral evolution, and there must have been a tendency, even at that early period, to distribute between kings and others the temporal and spiritual functions that had hitherto devolved upon the king alone, and so to pass into the stage in which the conduct of religious affairs is entrusted to those who were purely and simply priests. Indeed, the transition was in operation : the Latins, for example, had priests ; and the Germans, who had no clergy when Cæsar wrote, are credited with priests by Tacitus. And as for the general contention that a powerful and complicated priesthood is foreign to indogermanic temperament, here are the Kelts with their druids ; and in India, there are the Hindoos with their Brahmans.

It seems impossible, then, to name a period before which the Kelts could not have had priests, even though we admit, as I readily do, that a Keltic divine king preceded in point of time the Keltic priest pure and simple.

And let us consider another point. If the Kelts stole the idea of their priesthood from Britain, ought we not to find therein some evidence of the existence of a clergy as famous as that in Gaul ? It is strange that the next conquerors of our island, when they crossed the channel, seem to have been unimpressed, even though Keltic authority (according to this theory) had by that time been added to the native sacerdotal class. In fact, all the Romans troubled to record was that there were some wild creatures called

the effect that Brennus was too arrogant to use soothsayers ; and the significance of even this much is diminished by the next remark, which shows that the writer knew nothing at all about Keltic religion. The point, therefore, is, if Brennus had had druids with him, would the Greek historian have been thus ignorant ?

druids once seen exciting the defenders of Anglesey to a
final resistance.[1]   And nothing more is said of them, not
even at the time of the rebellion ; indeed, Boadicea seems
to have conducted sacrifices herself without the aid of
priests.

On the other hand, it is conceivable that a pre-Keltic
priesthood of the requisite authority existed in Ireland.
Legend, on the whole, presents the Irish druids as a less
highly organised class than the druids of Gaul, lacking, it
seems, a single arch-druid at their head ; and it presents
them rather as potent magicians than priests of the altar.
But I am alive to the possibility that legend, winnowed by
disapproving Christianity, may have left us with a very
imperfect residue of fact.   Therefore I will only say that
we have no knowledge that suggests the Irish priests as the
society upon which was modelled the powerful Gallic clergy.
Instead, the evidence hints the other way ; for surely it is
significant that the druids of Ireland were servants of the
primitive Keltic festival-system in its central European
form.   This last is a point that goes to the very heart of
the problem, for I think it well-nigh incredible that if these
Irish druids were pre-Keltic, they should have been at once
strong enough to impose themselves and their organisation
upon their conquerors, and yet so feeble that they accepted
for their principal ceremonies the two antique Keltic festivals of the old pastoral year.

But here Dr. Julius Pokorny intervenes with his argument of the oak.[2]   The cult of this tree, he observes, is
well attested as a general element of indogermanic religion,
and the Gallic druids were known to be its priests.   Therefore, if the Kelts already had druids when they crossed to
the British Isles, they would certainly have brought the
oak-cult with them, for there are plenty of oaks to worship
in that country.   But, strange though it may seem, the oak

[1] See p. 91.
[2] *Mitteilungen der anthrop. gesell. in Wien*, XXXVIII (1908),
p. 44.   This justly famous paper by Pokorny has been translated
into English, *Ann. Report*, Smithsonian Institution, 1910, p. 83, and
Celtic Review, V (1908-09), p. 1.

is rarely mentioned in the rich literature of early Ireland, no superstitions are connected with the oak, nor were the druids ever associated with it ; instead, their sacred tree was the mountain ash. There was *no* oak-worship, therefore, in Ireland, says Dr. Pokorny, and this can only be explained by the assumption that the druids in Ireland were originally priests of a people who did not know the oak-cult. That is to say, the Gallic druids were oak-worshippers merely because the Gauls among whom they lived were less under the influence of the pre-Keltic inhabitants of the British Isles than the conquerors of Britain and Ireland, and therefore preserved together with the new druidic doctrine this custom of their indogermanic ancestors. And if the druids were once the priests of a people that did not know the oak-cult, and the Kelts were oak-worshippers, as it is certain they were, then it follows that the druids cannot have been in the beginning a Keltic priesthood.

In archæology it is seldom that we can prove a point with argument so slick and simple as this, and it becomes us to be suspicious. But I myself have no new criticism to add to those that have already been made. For Dr. Much, in discussing Dr. Pokorny's paper, immediately remarked [1] that the absence of signs of oak-worship in a particular country was not an infallible proof of the former absence of the cult, because this absence might result easily from the loss of the oak's sacred character due to the plentifulness of the tree, on the principle, that is, that familiarity breeds contempt. And Dr. Goldman went further [2] and denied the premises, saying that there were, after all, some signs of the oak-cult in Ireland, such as the oak of St. Brigit, and the " churches of the oak " that may stand on the site of an earlier sacred grove.[3]   While as for England, I am tempted to ask, are not the boughs of oak strewn over the oaken coffin in the Bronze Age burial at Gristhorpe also admissible as signs of a special, and here pre-Keltic, reverence for the tree ?   And, finally, that most formidable of critics, Dr. Rice Holmes, completed the attack by remarking [4] that the conclusion is

[1] *Mitt. anthr.*, Wien, XXXVIII (1908), p. 46.
[2] *Ibid.*, p. 47.   [3] P. 124, above.
[4] *Cæsar's Conquest of Gaul*, Oxford, 1911, p. 524, n. 2.

unsound, even supposing the facts were correct ; for the most that can be proved from them is that the Keltic invaders of Ireland, who undoubtedly were oak-worshippers, were unable or unwilling to impose oak-worship upon the Irish aborigines.

Another point sometimes made is that if the druids were Keltic priests, then there should be druids wherever there were Kelts, instead of in one corner only of the Keltic world.

I am prepared to grant that it is virtually certain that some of the Kelts did not have druids, even though some writers have contested this.[1]   In my view, Cæsar's considered statement on druidism is a sufficient authority for the common belief that the druids were confined to Gaul and the British Isles ; for if Cæsar knew that there were druids in Cisalpine Gaul, where they would be already well known to the Romans, he would surely have omitted or reduced his own circumstantial account of them, because this seems to me to be intended for readers who knew nothing at all about the druids.   Moreover, if there were druids in Italy and the Danube valley and in Spain, there would be several sources of information about these priests, and not one only, available for other writers who chose to make mention of them ; yet although seventeen authors, beside Cæsar, did so, not one of them can be shown to have availed himself of the rival sources, nor to hint that there were druids outside Gaul and Britain.

But it will be asked whether it is conceivable that druids could be of Keltic origin, and yet confined to certain of the Kelts and not the common property of them all.   I think myself that it is not only conceivable that this should be so, but that it would be very astonishing if it were otherwise. The original Keltic province was the enormous tract between Switzerland and Hungary in which the La Tène culture was consolidated, and the people therein, although united by the bond of a common language and a common art, were far from being a homogeneous race.   In the period of expansion of these Keltic-speaking folk, who were sprung from

---

[1] See, for instance, MacCulloch, *Religion of the Ancient Celts*, p. 297.

mixed racial stocks, it is clear that there was a probability of a rapid divergence in customs as the various separate communities spread abroad ; and this not only in virtue of the varying tendencies in each party that were due to a lack of racial homogeneity, but also because of the new and varying influences to which each party was subject. In view of this potential disintegration of Keltic unity, it would be expecting too much of this people to demand universal identity in the organisation of their religion, and we can readily understand how the easy progress from the stage of the divine king to the stage wherein there was a distinct priesthood should have been achieved at different times and in different ways by the various sections of the Kelts.

There is nothing for it, therefore, but to allow common sense one of its rare victories by declaring our opinion that the complicated and powerful druidic priesthood in Gaul must have been of Keltic origin. And I repeat the simplest and most effective reason in favour of this opinion, namely, that the Gauls in one of the proudest moments of their history would never have tolerated, nor welcomed, the imposition of a foreign priestly caste able so thoroughly to dominate both their civil and religious life.

But doctrines and theology are another matter, and we must now consider the possibility of Keltic borrowings here. It has been argued, for example, that there is much in druidism, as known to us in the pages of the classical authors, that is opposed to Aryan or indogermanic sentiment. A great deal has been written upon the subject, but for my part, I am inclined to treat it cursorily and declare that I do not know a single item of druidic belief that was not also known to one or another of the indogermanic peoples.[1]

---

[1] Human sacrifice, of course, will not do ; and the best example I know is the doctrine of the redemption of one life by another. Dr. Pokorny (*loc. cit.*) adds that traces of cannibalism, matriarchy, and the couvade in legend and folklore are additional signs of the non-indogermanic religion in the British Isles from which druidism is derived. As a matter of fact, they are all three open to objections (see the discussion following the paper), but even if Dr. Pokorny were right and they do represent a pre-Keltic religion, what of it ? No one disputes that there was a pre-Keltic religion. We do not

The problem is difficult to discuss except at considerable length, since parallel customs are sometimes open to the rebuke that they followed, instead of preceded, the introduction of the same custom into the indogermanic world by the druids. But I feel very strongly that we do not know enough about primitive indogermanic thought to enable us to announce of any of the doctrines fully accepted by the Kelts of Gaul and Britain, as were all the druidic doctrines, that it was foreign to primitive Keltic sentiment, and so must have been taken over by them from a non-Keltic folk. Moreover, if it was foreign to the sentiment of the Kelts, why should they, being the then lords of western Europe, accept it ?

In what we have left us recorded of druidism, wrote Professor MacBain,[1] there is absolutely nothing that can be pointed to as non-Aryan. And he went on to say that the strong priestly caste, divided off from the nobles and the commons, can be paralleled in the Hinduism of India with its rigid caste of Brahmans, who monopolised all religious rites. Further, the human sacrifices of the druids can be matched, in some degree, by actual instances of such, or by rites which pointed to them as previously existent, among other Aryan nations, including those of Greece and Rome ; while the doctrine of the transmigration of the soul is a tenet of both Brahmans and Buddhists of Aryan India, and found its classical development in the views of Pythagoras.

There is not, therefore, much encouragement for enquiry on these lines, and the time has come to attempt another method of approach. But I should be false to the aim of this book if I attempted to disguise the nature of this other method, and I will say at once that it is merely a hypothetical reconstruction of events based on the little knowledge of the period that we have won. Rational reconstruction is a pretty name for the process ; but I fear that guesswork is another.

know that these items were included in *druidism*, and the point is, is there anything in *druidism* that must come from the pre-Keltic faith ?

[1] *Celtic Mythology and Religion*, Stirling, 1917.

Let us reconsider for a moment the picture of prehistoric Gaul and Britain that was presented to us in the second chapter. It was shown that in the Bronze Age, although we could identify various provinces in this great area, there was a general cultural unity achieved during a long period of relatively unadventurous prosperity. And the chief lesson of archæology is that there existed extraordinarily intimate trade-relations throughout the whole area of the three provinces of Gaul and the British Isles. Now, among such primitive societies we can reasonably suppose that the religion of one group must have been very nearly identical with that of its neighbours, and it is likely, therefore, that there would arise between those areas most intimately connected by the traffic of commerce a *consciousness* of unity in religious ideas. We can speak, therefore, of prehistoric *provinces of religious unity*.

One province would be western Gaul, Ireland, and western and south-western England. But a more important one was northern Gaul and south-eastern and eastern England. The cultural unity here goes right back to the Stone Age, for the districts together formed the " Flint-culture " that still lasted on in the Bronze Age, and the common religious bond was, therefore, one of high antiquity.

In the Bronze Age itself, the Gaulish portion of this province was affected by the Ligurian and the East German cultures, but the English portion was concerned to a much lesser degree. And also at the beginning of the Iron Age England was relatively more secluded from the new influences that were changing the face of Continental civilisation. Britain, therefore (and here I may speak for the western province too), was better enabled to maintain its ancient faith in an unaltered form, and as intercourse within the provinces was uninterrupted, it would automatically tend to acquire on the Continent a *religious distinction* because of its advantages in this respect. Moreover, we must add something on the score of native enterprise in an island, to which the prodigious development of the stone circles in the Stone and Bronze Ages bears witness.

Then the Kelts arrived in Eastern and North-Eastern

France. They were not merely raiders ; they settled in their new homes and became identified with the land itself ; and a great and special development of their La Tène civilisation was achieved in the Marne area. Therefore, whatever may have happened in the first conflict between native and Keltic religion, the result seems plain : in the end there was one pantheon and one faith.

Now, I have already given (p. 70) what I think is a very remarkable instance in this Marne area of the preservation of artistic tradition lasting from the Stone Ages through the Keltic period into the centuries of Roman rule ; and I suggested, and I now repeat, that there is an equal probability of the persistence of native religious tradition. Therefore, after the passing of a few generations of the first La Tène culture here the inhabitants would be as much conscious of the native faith of the land as they would be of the superposed elements of Keltic belief, if these differed, as I see no reason to suppose they did, in any notable way from the tenets of the local system. In a word, Keltic faith in the Marne area would be built upon native faith.

Then followed the invasion of England. But the Kelts who crossed to our shores were not the wanderers who had come from the Alpine lands into Northern France ; on the contrary, they were simply the Keltic-speaking descendants of these wanderers and the native Marne population. The advent into England of these mixed Keltic-Marne folk, therefore, would merely bring them into contact with what was recognised as the ancient faith of the Marne area in its unaltered form. The newcomers settled in England, and I venture to think they would unhesitatingly incorporate the native faith in their own, thus adding the authority of conquerors to a religion already celebrated as the purest source of the native element included in their own belief. Centuries passed, Keltic blood was thinning in the native veins, the antique religion still possessed the province, and the fame of Britain as the scene of its purest worship persisted. Small wonder, then, that when Cæsar asked the origin of Gallic faith or druidism, he was answered

*Disciplina in Britannia reperta atque inde in Galliam trans-
lata existimatur.*

But here is talk of the origin of druidism without a word
of the druids themselves ! How and when did they make
their appearance ? If I had any reason to suppose I could
answer that question to my own, or to anybody else's,
complete satisfaction, I would print what I have to say in
red ink. As it is, I have nothing to offer but another
hypothesis.

One method of finding out the origin of this priesthood
is to seek the condition most favourable for its formation,
and that is the line of enquiry I propose to follow. As I
see it, there are two main factors controlling this condition,
the first being *peace*, and the second *example*. That is to
say, the Kelts would not normally be likely to evolve a
priesthood in times of movement, war, or acute national
emergency ; but they would be likely to do so whenever,
as a settled and peaceful society, they found themselves
confronted with an efficient organised clergy of another and
more highly civilised people.

The first thing to consider, then, is whether there is a
probability that their priesthood was evolved in the old
Keltic home in the Alp lands and Central Europe before the
expansion period. One requirement is filled here, for the
origin of the La Tène or Keltic civilisation is one of slow
measured growth from Hallstatt beginnings, betokening
a period of long and tranquil prosperity ; and the second
factor is not by any means a negligible quantity, for Greece
was already in contact with the Keltic world in the 5th
century B.C., so that some of the Kelts may therefore have
been acquainted with the *priest-idea*. But I imagine that
only the southern fringe of the Keltic folk would be appreci-
ably affected by such influence. I conclude that in the
early stage of Keltic history, although the conception of a
priest and his function may have been familiar to some at
any rate of them, yet the generality of the Kelts had not
organised a priestly caste of their own at the time when
they were still concentrated within their ancient home.

Now, of all the Keltic-speaking peoples who set forth

on the great wanderings that eventually carried the La Tène culture from Scotland to Asia Minor, those who were soonest *settled* in their new territories were the first Keltic invaders of France and Italy. But of these, the French Kelts were, so far as we know, undisputed lords of the land they occupied, while the Italian Kelts, when at length they attempted to consolidate themselves in the northern plain, were perpetually engaged in the struggle to defend their precarious foothold against the jealous rivals pressing upon them from the south and east. Moreover, the French Kelts were soon familiar with a very high form of Greek corporate life, that of the colony of Massilia ; whereas nearly all that their Italian neighbours saw of higher civilisation was the battle array of Etruscans and Carthaginians. From this I conclude that opportunity, both as regards a settled life and conspicuous example, favoured the development of a priestly caste, the druidic hierarchy in other words, in Gaul.

It is no help to any hypothesis to pack it with corroborative detail, and although there is more that I should like to say here, I am content, if I have made my principal reasons clear, to say at once that I believe that the druids, as Keltic priests, originated in Gaul, and, therefore, that the druidic system was not common to all the Kelts. But by this I do not mean that the Kelts in Gaul specifically reorganised their society with the intention of creating a *new* caste of *new* officials ; on the contrary, I believe that the double opportunity of settled life and of example merely completed a gradual process inherent in this social life, a process whereby the functions of political chief and priest, hitherto united, became henceforward dissociated and relegated to separate individuals. The new priests, therefore, were new only in virtue of their specialised functions, so that they were invested, even at the period of their origin, with an ancient authority. Like the princes they too were the heirs of primitive patriarchal dynasties. Therefore, although we may say that the hierarchy was first of all established as late as the 4th, or even the 3rd, century B.C., the druids of the Kelts held in Greek eyes offices of high antiquity. What the druids now performed, Keltic kings had performed before them. And that is why so late a date for the origin of this clergy is consistent with their renown in the Greek world as early as 200 B.C.

This has led to what I hope will be the chief feature of this chapter, namely, the discovery that the origin of druidism and the origin of the druids are different events due to different causes. Druidism in Gaul is Keltic religion *after* its consolidation in the Gallic settlements and *after* the amalgamation with native faith that took place therein ; druidism in Britain is the inclusion in this Kelticised native faith of an autochthonous British religion that was in itself an unaltered expression of the Continental native element in druidism. Druidism, therefore, may properly be said to be Keltic, but it is only Keltic in as much as it is a *welding* under a new Keltic influence of the older Gallo-British religious unity.

On the other hand, the druids, as an organised hierarchy, were only subsequent Keltic servants of the Kelticised native faith in Gaul, a separate and accidental phenomenon of Gallic (not British) druidism.

Now let us try to understand the significance of this distinction. At the time when the druidic clergy was formed in Gaul, the mixed Keltic-native faith, i.e. druidism, was already established ; and in virtue of its partly (and I myself believe chiefly) indigenous character, it could only have been regarded as the universal religion of the land. Therefore, there is nothing surprising in that its newly-professed ministers ultimately attained to an extraordinary degree of authority ; nor is it remarkable that the priests should have taken advantage of the fact that a common religion lessened the significance of Keltic tribal divisions in the eyes of the merely Kelticised natives and their descendants, for they were thereby enabled to organise their system on an intertribal basis, and thus to secure for themselves, at any rate by the time of Cæsar, an undisputed control of the religious, as well as much of the civil, affairs of Keltic Gaul.

But the druids had not always dominated druidism. And at the time of the first Kelticisation of Britain, the time, that is to say, of the introduction of druidism into this country, I do not suppose that the migrating Keltic-speaking folk knew anything at all about the druids. Nor do I think that the rise of the druidic class in Gaul meant that henceforward British druidism was either administered by the Gallic college of druids, or controlled by an organisation of its own modelled on similar lines. As I read the evidence, I see no sign whatever of a corporate body of druids in this country; but on the contrary, a definite suggestion that the ritual of druidism in this island was always in the hands of those who had hitherto exercised the priestly functions, namely, the chieftains and kings. There would no doubt be minor changes; Gallic druids are said to have come to Britain for instruction in the original dogma of the island, and it is possible that the word *druid* would be introduced; more than that, it is possible that groups of British elders, who had constituted themselves the special repositories of the prized native lore, might call themselves by that name. But, for all that, there seems to have been no attempt at the inter-tribal organisation of a British clergy, and whatever tendency there may have been towards the formation of an effective national priesthood was abruptly terminated by the shattering blows of the Belgic occupation and the coming of the Romans. And thenceforward those who called themselves druids were only the magicians and soothsayers of a fugitive and desperate people.

It will be seen, then, that there may have been places of druidical worship in Britain, although the worship and sacrifices performed there were not conducted by druids in the Gallic sense of an organised and distinct priesthood. And for want of evidence to the contrary, therefore, I am disposed to dispossess the " ancient druids " of Britain in favour of the tribal leaders. That is to say, although I agree that the present temple at Stonehenge is druidic, in the sense that it was consecrated to druidism, I am not prepared to grant that the worship there was conducted by the white-robed druids of our accustomed imagining. The priests at Stonehenge were more probably the temporal rulers and the lesser chieftains of the great plain upon which it stands.

To revert once more to the question of the megaliths. Druidism, in Britain, if the name is to mean anything at all, is a form of religion not older than the Kelticisation of this island, and, accordingly, no temple site, be it stone circle or what not, can be fairly called druidic unless there is a probability that its use was continued after this Kelticisation. The present Stonehenge, I believe myself, was built during the dominion of druidism, but even this much will be challenged by most archæologists of to-day; and, as regards the stone circles, I freely admit it is quite beyond my power, and I suspect anyone else's, to prove for any one of them that it was still used as a temple after druidism was established. I can only say that, for my part, I think it is highly probable that some of them were so used, and that to this small extent popular opinion may be justified. But we must perforce rest content with this probability, without over-emphasising it or excluding it.

As for Ireland, it seems to me that the Kelticisation here is of sufficiently late date to make it probable that the branch of the Keltic-speaking folk responsible, and it was a branch quite distinct from those who had already crossed to England, may have already known something, before this migration, of the organised priestly caste in Gaul. It is reasonable, therefore, that although we should properly think of the introduction of druidism into Ireland in the terms of its introduction into England, that is as the completion of the Kelticisation of native religion in that province which included Gaul, South-Western England, and perhaps Wales and Ireland, yet we should add the difference that the Kelts in Ireland may have attempted to impose some kind of clergy upon the ancient faith. It seems likely, however, that the druidic caste in Ireland was never anything but a very faint reflection of the Gallic system, and one that speedily became isolated and degenerate. On these grounds, it is just a little more probable that some circle-sites in Ireland might truly have been places of worship of the ancient druids, though I would observe with all my force that the same uncertainty is present, and the same precaution necessary in adopting such a view.

And now I have done. I have dealt perhaps unsympathetically with theories of the origin of druidism that have won popular and academic approval, and instead I have been able to offer nothing better than what I know to be surmise. But I have written according to my lights. Long ago a young German scholar, Esaias Pufendorf, wrote a book on the same subject as this, and he begged the indulgence " of those who are distinguished for superior sagacity in antiquarian investigation " if he fell into error, because, he said, his way was difficult " by reason of the unrelieved darkness with which on various sides we are beset." Nearly three hundred years have passed, the lamps of many scholars have been turned upon these blank walls of obscurity, but still we are groping feebly and uncertain in the gloom. I repeat his plea. And I conclude in his words : " Now, if anyone votes in favour of these views we object not, nor do we object if he black-balls them, seeing that it is doubtful whether they can be confirmed by trustworthy evidence. And so here end our brief dissertation upon the druids." [1]

---

[1] Edmund Goldschmid's translation of E. Pufendorf's *Dissertation on the Druids*, Edinburgh, 1886, p. 61.

APPENDIX

PASSAGES RELATING TO THE DRUIDS AND DRUIDISM IN THE WORKS OF GREEK AND LATIN AUTHORS OF WHICH ENGLISH TRANSLATIONS ARE GIVEN IN CHAPTER III

DIOGENES LAERTIUS. *Vitæ, Intro.* 1

τὸ τῆς φιλοσοφίας ἔργον ἔνιοί φασιν ἀπὸ βαρβάρων ἄρξαι. γεγενῆσθαι γὰρ παρὰ μὲν Πέρσαις Μάγους, παρὰ δὲ Βαβυλωνίοις ἢ Ἀσσυρίοις Χαλδαίους, καὶ Γυμνοσοφιστὰς παρ' Ἰνδοῖς, παρά τε Κελτοῖς καὶ Γαλάταις τοὺς καλουμένους Δρυίδας καὶ Σεμνοθέους, καθάφησιν Ἀριστοτέλης ἐν τῷ Μαγικῷ καὶ Σωτίων ἐν τῷ εἰκοστῷ τρίτῳ τῆς Διαδοχῆς.

Vitæ, Intro. 5

οἱ δὲ φάσκοντες ἀπὸ βαρβάρων ἄρξαι φιλοσοφίαν καὶ τὸν τρόπον παρ' ἑκάστοις αὐτῆς ἐκτίθενται · καὶ φασι τοὺς μὲν Γυμνοσοφιστὰς καί Δρυίδας αἰνιγματωδῶς ἀποφθεγγομένους φιλοσοφῆσαι σέβειν θεοὺς καὶ μηδὲν κακὸν δρᾶν καὶ ἀνδρείαν ἀσκεῖν.

CÆSAR. *Be Bello Gallico*, VI, 13

In omni Gallia eorum hominum qui aliquo sunt numero atque honore genera sunt duo. Nam plebes paene servorum habetur loco, quae nihil audet per se, nulli adhibetur consilio. . . . Sed de his duobus generibus alterum est druidum, alterum equitum. Illi rebus divinis intersunt, sacrificia publica ac privata procurant, religiones interpretantur ; ad hos magnus adulescentium numerus disciplinae causa concurrit, magnoque hi sunt apud eos honore. Nam fere de omnibus controversiis publicis privatisque constituunt, et si quod est facinus admissum, si caedes facta, si de hereditate, de finibus controversia est, idem decernunt, praemia poenasque constituunt ; si qui aut privatis aut populus eorum decreto non stetit, sacrificiis interdicunt. Haec poena apud eos est gravissima. Quibus ita est interdictum, hi numero impiorum ac scelera-

torum habentur, his omnes decedunt, aditum sermonemque de-
fugiunt, ne quid ex contagione in commodi accipiant, neque iis
petentibus ius redditur neque honos ullus communicatur. His
autem omnibus druidibus praeest unus, qui summam inter eos
habet auctoritatem. Hoc mortuo aut si qui ex reliquis excellit
dignitate succedit, aut, si sunt plures pares, suffragio druidum, non-
numquam etiam armis de principatu contendunt. Hi certo anni
tempore in finibus Carnutum, quae regio totius Galliae media
habetur, considunt in loco consecrato. Huc omnes undique qui
controversias habent, conveniunt eorumque decretis iudiciisque
parent. Disciplina in Britannia reperta atque inde in Galliam
translata existimatur, et nunc qui diligentius eam rem cognoscere
volunt plerumque illo discendi causa proficiscuntur.

De Bello Gallico, VI, 14

Druides a bello abesse consuerunt neque tributa una cum reliquis
pendunt ; militiae vacationem omniumque rerum habent immuni-
tatem. Tantis excitati praemiis et sua sponte multi in disciplinam
conveniunt et a parentibus propinquisque mittuntur. Magnum
ibix numerum versuum ediscere dicuntur. Itaque annos non nulli
vicenos in disciplina permanent. Neque fas esse existimant ea
litteris mandare, cum in reliquis fere rebus, publicis privatisque
rationibus, Graecis litteris utantur. Id mihi duabus de causis
instituisse videntur, quod neque in vulgus disciplinam effere velint
neque eos qui discant litteris confisos minus memoriae studere ;
quod fere plerisque accidit ut praesidio litterarum diligentiam in
perdiscendo ac memoriam remittant. In primis hoc volunt per-
suadere, non interire animas, sed ab aliis post mortem transire ad
alios, atque hoc maxime ad virtutem excitari putant metu mortis
neglecto. Multa praeterea de sideribus atque eorum motu, de
mundi ac terrarum magnitudine, de rerum natura, de deorum
immortalium vi ac potestate disputant et iuventuti tradunt.

De Bello Gallico, VI, 16

Natio est omnis Gallorum admodum dedita religionibus, atque
ob eam causam qui sunt adfecti gravioribus morbis quique in proeliis
periculisque versantur aut pro victimis homines immolant aut se
immolaturos vovent, administrisque ad ea sacrificia druidibus
utuntur, quod, pro vita hominis nisi hominis vita reddatur,
non posse deorum immortalium numen placari arbitrantur, pub-
liceque eiusdem generis habent instituta sacrificia. Alii immani

magnitudine simulacra habent, quorum contexta viminibus membra vivis hominibus complent ; quibus succensis circumventi flamma exanimantur homines.¹ Supplicia eorum, qui in furto aut in latrocinio aut aliqua noxia sint comprehensi, gratiora dis immortalibus esse arbitrantur ; sed, cum eius generis copia defecit, etiam ad innocentium supplicia descendunt.

De Bello Gallico, VI, 18, 1

Galli se omnes ab Dito patre prognatus praedicant idque ab druidibus proditum dicunt.

De Bello Gallico, VI, 21, 1

Germani multum ab hac consuetudine differunt. Namque neque Druides habent, qui rebus divinis praesint, neque sacrificiis student.

CICERO. *De Divinatione*, I, xli, 90

Eaque divinationum ratio ne in barbaris quidem gentibus neglecta est, siquidem et in Gallia Druidae sunt, quibus ipse Divitiacum Aeduum, hospitem tuum laudatoremque, cognovi, qui et naturae rationem quam φυσιολογίαν Graeci appellant, notam esse sibi profitebatur et partim auguriis, partim coniectura, quae essent futura, dicebat.

DIODORUS SICULUS. *Histories*, V, 28, 6

Ἐνισχύει γὰρ παρ' αὐτοῖς ὁ Πυθαγόρου λογος, ὅτι τὰς ψυχὰς τῶν ἀνθρώπων ἀθανάτους εἶναι συμβέβηκε\καὶ δι' ἐτῶν, ὡρισμένων πάλιν βιοῦν εἰς ἕτερον σῶμα τῆς ψυχῆς εἰσδυομένης.

V, 31, 2-5

εἰσὶ δὲ παρ' αὐτοῖς καὶ ποιηταὶ μελῶν, οὓς βάρδους ὀνομάζουσιν. οὗτοι δὲ μετ' ὀργάνων ταῖς λύραις ὁμοίων ᾄδοντες οὓς μὲν ὑμνοῦσιν, οὓς δὲ βλασφημοῦσι.

φιλόσοφοί τέ τινές εἰσι καὶ θεολόγοι περιττῶς τιμώμενοι, οὓς δρουίδας ὀνομάζουσι. χρῶνται δὲ καὶ μάντεσιν, ἀποδοχῆς μεγάλης ἀξιοῦντες αὐτούς · οὗτοι δὲ διά τε τῆς οἰωνοσκοπίας καὶ διὰ τῆς τῶν ἱερείων θυσίας τὰ μέλλοντα προλέγουσι, καὶ πᾶν τὸ πλῆθος ἔχουσιν ὑπήκοον. μάλιστα δ' ὅταν περί τινων μεγάλων ἐπι σκέπτωνται, παράδοξον καὶ ἄπιστον ἔχουσι νόμιμον · ἄνθρωπον γὰρ κατασπείσαντες τύπτουσι μαχαίρᾳ κατὰ τὸν ὑπὲρ τὸ διά-

φράγμα τόπον, καὶ πεσόντος τοῦ πληγέντος ἐκ τῆς πτώσεως καὶ τοῦ
σπαραγμοῦ τῶν μελῶν, ἔτι δὲ τῆς τοῦ αἵματος ῥύσεως τὸ μέλλον νόοῦσι,
παλαιᾷ τινι καὶ πολυχρονίῳ παρατηρήσει περὶ τούτων πεπιστευκότες. ἔθος
δ᾽ αὐτοῖς ἐστι μηδένα θυσίαν ποιεῖν ἄνευ φιλοσόφου · διὰ γὰρ τῶν ἐμπείρων
τῆς θείας φύσεως ὥσπερεί τινων ὁμοφώνων τὰ χαριστήρια τοῖς θεοῖς φασι
δεῖν προσφέρειν, καὶ διὰ τούτων οἴονται δεῖν τἀγαθὰ αἰτεῖσθαι. οὐ μόνον
δ᾽ ἐν ταῖς εἰρηνικαῖς χρείαις, ἀλλὰ καὶ κατὰ τοὺς πολέμους τούτοις μάλιστα
πείθονται καὶ τοῖς μελῳδοῦσι ποιηταῖς, οὐ μόνον οἱ φίλοι, ἀλλὰ καὶ οἱ
πολέμιοι · πολλάκις δ᾽ ἐν ταῖς παρατάξεσι πλησιαζόντων ἀλλήλοις τῶν
στρατοπέδων καὶ τοῖς ξίφεσιν ἀνατεταμένοις καὶ ταῖς λόγχαις προβεβλη-
μέναις, εἰς τὸ μέσον οὗτοι προελθόντες παύουσιν αὐτούς, ὥσπερ τινὰ θηρία
κατεπᾴσαντες. οὕτω καὶ παρὰ τοῖς ἀγριωτάτοις βαρβάροις ὁ θυμὸς εἴκει
τῇ σοφίᾳ καὶ ὁ Ἄρης αἰδεῖται τὰς Μούσας.

STRABO. *Geographica*, IV, 4, c. 197, 4

παρὰ πᾶσι δ᾽ ὡς ἐπίπαν τρία φῦλα τῶν τιμωμένων διαφερόντως ἐστί,
βάρδοι τε καὶ οὐάτεις καὶ δρυΐδαι · βάρδοι μὲν ὑμνηταὶ καὶ ποιηταί, οὐάτεις
δὲ ἱεροποιοὶ καὶ φυσιολόγοι, δρυΐδαι δὲ πρὸς τῇ φυσιολογίᾳ καὶ τὴν ἠθικὴν
φιλοσοφίαν ἀσκοῦσι · δικαιότατοι δὲ νομίζονται καὶ διὰ τοῦτο πιστεύονται
τάς τε ἰδιωτικὰς κρίσεις καὶ τὰς κοινάς, ὥστε καὶ πολέμους διῄτων πρότερον
καὶ παρατάττεσθαι μέλλοντας ἔπαυον, τὰς δὲ φονικὰς δίκας μάλιστα τούτοις
ἐπετέτραπτο δικάζειν. ὅταν τε φορὰ τούτων ᾖ, φορὰν καὶ τῆς χώρας νομί-
ζουσιν ὑπάρχειν. ἀφθάρτους δὲ λέγουσι καὶ οὗτοι καὶ ἄλλοι τὰς ψυχὰς
καὶ τὸν κόσμον, ἐπικρατήσειν δέ ποτε καὶ πῦρ καὶ ὕδωρ.

Geographica, IV, 4, c. 198, 5

καὶ τούτων δ᾽ ἔπαυσαν αὐτοὺς Ῥωμαῖοι, καὶ τῶν κατὰ τὰς θυσίας καὶ
μαντείας ὑπεναντίων τοῖς παρ᾽ ἡμῖν νομίμοις.
ἄνθρωπον γὰρ κατεσπεισμένον παίσαντες εἰς νῶτον μαχαίρᾳ ἐμαντεύοντο
ἐκ τοῦ σφαδασμοῦ. ἔθυον δὲ οὐκ ἄνευ δρυϊδῶν. καὶ ἄλλα δὲ ἀνθρω-
ποθυσιῶν εἴδη λέγεται · καὶ γὰρ κατετόξευόν τινας καὶ ἀνεσταύρουν ἐν τοῖς
ἱεροῖς καὶ κατασκευάσαντες κολοσσὸν χόρτου καὶ ξύλων, ἐμβαλόντες εἰς
τοῦτον βοσκήματα καὶ θηρία παντοῖα καὶ ἀνθρώπους ὡλοκαύτουν.

AMMIANUS MARCELLINUS, XV, 9, 4

Drasidae memorant revera fuisse populi partem indigenam, sed
alios quoque ab insulis extimis confluxisse et tractibus trans-
rhenanis, crebritate bellorum et adluvione fervidi maris sedibus
suis expulsos.

AMMIANUS MARCELLINUS, XV, 9, 8

Per haec loca hominibus paulatim excultis viguere studia laudabilium doctrinarum, inchoata per bardos et euhagis et drasidas. Et bardi quidem fortia virorum illustrium facta heroicis composita versibus cum dulcibus lyrae modulis cantitarunt, euhages vero scrutantes seriem et sublimia naturae pandere conabantur. Inter eos dryaridae ingeniis celsiores, ut auctoritas Pythagorae decrevit, sodaliciis adstricti consortiis, quaestionibus occultarum rerum altarumque erecti sunt et depectantes humana pronuntiarunt animas immortales.

SUETONIUS. *Claudius*, 25

Druidarum religionem apud Gallos dirae immanitatis et tantum civibus sub Augusto interdictam penitus abolevit.

POMPONIUS MELA. *De Situ Orbis*, III, 2, 18 and 19

Manent vestigia feritatis iam abolitae, atque ut ab ultimis caedibus temperant, ita nihilominus, ubi devotos altaribus admovere, delibant. Habent tamen et facundiam suam, magistrosque sapientiae druidas. Hi terrae mundique magnitudinem et formam, motus caeli ac siderum, et quid dii velint scire profitentur. Docent multa nobilissimos gentis clam et diu vicenis annis, aut in specu aut in abditis saltibus. Unum ex his quae praecipiunt in vulgus effluxit, videlicet ut forent ad bella meliores, aeternas esse animas vitamque alteram ad Manes. Itaque cum mortuis cremant ac defodiunt apta viventibus. Olim negotiorum ratio etiam et exactio crediti deferebatur ad inferos : erantque qui se in rogos suorum velut una victuri libenter immitterent.

LUCAN. *Pharsalia*, I, 450-8

Et vos barbaricos ritus moremque sinistrum
sacrorum, Druidae, positis repetistis ab armis.
solis nosse deos et caeli numina vobis
aut solis nescire datum : nemora alta remotis
incolitis lucis : vobis auctoribus umbrae
non tacitas Erebi sedes Ditisque profundi
pallida regna petunt : regit idem spiritus artus
orbe alio : longae—canitis si cognita—vitae
mors media est.

Pliny. *Nat. Hist.*, XVI, 249.

Non est omittenda in hac re et Galliarum admiratio. Nihil habent Druidae (ita suos appellant magos) visco et arbore, in qua gignatur, si modo sit robur, sacratius. Iam per se roburum eligunt lucos, nec ulla sacra sine earum fronde conficiunt, ut inde appellati quoque interpretatione Graeca possint Druidae videri. Enimvero quidquid adnascatur illis e caelo missum putant signumque esse electae ab ipso deo arboris. Est autem id rarum admodum inventu et repertum magna religione petitur et ante omnia sexta luna, quae principia mensum annorumque his facit et saeculi post tricesimum annum, quia iam virium abunde habeat nec sit sui dimidia. Omnia sanantem appellant suo vocabulo. Sacrificio epulisque rite sub arbore comparatis, duos admovent candidi coloris tauros, quorum cornua tum primum vinciantur. Sacerdos candida veste cultus arborem scandit, falce aurea demetit, candido id excipitur sago. Tum deinde victimas immolant precantes, suum donum deus prosperum faciat iis quibus dederit. Fecunditatem eo poto dari cuicumque animalium sterili arbitrantur, contra vènena omnia esse remedio. Tanta gentium in rebus frivolis plerumque religio est.

Nat. Hist., XXIV, 103-104

Similis herbae huic Sabinae est selago appellata. Legitur sine ferro dextra manu per tunicam qua sinistra exuitur velut a furante candida veste vestito pureque lautis nudis pedibus, sacro facto prius quam legatur pane vinoque. Fertur in mappa nova. Hanc contra perniciem omnem habendam prodidere Druidae Gallorum et contra omnia oculorum vitia fumum eius prodesse Iidem samolum herbam nominavere nascentem in umidis, et hanc sinistra manu legi a ieiunis contra morbos suum boumque, nec respicere legentem, nec alibi quam in canali deponere, ibique continere poturis.

Nat. Hist., XXIX, 52

Praeterea est ovorum genus in magna fama Galliarum omissum Graecis. Angues innumeri aestate convoluti salivis faucium corporumque spumis artifici conplexu glomerant, anguinum appellatur. Druidae sibilis id dicunt in sublime iactari, sagoque oportere intercipi ne tellurem attingat. Profugere raptorem equo, serpentis enim insequi donec arceantur amnis alicuius interventu.

Experimentum eius esse, si contra aquas fluitet vel auro vinctum. Atque, ut est Magorum sollertis occultandis fraudibus sagax, certa luna capiendum censent, tanquam congruere operätionem eam serpentium, humani sit arbitri. Vidi equidem id ovom mali orbiculati modici magnitudine, crusta cartalaginis, velut acetabulis bracchiorum polypi crebris, insigne Druidis. Ad victorias litium ac regum aditus mire laudatur, tantae vanitatis ut habentem id in lite in sinu equitem Romanum e Vocontiis a divo Claudio principe interemptum non ob aliud sciam.

PLINY. *Nat. Hist.*, XXX, 13

Gallias utique possedit, et quidem ad nostram memoriam. Namque Tiberi Caesaris principatus sustulit Druidas eorum et hoc genus vatum medicorumque per senatus-consultum. Quid ego haec commemorem in arte oceanum quoque transgressa et ad naturae inane pervecta ? Britannia hodieque eam attonita celebrat tantis caerimoniis ut dedisse Persis videri possit. Adeo ista toto mundo consensere quamquam discordi et sibi ignoto. Nec satis aestimari potest quantum Romanis debeatur, qui sustulere monstra, quibus hominem occidere religiosissimum erat, mandi vero etiam saluberrimum.

TACITUS. *Annals*, XIV, 30

Stabat pro litore diversa acies, densa armis virisque, intercursantibus feminis ; in modum Furiarum veste ferali, crinibus deiectis faces praeferebant ; Druidaeque circum, preces diras sublatis ad caelum manibus fundentes, novitate aspectus perculere militem, ut quasi haerentibus membris immobile corpus vulneribus praeberent. dein cohortationibus ducis et se ipsi stimulantes ne muliebre et fanaticum agmen pavescerent, inferunt signa sternuntque obvios et igni suo involvunt. praesidium posthac inpositum victis excisique luci saevis superstitionibus sacri : nam cruore captivo adolere aras et hominum fibris consulere deos fas habebant.

Histories, IV, 54

Captam olim a Gallis urbem, sed integra Iovis sede mansisse imperium : fatali nunc igne signum caelestis irae datum et posessionem rerum humanarum Transalpinis gentibus portendi superitione vana Druidae canebant.

Dion Chrysostom. *Orations*, XLIX (*Teub.*, 1919, pp. 123, 124)

Πέρσαι μὲν οἶμαι τοὺς καλουμένους παρ' αὐτοῖς μάγους . . . Αἰγύπτιοι δὲ τοὺς ἱερέας . . . Ἰνδοὶ δὲ βραχμᾶνας . . . Κελτοὶ δὲ οὓς ὀνομάζουσι Δρυΐδας, καὶ τούτους περὶ μαντικὴν ὄντας καὶ τὴν ἄλλην σοφίαν. ὧν ἄνευ τοῖς βασιλεῦσιν οὐδὲν ἐξῆν πράττειν οὐδὲ βουλεύεσθαι, ὥστε τὸ μὲν ἀληθὲς ἐκείνους ἄρχειν, τοὺς δὲ βασιλέας αὐτῶν ὑπηρέτας καὶ διακόνους γίγνεσθαι τῆς γνώμης ἐν θρόνοις χρυσοῖς καθημένους καὶ οἰκίας μεγάλας οἰκοῦντας καὶ πολυτελῶς εὐωχουμένους.

Lampridius. *Alex. Severus*, LIX, 5

Mulier Dryas eunti exclamavit Gallico sermone, " Vadas, nec victoriam speres, nec te militi tuo credas."

Vopiscus. *Numerianus*, XIV

Cum (inquit) Diocletianus apud Tungros in Gallia quadam in caupona moraretur, in minoribus adhuc locis militans, et cum dryde quadam muliere rationem convictus sui cotidiani faceret, at illa diceret, " Diocletiane, nimium avarus, nimium parcus es." Ioco non serio Diocletianus respondisse fertur, " Tunc ero largus, quum imperator fuero." Post quod verbum dryas dixisse fertur, " Diocletiane, iocari noli : nam imperator eris cum Aprum occideris."

Aurelianus, XLIII, 4 and 5

Dicebat enim, quodam tempore Aurelianum Gallicanas consuluisse druidas, sciscitantem utrum apud eius posteros imperium permaneret : tum illas respondisse dixit nullius clarius in republica nomen quam Claudii posterorum futurum. Et est quidem iam Constantius imperator eiusdem vir sanguinis, cuius puto posteros ad eam gloriam quae a dryadibus praenuntiata sit, pervenire.

Ausonius. *Commen. professorum*, IV, 7-10

Tu Baiocassi stirpe Druidarum satus,
    Si fama non fallit fidem,
Beleni sacratum ducis e templo genus,
    Et inde vobis nomina.

AUSONIUS.   *Commen. professorum,* X, 22-30

Nec reticebo senem
Nomine Phoebicium,
Qui Beleni aedituus
Nil opis inde tulit ;
Set tamen, ut placitum,
Stirpe satus Druidum
Gentis Aremoricae,
Burdigalae cathedram
Nati opera obtinuit.

NENNIUS.   *Historia Britonum,* 40

Et postea rex ad se invitavit magos suos, ut quid faceret, ab eis interrogaret.

HIPPOLYTUS.   *Philosophumena* (*Refutatio Omnium Haeresium*), I, xxv

Δρυίδαι οἱ ἐν Κελτοῖς τῇ Πυθαγορείῳ φιλοσοφίᾳ κατ' ἄκρον ἐγκύψαντες, αἰτίου αὐτοῖς γενομένου ταύτης τῆς ἀσκήσεως Ζαμόλξιδος δούλου Πυθαγόρου, γένει θρᾳκίου· ὃς μετὰ τὴν Πυθαγόρου τελευτὴν ἐκεῖ χωρήσας αἴτιος τούτοις ταύτης τῆς φιλοσοφίας ἐγένετο. τούτοις Κελτοὶ ὡς προφήτας καὶ προγνωστικοὺς δοξάζουσιν, διὰ τὸ ἐκ ψήφων καὶ ἀριθμῶν Πυθαγορικῇ τέχνῃ προαγορεύειν αὐτοῖς τινα, ἧς καὶ αὐτῆς τέχνης τὰς ἐφόδους οὐ σιωπήσομεν ἐπεὶ καὶ ἐκ τούτων τινὲς αἱρέσεις παρεισάγειν ἐτόλμησαν. χρῶνται δὲ δρυίδαι καὶ μαγείαις.

CLEMENT OF ALEXANDRIA.   *Stromata,* I, xv, 70, 1

'Αλέξανδρος δὲ ἐν τῷ Περὶ Πυθαγορικῶν συμβόλων Ζαράτῳ τῷ 'Ασσυρίῳ μαθητεῦσαι ἱστορεῖ τὸν Πυθαγόραν . . . ἀκηκοέναι τε πρὸς τούτοις Γαλατῶν καὶ Βραχμάνων τὸν Πυθαγόραν βούλεται.

Stromata, I, xv, 71, 3

φιλοσοφία τοίνυν πολυωφελές τε χρῆμα πάλαι μὲν ἤκμασε παρὰ βαρβάροις κατὰ τὰ ἔθνη διαλάμψασα, ὕστερον δὲ καὶ εἰς Ἕλληνας κατῆλθεν. προέστησαν δ' αὐτῆς Αἰγυπτίων τε οἱ προφῆται καὶ 'Ασσυρίων οἱ Χαλδαῖοι καὶ Γαλατῶν οἱ Δρυίδαι καὶ Σαμαναῖοι Βάκτρον καὶ Κελτῶν οἱ φιλοσοφήσαντες καὶ Περσῶν οἱ Μάγοι . . .

APPENDIX 221

Valerius Maximus, II, 6, 10

Horum moenia egressis vetus ille mos Gallorum ocurrit, quos memoria proditum est pecunias mutuas, quae his apud inferos redderentur, dare, quia persuasum habuerint animas hominum immortales esse. Dicerem stultos, nisi idem bracati sensissent, quod palliatus Pythagoras credidit.

INDEX